The

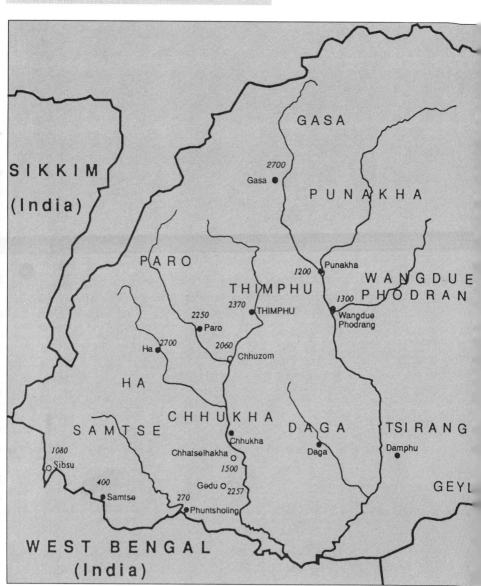

Map of Bhutan

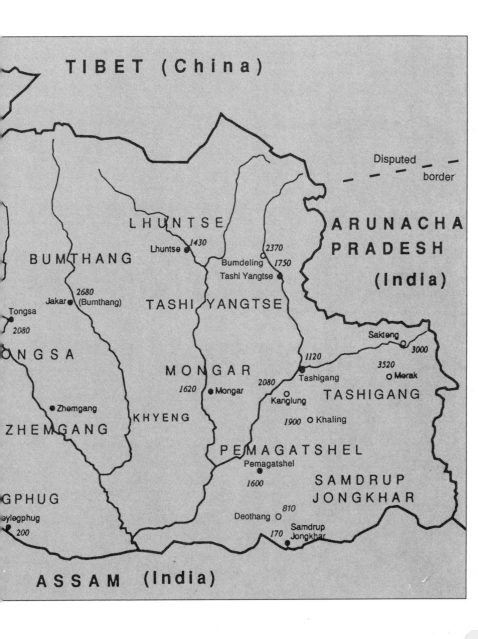

TIBET (China)

Disputed border

LHUNTSE

ARUNACHA PRADESH (India)

BUMTHANG

Lhuntse ● *1430*

2370

Bumdeling *1750*

Tashi Yangtse

Jakar ● *2680* (Bumthang)

Tongsa

2080

TASHI YANGTSE

Sakteng *3000*

NGSA

1120

3520 ○ Merak

MONGAR

2080

Tashigang

1620 ● Mongar

Kanglung

TASHIGANG

● Zhemgang

1900 ○ Khaling

ZHEMGANG

KHYENG

PEMAGATSHEL

Pemagatshel

1600

SAMDRUP JONGKHAR

GPHUG

810

aylegphug

Deothang ○

200

170 Samdrup Jongkhar

ASSAM (India)

Western Bhutan and adjoining region

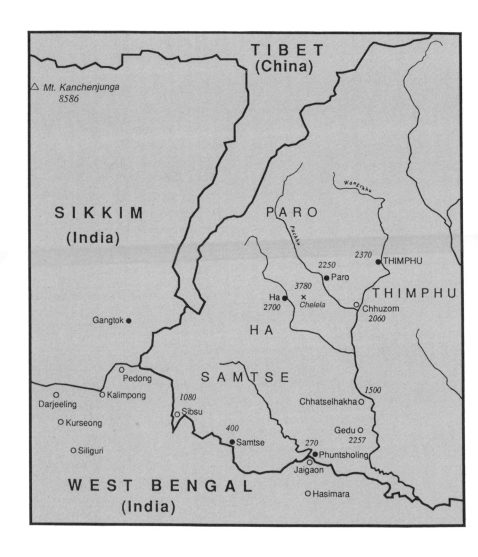

TIBET
(China)

△ Mt. Kanchenjunga
8586

SIKKIM
(India)

PARO

Wangchhu

Pachhu

2370 ●THIMPHU

2250

● Paro

3780

Ha   × Chelela

2700

THIMPHU

○ Chhuzom
2060

Gangtok ●

HA

○
Pedong

SAMTSE

○   ○ Kalimpong   1080
Darjeeling

1500

○ Sibsu

Chhatselhakha ○

○ Kurseong

400

Gedu ○
2257

○ Siliguri

● Samtse   270

● Phuntsholing
○
Jaigaon

WEST BENGAL

○ Hasimara

(India)

Eastern Bhutan (prior to 1993)

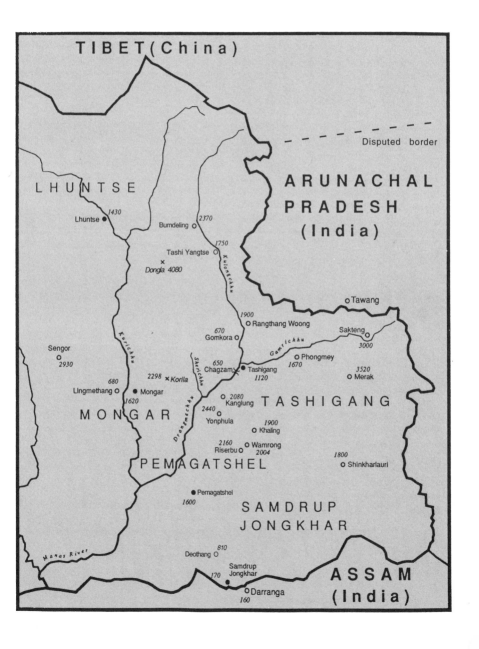

Other books you may enjoy from this publisher:

The Empty Cathedral, by Jean-Paul Lefebvre
Zen & the Art of Post-Modern Canada, by Stephen Schecter
The Last Cod Fish, by Pol Chantraine
No Mud on the Back Seat, by Gerald Clark
*A Canadian Myth: Quebec, between Canada and the
Illusion of Utopia,* by William Johnson
Economics in Crisis, by Louis-Philippe Rochon
Dead-End Democracy?, by Yves Leclerc
Voltaire's Man in America, by Jean-Paul de Lagrave
Moral Panic: Biopolitics Rising, by John Fekete

CANADIAN CATALOGUING IN PUBLICATION DATA

Solverson, Howard M. (Howard Marvin)

The Jesuit and the dragon : the life of Father William Mackey in the
Himalayan Kingdom of Bhutan.

Includes bibliographical references; includes glossary

ISBN 1-895854-37-7

1. Mackey, William.   2. Bhutan.   3. Jesuits — Missions — Bhutan —
Biography.   4. Missions, Canadian — Bhutan — Biography   5. Mission-
aries — Canada — Biography.   6. Missionaries — Bhutan — Biography.
I. Title.

BX4705.M32S64 1995   266'.0092   C95-940418-X

To receive our current catalogue and be kept on our mailing list for
announcements of new titles, send your name and address to:

Robert Davies Publishing,
P.O. Box 702, Outremont, Quebec, Canada H2V 4N6

Howard Solverson

The Jesuit and the Dragon

The life of Father William Mackey
in the Himalayan Kingdom of Bhutan

ROBERT DAVIES PUBLISHING
MONTREAL—TORONTO—PARIS

This book may be ordered in Canada from
General Distribution Services,

☎1-800-387-0141 / 1-800-387-0172 FAX 1-416-445-5967;

in the U.S.A., from Associated Publishers Group,
1501 County Hospital Road, Nashville, TN 37218
dial toll-free 1-800-327-5113;

or call the publisher, toll-free throughout North America,

1-800-481-2440, FAX 1-514-481-9973;

In the UK, order from Drake International Services,
Market House, Market Place, Deddington, Oxford OX15 OSF
Telephone/Fax 01869 338240

The publisher takes this opportunity to thank the
Canada Council and the *Ministère de la Culture du Québec*
for their continuing support.

*Dedicated to
Father Mackey*

Table of Contents

Part IV - Peak of learning

Part V - No twilight years

Maps

Acknowledgements

This book is based almost completely on stories told to me by Father Mackey. But whenever possible, I have tried to verify or cross-check details. Many people have assisted me in trying to track down information, some providing material directly. Others have helped facilitate my work, especially by offering generous hospitality for sometimes extended periods. Still others have offered valuable advice and encouragement. I would like to thank all these people and will name as many as I can.

First, my sister Betty and her husband Tony Pletcher have helped immeasurably in a variety of important ways, including providing a comfortable home in Vancouver for much of the time this book has been inching forward. Brigadier and Mrs. Amarjit Singh and Padmesh, in Delhi, have also provided me with a much appreciated home from time to time. In Thimphu, I am grateful for the care provided by Kunzang Chhoedron and Mindu while I stayed with Father Mackey. I'd also like to mention Pat Cupiss in Toronto for her help and hospitality.

Regarding my visits to Bhutan after I no longer lived there, I would like to thank Lyonpo Dawa Tshering and Dasho Thinley Gyamtsho. And for helping me track down information, I want to thank Dasho Sonam Tobgye, Dasho Tenzin Dorje, Dasho Kunzang Tangbi, Minyak Tulku, Mr. Ugyen Tshering, Mr. Lhatu Wangchuk, Aum Dago Beda and Miss Nancy Strickland. I also wish to thank Mr. Francis Fanthome in Delhi. For photographs and help with photography, I wish to thank Teresa Mackey and Mike Heney.

Many members of the Jesuit community have been helpful and as a way of thanking them all, I wish to mention Father Edward Dowling, Father James McCabe and Father Richard Sherburne.

I wish to thank my editor, Ken McGoogan, not only for his work, which so impressed me, but for his enthusiasm for the book and for being so easy to work with.

Many people have been generally supportive, but among them I want to thank Daniel Wood for his instruction, advice and encouragement.

Thanks to Robert Davies for taking a chance on a new writer and to Alexa LeBlanc for the introduction.

In all the categories above, and more, especially her scholarly expertise, Dr. Françoise Pommaret has been a tremendous support, for which enough thanks cannot be given.

The key to this book is, of course, Father Mackey. For letting me tell his story, for telling it to me and for his patience in trying to deal with my apparently endless string of questions I want to express my great thanks to him.

A Note on Bhutanese Names

Traditionally there was no system of family names in Bhutan. When a child was named, he or she would be given one, two or three, but usually two, names, normally by a lama. These names in combination would have a religious meaning. Both names would be used together for properly referring to or addressing the person, but the first name by itself would usually come to be used more commonly, especially in close personal relations. This leads to great frustration for foreigners who have no knowledge of the kinship of the people they deal with, having no family names to guide them and not having the knowledge or sense of genealogy that the Bhutanese seem to have. However, a very small number of "big" families have adopted the use of family name. Most notable is the royal family of Wangchuck. Next would come the Dorji family.

While both names are properly used in referring to or addressing people, it is quite common to use only their first name along with their title. For example, the foreign minister is Lyonpo (minister) Dawa Tshering. However, he is quite commonly referred to as Lyonpo Dawa. But not Lyonpo Tshering.

Names in common use often incorporate an aspect of the individual, such as the place he or she comes from. This helps somewhat in situations where there is more than one person by the same name (and Bhutan has a relatively small number of personal names). Hence, the boy Jigme Tshultim, from the village of Radi, was known at school as Radi Jigme.

The spelling of names can add to the outsider's difficulty. All Bhutanese names and other words which have come to be written in

Romanized form, came originally, of course, from languages (principally Dzongkha) that used another script. Hence transcription was required. Unfortunately, such processes have not been uniform and we find a variety of ways of spelling even very common and prominent words. For very simple and obvious examples we need look only as far as Wangchuck and Dorji. To the author's knowledge, the basic forms of these two names would be Wangchuk and Dorje. But the royal family has changed the spelling of its name to Wangchuck and their in-laws adopted Dorji as the spelling of their name.

Throughout the country one may find persons whose name also happens to be Dorje/Dorji, for example, spelling their name either way and occasionally both ways from time to time. It can also be noted that the third King and the Prime Minister had the same first name, the basic form of which (to the author's knowledge) is Jigme. But Jigmi is also often used, and Jigmie, the spelling of the Prime Minister's name, was apparently adopted deliberately to be distinguished from the King.

PROLOGUE

In the summer of 1989, in the kingdom of Bhutan in the Eastern Himalayas, two hundred Bhutanese citizens gathered late one afternoon to await the arrival of a 74-year-old Canadian Jesuit priest. When Father William Mackey arrived, in traditional Bhutanese costume of rich, hand-woven fabric, the Royal Bhutan Army pipe band — unique in their dress and music — piped him into the compound.

Father Mackey made his way from the gate to the hall, chatting and waving as well-wishers, some of whom had known him for forty years, came forward to drape ceremonial white silk scarves around his neck. He was vibrant and good-looking: lean and fit, lively in spirit, mind and body, and only his white hair betrayed his age.

At the steps of the hall, surrounded by foreign dignitaries, friends and former students — among them teachers, businessmen, government ministers — Father Mackey paused for photographers. Then he led the procession into the hall and a night-long party — his "Platinum Jubilee Birthday Celebration." Father Mackey, who was 75 by Bhutanese reckoning, had already received the two highest, and most rare, official honours that Bhutan could award him: the Druk Zhung Thuksey medal and Bhutanese citizenship. But in human terms, the unprecedented outpouring of sentiment by Bhutanese of all walks of life at this August celebration was the clearest evidence of Bhutan's appreciation of the pioneering priest from Canada.

Twenty-six years before, expelled from his beloved Darjeeling hills after seventeen years, Father Mackey had waited on the hot Indian plain for word that he could enter Bhutan. This small mountain kingdom —

Druk Yul, to the Bhutanese — mysterious, reclusive and closed to the outside world, wanted a Jesuit Father to establish its first high school. Once within this Land of the Dragon, sandwiched between Tibet and northeast India, Father Mackey took his mandate to the remote Eastern region of the country, hiking a dusty mountain trail to the imposing fortress of Tashigang Dzong.

There he stepped back centuries and entered what was essentially a feudal society. During the next two decades, the 1960s and '70s, while living among the people of Bhutan, Father Mackey established and ran three high schools, almost single-handedly laying the foundations for the development of modern education in Bhutan. His was a simple life of hard work and fun, some sadness and a great deal of laughter.

Back in Canada, Father Mackey was called a missionary. But not in Bhutan. The official religion of Bhutan, practised by the majority of the population, is Tibetan Buddhism, though the Hinduism of the ethnic Nepali people in the southern border area of the country is respected. But the Bhutanese tolerate no conversion efforts by any religion, making their acceptance, and indeed adoration, of a Jesuit priest all the more remarkable.

Father Mackey was never an ordinary missionary. Still in Bhutan today, he remains comfortable with not having converted a single Bhutanese to Catholicism, and admits that he has been profoundly influenced by Buddhism: "Bhutan has taught me how to pray." Whether it was the mix of people he encountered in and around his Irish Montreal neighbourhood, his upbringing in a Catholic-Protestant home, his time in French-Canadian Jesuit institutions or what he learned later, from people in his adopted homes, Father Mackey's spiritual outlook is broad, even universal.

His work, personality and spirituality have won him heroic status in Bhutan, where he is unique as a subject of love and respect. "Travelling with him in the capital," a Canadian reported in the 1980s, "through the villages or [across the main interior road] of the country, he is greeted with warmth and laughter by shopkeepers, border guards, immigration officers, teachers, government officials and cabinet ministers." But Father Mackey's name is also known to people who never attended any of his schools, who never went to school at all, and who may have never even seen him.

Having earned the acceptance of the people, Father Mackey became the most important figure in bringing secular education from its bare existence in the early 1960s — a handful of primary schools — to its highly respectable situation today, with some 64,000 students enrolled in 143 primary schools (plus ninety-two one-room community schools), seventeen junior high schools, eight high schools, two teacher-training institutes, two technical schools and a college. As one observer put it: "No other country has experienced such an education explosion: Bhutan has done in 25 years what other countries have taken centuries to accomplish."

Father William Mackey, Canadian Jesuit, is at the heart of this transformation. For almost five decades he has lived far away from his native land, contributing to each of his adopted communities, but also gaining immeasurably from them. His treasures include a wealth of stories that are the basis for this book.

1/

The kingdom of Bhutan lies between India and Tibet (China). Roughly the size of Switzerland, it measures 300 kilometres east to west and 175 kilometres north to south. Located in the Eastern Himalayas, east of Nepal and north of Bangladesh, it is entirely mountainous except for a sliver of sub-continental plain along its southern border. Mountain chains running north-south define the kingdom's geography and demographics.

This is not a book of anthropology and the use of difficult, academic and foreign words will be kept to a minimum. However, an occasional paragraph of solid background will help the reader appreciate the stories better. On these occasions, the aim is for accuracy, while keeping things simple and general (not an easy balance to strike).

Today, Bhutan's population of about 600,000 comprises two main groups, generally speaking — the Drukpa, people traditionally of the interior, and the Lhotsampa, those of the southern border area. These latter are of Nepali origin and arrived in Bhutan from the end of the 19th Century. The Drukpa, of Mongoloid stock, are made up of three main linguistic groups: from Western Bhutan, the Ngalong, who speak Dzongkha; from Eastern Bhutan, the Sharchopa, who speak Tsangla; and from Central Bhutan, the people of Tongsa, Bumthang and Khyeng.

The people of the western and central interior are descended from Tibetans who moved into Bhutan from the 7th Century. Historians and cultural anthropologists are still studying the origins of the much more numerous Sharchopas of Eastern Bhutan, but they may have arrived much earlier, perhaps from eastern Tibet. Except for a significant number of Hindus in the south, the Bhutanese are Buddhists, following one or other of the Tibetan schools.

Prior to 1960, which marks its emergence, Bhutan remained isolated from most of the world. Administratively, it functioned as it had for three hundred years — or for countless centuries, as far as the peasant farmers were concerned. Bhutan gave up its policy of isolation in 1959, and created its first five-year plan for development in 1961.

These changes came under King Jigme Dorji Wangchuck, who ascended the throne in 1952. His partner in these early efforts was his Prime Minister, Jigmie Palden Dorji (commonly called Jigmie Dorji), who was also his wife's brother. In 1959-60, they undertook to build the first roads into the interior of Bhutan.

Until this time, except for high-priority helicopter flights by senior government officials, people travelled over mountain trails. The main route to the western Bhutan centres of Ha, Paro and Thimphu was a mule track that ran north from Samtse. Travellers from the south destined for Thimphu would trek north to Ha, then east to Paro and then on to Thimphu. Similar tracks from India followed river valleys to other centres further east, among them Tashigang, the most easterly centre.

The first road in Western Bhutan ran from Phuntsholing to Thimphu, and in Eastern Bhutan from Samdrup Jongkhar to Tashigang. Building them posed a monumental challenge. The mountains of Bhutan provided a base that varied from sand and shifting scree to solid rock. The slopes to be traversed — those that were not vertical cliffs — were covered with vegetation ranging from tropical jungle to thick temperate forest.

The Bhutanese leaders launched another major initiative in 1963, when they undertook to establish the country's first high school. Up to this time, although monastic schools had existed for centuries, Bhutan's secular education system consisted of only primary schools (about twenty in 1963). Students with the means (perhaps government support), the qualifications and the desire to attain higher education had to leave the country to pursue this goal. Most attended schools in the Darjeeling district of northern India and some of the most respected of these schools were run by Jesuits — members of the Society of Jesus, a Catholic religious order known for its quality work in education.

The Bhutanese government wanted a first-rate high school, and they wanted a Jesuit to establish and run it. When Prime Minister Jigmie Dorji approached the Jesuit Superior, Father Jim McCabe, his timing was perfect. One of the Jesuits' most outstanding educators, Father William Mackey, was being expelled from Darjeeling.

The prime minister had met this Canadian Jesuit, knew his exemplary work, and now invited him to Bhutan to establish its first high school. While not a total consolation for having to leave a district whose people he loved, and in which he had served seventeen years, this was just the challenge Father Mackey had been preparing for all his life.

Besides having a cross-cultural Canadian background, the forty-seven-year-old Jesuit had come to know something of the Bhutanese. South of Darjeeling, in the town of Kurseong, he had taught a few Bhutanese boarders, most of them from south-western Bhutan. Later, in Darjeeling itself, he'd taught Bhutanese students from the interior, and worked with yet another group of boys from the aristocracy, including branches of the royal family.

Father Mackey had no trouble deciding to go to Bhutan.

Getting there, however, would not be so easy. Indian administration and the ruggedness of the terrain posed something of a challenge. But at least he did not have to experience travel quite as rough as some of his students had. Bhutanese students from the southern border areas travelled easily through Bengal to get to Kalimpong, Kurseong or Darjeeling, but students from the interior of Bhutan had to cut across the western end of the country.

This was a rigorous trip, especially at the beginning of the school year in late winter. As there were no roads into the interior of Bhutan prior to the 1960s, people travelled by foot or on horseback or, in the case of the high northern regions, perhaps on yaks. Horses, donkeys, mules and yaks were used to transport goods.

Darjeeling-bound students from Bhutan's interior would gather in Paro. They would then hike over the mountains that formed the west side of the Paro valley, usually crossing the 3,800 metre pass, Chelela, to the next major valley and its principal community, Ha.

If travellers — merchants, for example — were bound for the plains of India, they would turn south at this point and follow the valleys to the border towns of Samtse or Sibsu. Students heading for Darjeeling, however, would proceed over the mountains, first west into the nub of Tibet that extends along the north-western border of Bhutan, and then to Gangtok, Sikkim, crossing the West Bengal border to Pedong, and continuing on south-west to Kalimpong.

The trip over snow-covered passes and trails was a gruelling one that took a week, ten days, even two weeks if the weather was bad. The upper-class students must have been a fine-looking bunch by the time they reached Bhutan House in Kalimpong. There they would clean up and get road transport west into Darjeeling. Father Mackey would be able to travel into Bhutan by road, albeit new and rough. But he faced a second major hurdle. The mountain kingdom, while sovereign, had arrangements with India — its giant neighbour and, in many ways, benefactor — that included Indian involvement in Bhutan's relations with the outside world. This extended to India's partial control over foreigners entering the kingdom. They required specific permits to pass through the restricted area of India that bordered Bhutan on the south.

Given that Father Mackey had just been expelled from Darjeeling, this permission was not automatically forthcoming. While he had every expectation that his permit would be issued, as the official application came from the Bhutanese prime minister, this would take some time and diplomacy.

While waiting for his permit, Father Mackey was exiled to Jamshedpur in Bihar state. He left Darjeeling at the end of June 1963, and took up a temporary position as Secretary to Bishop Picachy of Jamshedpur. During the next few months, he not only cleaned up the Bishop's correspondence and book-keeping, but also worked with Mother Teresa of Calcutta.

Father Mackey picked up his travel permit in Calcutta on October 14th. On his way to Bhutan, he stopped in Darjeeling and met up with Father McCabe, the Jesuit Superior who would initially accompany him. At dawn on the 17th, the two Jesuits set out to meet a Bhutan government jeep just outside Darjeeling. Twelve hours later, at what seemed an obscure spot in the dark, the guide pulled over and said, "We're here."

The town of Phuntsholing, which was to grow into the financial and commercial centre of Bhutan, consisted of a few simple shops and some government buildings. It served as the supply point for goods from India — diesel fuel, petrol, non-perishable food, basic hardware and household supplies — mostly for the road-building project.

In this part of the world, where Western technology was not readily available, the model for road-building was Indian — a basic, labour-intensive method using dynamite, perhaps a bulldozer and, most importantly, hundreds and hundreds of labourers. It was a process not unknown to Father Mackey, but as they proceeded north he marvelled at the magnitude of the job and the raw reality of cutting the first road through virgin mountain terrain.

The road north began to climb from the town itself, winding up through the surrounding forest. The first stretch was rough but not problematic. But after about twenty kilometres, the road traverses a very steep slope with less forest cover. This area was, and still is, very prone to rock and mud slides.

The jeep carrying the two Jesuits proceeded slowly along this section through the rain, following a zigzag pattern up the mountain side. They soon met their first "slip," a minor landslide that delayed them an hour while workers cleared it. But a little further, they encountered another, more serious blockage: a slide of rock and mud had carried away part of the road. This would take many hours to rectify.

Fortunately, three kilometres further, beyond the slide, the travellers learned, a south-bound government jeep sat blocked. Now Father Mackey had his first experience of "trans-shipping." The Jesuits scrambled over the rubble that blocked the road and hiked up to the other jeep. The people from that jeep brought their things down the road. Both jeeps had government drivers, and they remained with their own vehicles. Each group of people got into the other's jeep with their baggage, the drivers turned around and the travellers continued their journeys.

A few hours up the road, near the village of Gedu, the Jesuits had to trans-ship again. Finally they reached Chhatselhakha, and a guest house reserved for the Royal Family and high officials. It was well-outfitted and supplied with food, and there they stayed overnight.

The next day's travelling was similar in some ways, different in others. The Jesuits were now well into the river valley that took them north. They were at a considerable altitude, over 2,000 metres, on the west side, travelling through lush forest with a magnificent view of the valley. They journeyed north and gradually downward to the river, which they crossed on a wooden bridge, then began climbing the valley's east side.

The road was very rough, having been carved from the rock with dynamite, bulldozers and hand labour, but the Jesuits lost less time to stoppages than the day before. They marvelled at a stretch of road cut into a cliff face, and then, emerging from the mist that shrouded parts of the valley, reached peak elevation around 3,000 metres, where the day grew bright and warm.

The Jesuits descended again to the river, gradually at first, and then abruptly, through a series of switch-backs. Now they stayed close to the river. They reached a place called Chhuzom or The Confluence, where the Pachhu (*chhu* being river) running down the Paro Valley joins the Wangchhu, which comes down past Thimphu and which they had been roughly following since Gedu.

They crossed the Wangchhu on a Bailey bridge immediately below the confluence, and headed west towards the Paro Valley. Here the altitude and afternoon sun made for a pleasant drive. The Jesuits reached the town of Paro at five o'clock, and dined that evening with the Prime Minister. They would be guests of the Dorji family, who had property in Paro.

The next day, after a meeting with the Prime Minister and senior education officials, the Jesuits toured Paro, which had recently become an administrative centre. In 1952-53, when Bhutanese leaders began modernizing the country, they had moved the seat of central power from Punakha to Tashichoedzong ("the fortress of the auspicious religion"), which is the great *dzong* or fortress in Thimphu, still the capital of the country today.

When development activities began in the early 1960s, however, they observed that Thimphu lacked the facilities to accommodate them. The leaders also wondered whether such activities, largely secular and involving strangers from outside, should be based near Tashichoedzong. It was not only the seat of government but also the summer headquarters for the Monk Body, and as such a very sacred place.

They decided to administer development from Paro, a significant historical site with its own *dzong*, Rinpung Dzong, and — because of its layout and somewhat lower elevation — a slightly more hospitable climate than Thimphu.

Besides the *dzong*, Paro had administrative offices for education, agriculture, health and road construction. There was a small primary school, offering the first four or five years of schooling, in English. There were also a few small shops selling simple items like soap, pots and pans, matches, liquor, cloth and yarn, all from India. As Father Mackey would soon learn, this was one of the few towns in Bhutan with any commercial centre.

Next day, the Jesuits visited Thimphu, a three-hour drive on a rough dusty road. It did not look much like a capital city. The former Tashichoedzong had been torn down and a new one was being built. Part of the old *dzong* remained and would be incorporated into the new construction.

Father Mackey was intrigued by the scene. The immense *dzong*, ranging from three to more than five storeys in height, would be built in traditional style using hand-hewn wooden beams and stone, assembled and held together by traditional, medieval means. Across the river, a little upstream from the *dzong*, a small hospital and a primary school shared a U-shaped building. Back on the way to Paro lay an army cantonment. There was little else.

The final stop on the tour was Dechenchoeling, a few kilometres up river beyond Thimphu, where the Royal Palace was located. The King was there, but had recently suffered a heart attack and was still not well. The Jesuits admired the Palace from the roadway, then started back the way they'd come, reaching Paro at six that evening.

The visit wound up the next day and Father Mackey had his basic mandate. The Bhutanese wanted a high school comparable to the better schools in Darjeeling. It would be in Eastern Bhutan, but they hadn't decided precisely where to situate it. Father Mackey had little knowledge of the geography of Bhutan, much less the demographics and culture. But he would go where they sent him and get the job done. His entire life, after all, had prepared him to do exactly that.

2/

William Joseph Mackey has spent his life straddling dualities. In India, where he lived for seventeen years, these included Bengali-Nepali and Hinduism-Catholicism. In the kingdom of Bhutan, his home for the past three decades, the Jesuit priest added Drukpa-Nepali, Drukpa-Sharchopa and Buddhism-Catholicism. But this pattern began much further back, when as a boy William Mackey confronted those quintessentially Canadian dichotomies — French-English and Catholic-Protestant.

Born in Montreal on August 19, 1915, "Billy" Mackey was the son of first-generation immigrants. His mother, Kitty Murphy — raised as an Irish Catholic — trained as a teacher and moved to England as a young woman. His father, Herbert Mackey, was a Protestant of Irish descent, though his family had lived in England for several generations.

The two met in a London bakery and moved to Canada after Herbert, who was athletic and solidly built, answered an advertisement for farm hands. A farmer in Danville, Quebec, paid his passage and Herbert worked for him for two years. Then he got a job as a motorman or streetcar driver in Montreal. Over the years, he worked his way up to inspector and supervisor of traffic, until a bad leg forced an early retirement.

Kitty Murphy followed Herbert to Canada, working first in a convent in Richmond, Quebec, then on a farm at Melbourne, a half-hour buggy ride away, which happened to be owned by a family also named Murphy. Herbert converted to Catholicism and married Kitty in Richmond in 1910. Over the next several years, Kitty bore seven children, only four of whom survived childhood. Billy came third after sister Teresa (Tess) and brother James (Jim), and was followed by sister Isabel (Bella). The Mackeys lived in the district of St. Henry. It boasted a rich mix of people — many Irish Catholics, but French and Italians, and English Protestants as well. Each community kept to itself, and animosities were confined to playing fields, courts and rinks, where rivalries thrived.

For these lower-middle-class or working-class people, the home was the focal point for activity. Entertainment consisted largely of Saturday night gatherings at the home of one family or another. Adults played card games like euchre, at which Herbert Mackey excelled. There was singing, friendly conversation and plenty of "horsing around," as Father Mackey now describes it. Nobody drank much — just the occasional glass of Molson's beer.

The younger people had dance parties, which again tended to be dry. As a boy, Billy Mackey watched and enjoyed these activities from the sidelines, but when his sister's bridge club was short of players he could be conscripted, lured by the prospect of tasty snacks.

The Mackey home life, while not without the occasional squabble, was a model of activity, love and warmth. Herbert's salary from the tramways supported the family adequately, and Kitty was good at the sewing machine and made many of the family's clothes. The family had to be careful about money, but managed occasionally to visit an amusement park or go for a day's fishing.

Both parents, conscientious in their traditional roles, nurtured two main aspects of Billy's future life. Kitty used her teaching background in helping the children with their school work. And while Herbert did not have Kitty's formal education, he did have broad interests and a love of good books. Even as a child, Billy would read the books his father brought home from the library.

That Billy became a Jesuit priest suggests the influence of his Catholic mother. But while he was raised as a Catholic, he credits the religious mix at home, his father being essentially Protestant, with engendering the broad religious views he would hold in later life. The variety of religious, ethnic and language groups outside the home also played a part. Catholics and Protestants each felt they were travelling the one true path to salvation, and that members of the other group were destined for hell. The French-English division could get heated, too. But most differences were acted out and dissipated in neighbourhood sports.

* * *

As a boy, Billy Mackey devoted himself completely to "boy" things like scouting and sports — especially sports, at which he excelled. He began playing the North American Indian game of lacrosse while at primary school, where lacrosse sticks sold for seventy-five cents each. He stayed with lacrosse on into high school and played for the St. Henry Shamrocks, a senior community team. A good runner, with good speed, he played centre forward and became a leading scorer. In 1932, before he joined the Jesuits, he captained the team that cleaned up the senior lacrosse league in Montreal, then went on to become provincial and national champions.

Billy's main sport, however, was ice hockey. Starting in bantam league, he played throughout his school years at the various levels organized by the Quebec Hockey Association. Early on, he played mostly forward, but in high school he became a defenceman. He played for championship teams in both junior and senior high school leagues, and played for Loyola College in the juvenile league.

For the Montreal Junior Canadiens, Billy Mackey was a prospect. Every once in a while a scout would slip him and other promising players a bit of cash, or perhaps pieces of hockey equipment — shin pads, hockey pants, sweaters. College students, older than Billy, played at the junior level in the Montreal Forum, and occasionally Billy would be called up to fill a vacant spot. It was a big thing to play in the Forum.

If he had stayed with hockey, probably he would have played many more games there. He was one of the leading scorers at the juvenile level, even though he played defence. He was fast and known for his rushes down the ice. Two or three times a game he'd catch a pass, break away and score. Nobody could catch him.

*   *   *

Young Billy Mackey received a Catholic primary education — first at St. Michael's and then at St. Thomas Aquinas. Among his early teachers, he remembers a Mr. Kelly, who imparted a love of mathematics. The teacher's comic approach to discipline also rubbed off on the young teacher-to-be. Mr. Kelly carried a wooden stick and when he assigned a piece of work, he'd say, "Hmm, Quebec is noted for its lumber . . . I'm getting the medicine out." He'd take out a pen knife and scrape the stick a bit. And if you weren't minding your Ps and Qs, "Now watch out!"

Then, as Father Mackey put it, "Snap! He'd give you one sharp little crack. Nothing serious."

Had Billy left school after St. Thomas Aquinas, his friends would have considered him decently educated. Most dropped out after primary school and went to work. But, being a good student with parents who believed strongly in education, Billy went on to high school — one of six or seven from a class of thirty-five. Of those who made the transition, a high percentage went on to college.

Not being well-off financially, Billy tried for a scholarship. He wrote English and maths exams for a full day at Loyola College — which included a high school — and won a half scholarship: fifty dollars towards the year's tuition, a fair sum of money in those days. So began his life-long association with the name Loyola.

A bright young man, Billy Mackey stayed in the top ten of his class. He had little problem with maths, science, history, English and even Latin and Greek, though he was weak in French. In sports, he captained hockey and football teams. And in the cadet corps, which was compulsory, he found a niche and did well. First he became a signaller, and then, at artillery camp in Petawawa, a range finder.

He understood the mathematical principles involved and quickly developed the technical skill required to find the range of prospective artillery targets. He carried his equipment around like a golfer carries his clubs and he learned how to camouflage his instrument set-up. Best of all, for the youth wanting to avoid rifle drill and the slogging of the foot-soldiers, he got to ride around with the officers in a jeep. This specialization carried on through his fourth year of high school and the following summer. The training involved, more advanced than that which the other cadets got, helped get Billy promoted to captain of his corps.

The two-week cadet camps were held in late June, kicking off a busy summer vacation. The Murphys for whom Kitty had worked many years before had remained family friends, and Billy had often stayed on the farm at Melbourne, working with the animals and machinery. Once in high school, however, Billy spent most of each summer working at one job or another, and seldom managed to visit the farm.

Billy got his first summer job in 1927, when he was still in primary school. His father mentioned a man who owned a newspaper stand and needed people to deliver newspapers. Billy piped up, "Hey, I'll do that!" And so went to work. Mornings he would sell *The Gazette* at the corner of Victoria and Sherbrooke. Afternoons, he would deliver *The Montreal Star* to homes in Westmount. Then he'd walk down the hill to St. Henry, a satisfied working man. He earned ten dollars a week — fantastic money for such a young fellow.

The next summer, Billy landed the dream job of all young teenagers: soda jerk at Tremblay's Drug Store, which was situated downtown on St. Catherine Street opposite Simpson's department store. His first day at work, the owner said: "Now, one rule here is: you take and eat as much as you like." For three days, Billy stuffed himself with sundaes and ice cream sodas — then hardly touched ice cream for the rest of the summer.

Billy moved up the ladder in the restaurant business the next summer, when he worked at Murray's Sandwich Shop near the Lowe's theatre. Here he did everything from handing out menus and order slips to running messages and filling in for the cashier. He enjoyed the variety and extra responsibility.

The following summer, Billy became an usher at the Seville Theatre near the Forum. Legally, he was too young, but he was big for his age, five foot nine or ten, and showed he could handle the job. The days were long, from eleven in the morning until eleven at night. But Billy got time off for meals and filled in at the door when the ticket taker was on supper break. Billy enjoyed working with people and learned some common psychology as he dealt with unpleasant complainers and smart-alecks as well as those who needed help.

The summer before his final year, Billy worked as a waiter in the prestigious Seigneury Club at Montebello, where his sister Tess was secretary. He acquitted himself well, being pleasant and conscientious, and quite mature for just turning sixteen.

*　*　*

While his work experience taught Billy how to deal with people, Loyola College prepared him for the ministry in other ways. He owed his ability to give sermons, for example, to high-school elocution classes during which, in his last year, he had to give impromptu speeches to an auditorium full of students. A boy's name would be called out and, on his way up to the stage, a teacher would give him a topic on which he would have to speak for five minutes.

Loyola was a Jesuit institution with a faculty and staff comprising both ordained members of the order and those not yet ordained (called "scholastics"). Billy Mackey was particularly inspired by a Father McInerney who taught English literature. A scholastic in his thirties, Father McInerney was a great speaker and actor, but also a sickly man who had two club feet and wore special boots. He impressed Billy with his love of teaching, his patience, his kindness and his devotion to his religion.

Most scholastics were younger than Father McInerney. Though they were called "Father," they were not yet ordained, and were teaching for three years as part of their training and preparation for the priesthood. Boys could talk easily to the scholastics, who were not only closer in age but didn't have to be treated with as much reverence as a priest. The scholastics tended to be enthusiastic teachers who knew their subjects.

Many were also fine athletes, which appealed to Billy Mackey. The man he saw wearing a cassock in the classroom might be coaching hockey a few hours later. Sometimes a young Jesuit would come back after his ordination and say Mass for the boys. That was particularly impressive, and it helped attract young Billy to the order.

All through his childhood, Billy Mackey had also been in contact with priests not directly involved with his schooling. Father Tom Heffernan, Father Martin Reid and Father Wilf O'Kane had been parish priests in St. Thomas Aquinas parish. Billy had served Mass for Father Reid and when he'd come into the parish church early on cold winter mornings for the seven o'clock Mass he'd find Father Reid walking up and down the aisle, praying and meditating. Billy admired the priest's thoughtful character, but it was the holiness that he saw in the man that most impressed him.

By the time Billy Mackey entered his third year of high school, he was considering joining not just the priesthood, but the Jesuits. He had already been involved in the Sodality, a Jesuit social and service group whose members were interested in living a religious life beyond Sunday church. And at the beginning of each high school year, Billy attended a three-day retreat during which priests led discussions on future vocations.

Yet, if they knew of Billy's ponderings, they exerted no overt influence. The only other option Billy wished to consider was hockey. He not only loved the game, but had the talent required for a professional career, perhaps with even the Montreal Canadiens. In the end, the hockey-playing ability of the scholastics may have tipped the balance. Why couldn't he become a priest and still play hockey?

By 1931, when he attended the retreat at the beginning of his fourth and final year of high school, Billy Mackey knew he wanted to be a Jesuit. This hadn't come to him like a bolt out of the blue, but just seemed natural and obvious. He'd grown into it through influences that were a natural part of his life.

Billy had spoken of his desire to be a priest, and particularly a Jesuit, with his former parish priest, Father Reid, who told him: "Billy, go right ahead. You go where you like. There's no worry about whether you join the Society or the secular clergy under the Bishop. You go where God is calling you. You'll do well no matter where you go."

At the retreat, Billy approached Father McInerney and told him he wanted to join the Society of Jesus. The Jesuit told him to think over the other aspects of his life, that the decision involved his interests and not just his desire. Billy mentioned his love of sports, and the priest counselled further consideration. Billy asked some practical questions about joining, and Father McInerney explained that a candidate was usually interviewed by a number of Jesuits before being admitted into the novitiate. He also said that Billy should meet the head of the English-speaking Jesuits, the Provincial, and offered to arrange this when an opportunity arose.

The following spring, when the Provincial visited the school from Toronto, he arranged a meeting. When Billy arrived and sat down, the Provincial, Father Hingston, handed him a Latin breviary and asked if he could translate it. Billy, who was reasonably competent for a high school boy, opened the breviary and found it easier to translate than Cicero's speeches or stories of Caesar's Gallic wars. The priest seemed pleased, and then asked about Billy's Greek. Billy said it wasn't as good as his Latin, but he guessed it was okay.

Billy had been asked to bring a record of his high school marks. The latest complete set included four or five prizes in various subjects, but Billy excelled in maths. His overall average was very high. The Provincial said he would proceed, but that Billy would have to have interviews with other Jesuits.

A month or so later, on a Saturday afternoon, Billy went to Loyola College and was interviewed by four Jesuits, one after another. He knew all four, and two from the high school he knew very well. Among other things, they asked Billy if he understood the three Jesuit vows of poverty, chastity and obedience. Could he live without belongings? Could he live without marriage? Could he do whatever he was told? Billy answered in his natural, unaffected way. When the last interview was over, Father McInerney told him: "You'll hear from us."

Shortly after he graduated from high school, Billy received a letter from Toronto, from the Society of Jesus. He had been accepted. He should present himself at the novitiate in Guelph, Ontario, on the fourteenth of August. It mentioned a short list of things he should bring with him.

By this time, June of 1932, Billy's mother was deathly ill. She had contracted Spanish influenza many years before and this had badly affected her heart. She was in St. Mary's Hospital, about ten minutes walk from the Mackey home on Souvenir. Billy had already shown her his graduation certificate and the prizes he had won. Now, with his letter of acceptance, he went straight to the hospital with his father and sister and showed it to his mother. Her son was going to be a Jesuit priest. It was a great consolation to her as she lay on her death bed. A few days later, on June 24th, 1932, Kitty Mackey died.

The wake was held in the Mackey home and lasted three days. Billy was upset by his mother's death, but he also felt relieved that her suffering was over, and that she'd gone to heaven. After the wake came the Mass and then interment at the cemetery. When the Mackeys returned home, they found that the Protestant family from across the street had come in, cleaned the house from top to bottom, and now invited them for dinner.

3/

On the thirteenth of August 1932, six days before he turned seventeen, Bill Mackey caught the evening train at Windsor Station. He was bound for Guelph, Ontario, where the Society of Jesus had its St. Stanlislaus Novitiate. There, on the outskirts of town, Bill would spend the next four years, living in an old farm house that had been converted to house sixty young Jesuits.

The first two years, called the Novitiate, focused on spiritual training. The intention was to get the young Jesuit well-grounded and to determine as early as possible if he was suited to a spiritual life. The main feature of this training was a thirty-day retreat, which Bill took that first October: thirty days of what the Jesuits call "the Spiritual Exercises" consisting of a guided series of instruction, prayer and meditation. These exercises, common to Jesuits the world over, were written by Ignatius Loyola, who founded the Jesuit order, the Society of Jesus, in 1534.

The key exercises start from the premise that man is created to love, praise and serve God, and thereby save his soul. Novices meditate on developing talents received from God; and also on the kingdom of God, with Christ as a king with a plan for salvation, and Christians as followers who help in carrying out God's plan. Then come the three main meditations — the first on the opposing strategies of God and the devil, the second on approaches to dealing with one's failings, the third on degrees of humility and love of God. The final meditation, on obtaining divine love, focuses on a prayer that begins: "Take and receive, oh Lord, all my liberty."

The training of the whole first year is meant to help an individual decide whether he wants to be a Jesuit. It stresses the pros, cons and difficulties, as the Society of Jesus is not interested in recruiting individuals who are not suited and cannot fulfill their commitment.

Besides the main retreat, novices undertook a variety of other exercises or "experiments." Bill worked in the tailor shop, helped on the farm (where he felt much at home), taught catechism in nearby schools and worked in the kitchen with the lay brothers. He also served as The Bell Ringer, who not only rang bells but cleaned all the toilets. This training was meant to strengthen the novices' humility and respect for physical labour. It stressed servitude and thinking less of one's self.

One of the most interesting experiments was the "pilgrimage." The novice would set out on foot on a two-week journey, with daily destinations provided in a set of envelopes without a cent in his pocket. From one day to the next, he didn't know what would happen, but had to let Providence take care of him.

Each morning, novices would spend half an hour reading prescribed spiritual texts like those of Rodriguez, the Portuguese Jesuit author. They also attended some formal classes, including one a day in Latin or Greek, especially for those who hadn't had them before. Bill, though a young novice with only high school, had Latin and Greek already, and he was called upon in his second year to teach these classic languages to first-year novices.

As a "professor" of Latin and Greek, he had college graduates and other young Jesuits senior to himself as his students. Some of these young men knew more about the classical languages than he did and didn't have to concentrate. This led to pranks and smart-alecky remarks that would have unnerved most young men. Bill Mackey took them in good humour and learned from his mistakes.

Also in his second year, Bill Mackey was made beadle. The beadle was a novice who acted as a spokesman or liaison between the novices and the authorities. He was a kind of "head Jesuit" at this level, even though he was young compared to many of the others.

At the end of each year's programme the novices enjoyed a proper holiday, called "villa," at a place on the nearby Speed River that was also called "the villa." It was just another old farm house crowded with young men sleeping dormitory-style. But they filled their days with swimming, baseball, volleyball, picnics, walks and visits into Guelph, away from the scrutiny of the senior Jesuits. This break lasted three weeks, and was followed by the annual eight-day retreat which ended with the Feast of

St. Ignatius on the 31st of July. Special summer courses occupied the month of August.

Two years after joining the Jesuits, on August 15, 1934, the Feast of Our Lady's Assumption, Bill Mackey completed his Novitiate and took his first vows. Now he could add S.J., for Society of Jesus, after his name.

His enjoyment of this signal event was muted, however, because he'd recently developed a large and extremely painful carbuncle on the calf of his leg. He ended up hobbling down the aisle of the chapel on crutches. A dozen or so novices were taking their vows that day and they occupied the first two rows of the Novitiate chapel. Bill sat in the front row with his leg stretched out in front of him. Each of the others got up, went to the altar, knelt down and pronounced his vows, and then received communion. There was no question of Bill kneeling. He was probably the only novice in Guelph to say his vows sitting down.

At Guelph, after the spiritual grounding of the two-year Novitiate came the Juniorate. This also lasted two years, but included more formal academic studies concentrating on English and the classics. The English course, designed to produce men who could communicate well, included not only literature but a lot of writing and speaking. The study of Greek and Latin occupied less of the programme but also focused on reading and writing. The Greek would be used for the study of scriptures. But Latin was particularly important, as it was still the working language of the Catholic Church.

Even though he was from Montreal, Bill had lived in an English-speaking neighbourhood and taken all his schooling in English. He was as weak in French as he was strong in the classics. So when a summer course in French was provided at Guelph, he was signed up for it. Unfortunately, the August scheduling of the course conflicted with harvest time at the Jesuits' nearby farm, where crops like oats, hay and fruit had to be taken in.

With his love of the outdoors and experience at the Murphy farm, Bill was quick to volunteer for the harvest with a fellow "junior." The Jesuit instructor who had come up from Loyola College was furious, as the two young men could ill afford to miss French class for two or three days at a time. But at the farm, Bill was readily embraced as his experience and strength made him especially useful. He could drive a team of horses and operate farm equipment, like the horse rake, used for gathering hay. His tan and his muscles developed better than his French that summer.

The studies at Guelph amounted to a very sound university arts programme with a major in English. Bill passed his exams with no difficulty. His successful completion of the Juniorate provided him with part of the requirements of a Bachelor of Arts degree that he would receive a few years later.

* * *

In 1936, following his annual retreat, Bill went to Toronto. He would spend his next three years at Christi Regis College in the old Loretto Abbey at 403 Wellington Street, opposite the railway yards, near the Willard chocolate and Salada tea factories. At "403," Bill, now in his early twenties, would study philosophy. When winter came, he learned why his dorm on the third floor was called Eskimo Flat. The huge building was impossible to heat, especially with restricted funding, as the cold wind blew off nearby Lake Ontario.

Now the programme consisted of pure philosophy — four classes a day and a lot of reading. Fortunately, the young Jesuits had Sundays and Thursdays off, as well as half days on Tuesdays and Saturdays. The scholastics, as they would be called until their ordination, were expected to use this time to pursue special interests related to their vocations. Bill gravitated towards teaching, and on Tuesdays and Thursdays he caught a streetcar to an Italian parish north-west of Toronto where he taught catechism at one of the poorer schools. He found that he enjoyed being with the children, and had a talent for teaching.

In their "spare time," the scholastics were also expected to write a thesis focusing on history, literature, language, scripture, preaching, psychology or pedagogy. They had to present this in manuscript form at the end of the philosophy studies. The schedule gave them the opportunity to attend conferences or take courses at the University of Toronto. Bill Mackey decided to write about the Spiritual Exercises of St. Ignatius, the basis for retreats. He took every opportunity to study the history and analyze the essential components, to hear people preaching on the topic or to speak or preach on it himself.

Bill had not left hockey completely behind. And twice a week in winter, after the other scholastics went to bed, Bill and a couple of other enthusiasts would go out and flood the rink. They'd attach borrowed fire-department hoses to the hydrant just outside the gate. It was cold work but dear to the hearts of the hockey players. When they'd finished flooding, they'd go into the kitchen and make toast and hot chocolate. Finally, at eleven o'clock, they'd sneak up to bed.

Father Mackey credits this unacademic activity with keeping him sane. Even at Guelph, sports had kept him going when the training got tough. The summer holidays helped too. In June, when the academic year ended, the scholastics would head to Muskoka. The Jesuits owned a villa on St. Joseph's Lake called Stanley House. It was an old hotel situated on a lovely piece of land jutting out into the lake. Here the young men enjoyed three weeks of sun, swimming, canoeing, fishing and relaxing. They also made their annual retreat here before returning to Toronto and regular classes at "403."

By completing the philosophy programme in 1939, Bill Mackey earned two degrees. His juniorate studies, along with further work at Regis, qualified him for a BA (summa cum laude) from University of Montreal. He also received a Licentiate in Philosophy from Gregorian College, the main Jesuit college in Rome.

The next step in the long process of becoming a Jesuit priest was called Regency. This was a period of teaching, normally for three years. The scholastics could be sent to any of about seven Jesuit colleges in Canada, and Bill was surprised — and a little dismayed — to find himself posted to teach at Collège Jean-de-Brébeuf in Montreal. The Society often posted scholastics where they would be forced to learn the other official Canadian language, and Bill's lack of good French earned him a job back in his home town.

Brébeuf was a posh, French-language boys' school, and his main job would be teaching English to senior-high and college students. The school had embarked on a plan to modernize the teaching of English, and he had to find books appropriate to the new programme. Bill plunged into the research with enthusiasm, talking to other educators and scanning the market to see what was available.

He centred his teaching on literature, even when the objective was mastering grammar or other language basics. He believed strongly in good literature and the exercise of writing compositions. He also had his students stage English-language plays.

At the college level, the first- and second-year English courses were called *belles-lettres* and *rhetorique.* Father Mackey remembers teaching the latter to Charles Trudeau, brother of Canada's future prime minister, Pierre Trudeau. He describes Charles as "a good guy, but a wild guy." Some of his pranks were fun even for Bill as teacher. On one occasion he was on the high platform from which the teachers taught, reading a passage of Shakespeare to his class of fifty boys, when someone shouted, *"Mon Père!"* Bill looked up just in time to see a small object flying through the air towards him. He wasn't sure what it was, but he knew this gang. He deftly reached up, caught it and placed it directly into the front of his cassock. By the feel of the object he was pretty sure he knew what it was. He kept reading, barely missing a beat.

At the end of the class, Charles Trudeau approached him and asked, "Father, may we have our mouse back?"

"What do you want to do with it?"

"The next teacher is going to jump."

Bill conjured up the image of their next teacher, and returned the mouse to the boy.

As *Père préfet chez les petits*, Bill's responsibilities included organizing sports and other extra-curricular activities for boys under sixteen. His enthusiasm and athletic ability won the boys over completely. At twenty-four, he was still an excellent athlete, able to play baseball, basketball and Canadian football, and excelling at hockey and lacrosse. Many of the French-Canadians were amazed to see "*un Anglais*" who could play lacrosse better than they could. Bill coached most of these sports, and started a basketball team that won the league championship. He also skied and, while at Brébeuf, even tried the pole vault.

In years to come, Bill would earn fame with another sport he took up at Brébeuf: gymnastics. In high school, playing Canadian football, he had learned how to tumble, how to fall, how to hit the ground and roll so he wouldn't hurt himself. He'd enjoyed that and jumped at the chance to go further with gymnastics. A trained gymnast, a Major St-Pierre from La Palestre Nationale, came to Brébeuf and introduced horse work and some other aspects of gymnastics.

Bill was keen to learn and very fit. He took to it naturally and learned quickly. After working every day for a week or so with Major St-Pierre, Bill was doing somersaults, front-flips, back-flips and horse work. He was particularly good on the parallel bars. He then took the Brébeuf team to La Palestre Nationale and continued to learn. Later, he added his own twists to the standard gymnastics, using rings of fire and designing circus-style events.

Gymnastics would become a career-long involvement for Bill Mackey, but pole-vaulting was a different story. He got interested in the sport during his last year at Brébeuf. He got a pole, learned how to use it, and got the students started. One noon hour, while the boys were having lunch, Bill went into the gym and got out the pole to practice. He tied up his black soutane, or cassock, to free his legs and went to the end of the runway. The bar stood at eleven feet (3.35 metres).

Bill started down the runway, hit his speed, and swung upwards on the pole. He raised his legs and arched his body to clear the bar, but before he reached the top of his arc, the pole broke. With his legs and feet above him, his shoulders hit the runway and his two knees came in and cracked a couple of ribs. He lost consciousness. The school of 400 boarders had its own tailor shop, and the tailor happened to be standing in the doorway of the gym watching. He shouted for help and came running. Bill regained consciousness as people gathered around him. He was not seriously hurt, but he did have to endure a lot of pain through the summer holidays that ensued.

At Brébeuf, Bill enjoyed both the sports and his involvement with the boys. But he gained much, also, in other ways, and later said that his years at Brébeuf were his best preparation for India and Bhutan: learning to value a new culture and learning a new language taught him to fit into strange environments and situations.

Also, the boys at Brébeuf were a mixed lot and he had to deal with all kinds. He learned to look for reasons behind behaviour, and to help boys get the most out of themselves. Perhaps the most important lesson he learned was that there was good in even the worst kid.

In addition to three very successful years of teaching and learning, Bill Mackey also managed to earn a diploma in physical education from Collège Jean-de-Brébeuf, mainly by taking summer courses. But he particularly enjoyed his out-of-class work with the younger boys, *les petits*, organizing their sports and other activities. Many became his life-long friends. When visiting Canada, he has always tried to pay a visit to Brébeuf, which he thinks of as a kind of second home.

By 1942, when Bill Mackey finished his Regency, the Jesuit Province of Upper Canada had its own theologate in Toronto, offering a "short" programme in theology. However, Bill and a few other English-speaking scholastics who had been working in the French-Canadian Jesuit province were placed in Montreal's Collège de l'Immaculée-Conception, near the Parc Lafontaine. The "Immaculate" provided both short and long programmes, and Bill took the long, which the better students tended to take.

This meant not only that Bill carried on in French, but that he enjoyed a more international environment. It was wartime, and the Immaculate attracted many theologians (as scholastics at this level were called) who would otherwise have completed their studies in Europe. In his group of forty or fifty, in addition to students from French and English-speaking Canada, Bill found a number of Americans and Europeans, even a few German Jesuits who happened to be outside Germany when the war started.

This variety suited Bill just fine. It added to his experiences with people different from himself. He found that those who spent all their time in the "English house" in Toronto tended to have a narrower vision than he and his colleagues at the Immaculate. His vision was going to be stretched considerably in the years to come, but he feels that the early days of cultural and intellectual mixing back in Montreal helped prepare him.

At the Immaculate, Bill fit in well. He was not French, but he had been brought up in Montreal with some contact with the French community, and now he was half way through seven years of working in French at French institutions. This added to his natural sense of tolerance (perhaps with its own roots in the mixed religious setting of his home) and his easy-going sense of humour. And he was bright enough to understand some of the differences in the mentalities of the two cultures.

Even the simplest insights seemed to escape some of the most intelligent theologians. An old school chum, Ed (Butch) Sheridan, had done a shorter Regency because of his studies and previous teaching experience, and had now jumped a year ahead of Bill. He was acknowledged to be brilliant, had a reputation as an outstanding science teacher, and now showed promise of becoming a great theologian. But he was not at ease in the French milieu. One day he told Bill that he'd been invited to a meeting of the Loyola old boys: "I want to go, but I don't know if I can."

Bill was always going to the old boys' association at Brébeuf, so he said, "That's no problem. Just go in and ask the Rector and he'll give you permission."

Butch was skeptical but went ahead. With proper deference, he said, "Father, I would like to go to the old boys' meeting at Loyola."

The Rector seemed distracted. "Old boys? What's that? No."

Bill happened to be coming by just as Butch emerged from the Rector's office. He was fuming. "Dammit, he won't let me go!"

"What did you ask him?"

"If I could go to the old boys' meeting at Loyola."

"In English?" Bill asked incredulously. "Butch, you're crazy. You go back in and ask if you can attend the meeting of '*les anciens*.'"

"What do you mean?"

"*Les anciens*' — the old boys! Just get in there and say it in French."

Butch tried again. *"Mon Père,"* he began, and this time used *"les anciens"* instead of "old boys."

Understanding the question immediately, the Rector responded, *"Certainement, Mon Père."*

All Butch had to say to Bill when he came out was, "Bloody French."

Because of the war and the extra students, the Immaculate was filled beyond its lodging capacity. The Rector decided that the English Canadians would rent three small apartment buildings about twenty-minutes' walk from the theologate. This was a great coup for the scholastics because it meant that they escaped, in part, from the medieval European routine of the Immaculate.

Among the many awkward aspects of that routine was the strict locking of the doors at nine o'clock every night. This particularly annoyed the young scholastics, but other parts of the routine were irksome to the more senior Jesuits who were there studying or teaching. One was Father Bernard Lonergan. He, too, was a graduate of Loyola (where he had been known as "Brains Lonergan"), and was now on his way to becoming the greatest Canadian theologian in three hundred years.

Father Lonergan was one of the professors teaching Bill and the other scholastics, and he made a deal with the English Canadians. If they gave him a key to their apartment, he'd give them a key to the Immaculate. This allowed him to get away from the oppressive confines of the theologate, and allowed them to sneak in and out or to spring one of their "inside" colleagues to attend a hockey game.

The apartments also had unexpected effects on the academic success of the occupants. The English-speaking Canadians were considered less intellectual than their French-speaking colleagues inside the Immaculate. But the anglophones were doing better on their exams. This baffled the French Canadians, especially the authorities, and it took Father Lonergan to point out what was happening: "It's very simple," he said. "These guys are relaxing. You people can't relax. You're too medieval in your whole routine here."

He cited the rigid routine, the sombre surroundings, the incessant Latin, even a certain tenseness which gripped the institution. His observations helped bring in a few changes in the Immaculate. But he failed to change one of the more comic aspects of the Immaculate rules. The old French regime required that scholastics do everything in their soutanes. Even skiing. Bill and the other young Jesuits must have looked a sight. They would tuck the soutane up high enough to free their legs, leaving two flaps flying out behind. For hockey, the scholastics cheated a bit. Instead of wearing a full soutane, they would cut out a large triangle of cloth from an old unused one and stitch it into the back of the hockey sweater, giving the sweater a tail. As long as they had something hanging out they were okay.

* * *

While teaching and studying in Montreal, Bill got to know many more of the churches. And during his second and third year at the Immaculate, he and some of the others were invited to preach in English in French parishes, as there was a shortage of priests. He gave his first sermon at Gesù Church, a big Jesuit church at Bleury and St. Catherine, and he let his sisters know he'd be preaching. Both Tess and Bella came to hear him. He'd never had any trouble speaking in front of people and wasn't at all nervous, but apparently his younger sister Bella was. Bill looked down from the pulpit and saw her busy with her beads. After Mass he asked her, "What were you doing?"

"I thought you were going to forget and I was praying for you."

On the 15th of August 1945, the day after the Second World War ended, Bill Mackey was ordained by Archbishop Charbonneau in the Immaculate Conception Church. Bill, now officially "Father Mackey," said public Masses for the next couple of days after his ordination. But for the following Sunday, his birthday, his home parish of St. Thomas Aquinas organized a high Mass to which many of his old friends would come. As he was vesting for this, his first high Mass, in which he would have to sing, the woman who was organist and choir mistress came to him. She had known him since he was a boy. She said, "Billy, what note shall we give you?"

He answered honestly: "You can give me any note you like, but you'll get another one back."

Bill Mackey was tone deaf and couldn't sing to save his soul.

After his ordination, Father Mackey was called upon from time to time to preach Masses and work in the parish. One Saturday, he came in from playing hockey on the Immaculate rink, took a shower and went to the dining room to pick up a cup of coffee. The Rector popped in and said, "Somebody over at the hospital is looking for a priest who speaks English."

There was a big hospital on the other side of Parc Lafontaine, about ten minutes walk from the theologate. Father Mackey headed over. At the reception desk, a nurse explained that a man was dying of cancer and she'd called for a priest. But there was a complication. "You see, he's a Catholic who divorced his first wife and married again. He's worried now that he's dying, but he didn't want to call a priest."

Father Mackey went in to the man and sat down. He said: "I was just passing by. I understand you're quite sick. Very bad, this cancer."

After a while, the man opened up. His first wife had died since the divorce. But in the eyes of the Church he was not really married to his present wife, as the divorce from his first wife could not be recognized. The man said: "I've been living with my present wife for years. I can't ask her to marry me now, a second time."

"I don't see why not," Father Mackey said. "But suppose I ask her."

The man considered this and agreed.

As Father Mackey was leaving, he met the man's wife in the hall. He explained the situation and she said, "Father, anything, anything."

The dying man had very little time left.

The wife was a Protestant, and the rules of the Catholic Church were very strict concerning mixed marriages. As well, the following week was Holy Week and a marriage could not be performed on Thursday, Friday or Saturday. That left only the first half of the week, and Father Mackey had to get special permission from the Bishop. He said to the nurses and the wife, "Very good, let's have the marriage Wednesday."

The man was not in a private room, but the nurses moved him into one for the occasion. They brought in flowers and fixed the room up as nicely as they could. The man's wife already had a wedding ring on her hand, but they managed to remove it, and it was placed on her finger again during the ceremony Wednesday evening. The next morning, Holy Thursday, the Feast of the Blessed Eucharist, Father Mackey gave them both communion.

Ten days later the man died. His wife said to Father Mackey, "Father, what can I do for a funeral?"

"Don't worry, leave it to me."

Father Mackey arranged a wake. As the man had lived among Protestants for many years, it was held in a Protestant funeral parlour. Father Mackey went, talked to the widow, and met the friends and family who came. He was the object of some curiosity in his cassock, but he did his best to put everyone at ease.

The next step was the funeral and burial. Father Mackey went to St. Dominic's Parish Church where he had helped out and knew the parish priest. He told him the man's story. The parish priest said, "No problem. You just come along."

Normally a funeral would cost a couple of hundred dollars, and Father Mackey mentioned that the family had little money.

"Don't worry about it, Father. We'll take care of that. I'll get a couple of singers and you say the Mass."

The priest arranged for a hearse and a couple of taxis, and had the body brought to the church. Fifty or sixty Protestants came. Father Mackey said Mass and gave a comforting talk. Everyone proceeded to the cemetery and the man was buried. The wife never ceased to be grateful to Father Mackey. When he left for India, she attended his departure ceremony and for years continued to write letters and send donations to the Mission.

* * *

The Jesuit order, from its inception, has been a missionary organization. And for just about as long as he had been a Jesuit, Father Mackey had been interested in missionaries. During his Novitiate in Guelph he had listened to the stories of a Jesuit working in a mission to Ojibway Indians in northern Ontario. He remembered the talk mainly for its humour, the missionary keeping his audience in fits of laughter for an hour. But in addition to the humour, something serious caught hold, and Bill Mackey got the idea of going to the missions.

At the Immaculate he had more contact with missionaries. The French Canadian Jesuit province, the Province of Lower Canada, had overseas missions in China and Ethiopia. Occasionally, Father Mackey would meet missionaries who came to spend periods of time at the Immaculate. He found them to be outstanding people, their experiences having produced a breadth and depth that were foreign to the milieu in which he found himself.

Father Mackey's interest in the missions grew on into his third year of theology, but his prospects looked poor. The overseas missions fell under the Province of Lower Canada. Although he had spent half a dozen years in the Society's "French Canadian" province, he technically belonged to the Province of Upper Canada, the mainly English-speaking province which had been established in 1939, after fifteen years as a vice-province.

That probably would not exclude him completely from the China or Ethiopia missions, but he was not very hopeful. Fortunately a change came that year, 1945. Since its establishment, being young and relatively small, the Province of Upper Canada had not been given a foreign mission. Now, however, they would have an overseas mission of their own. In his last year of theology, soon after he learned of this, Father Mackey applied. Writing to Rome through the Provincial, he explained how his interest had developed under the influence of French-Canadian missionaries based in China and Ethiopia.

At the time, the specific location or nature of the new mission had not been disclosed. Father Mackey was shooting in the dark, but he didn't care. He just knew he wanted to be a missionary. A few months later, in the spring of 1946, when word came out that the mission would be in the Darjeeling District of north-east India, he wrote again to emphasize his commitment.

Bill Mackey completed his studies at Collège de l'Immaculée-Conception in May of 1946 with more credentials: he was now Reverend Father William Mackey, S.J., Licentiate in Theology, Licentiate in Philosophy, Bachelor of Arts, Diploma in Physical Education. He immediately left for an Ontario town on Georgian Bay. He still did not know if he would be selected for the Darjeeling Mission, but his next assignment was Assistant at Martyrs' Shrine at Midland.

This shrine honours early Jesuit missionaries to this part of Canada who were killed by Indians and became known as the Canadian Martyrs. They'd got caught up in seventeenth-century wars involving the French, the British and various Indian tribes. Five were tortured to death in the Midland area. Father T.J. Lally, the director of the shrine, had bought the site from a farmer. As the land was not very good, the farmer sold it cheap, probably unaware of its historical value.

Father Mackey took an active interest in the history of the Martyrs and the area. While at Midland he spent as much time as he could with Professor Drury, an archaeologist from London, Ontario, who was trying to find the site of Fort St. Ignace, the original village at Midland. It was described in *Les Relations*, the seventy-two-volume book of letters sent to France by the early Jesuit missionaries.

Father Mackey found the search fascinating. The archaeologist traced the outline of the palisade walls and buildings by using a metal rod to find soft spots left by rotted wooden posts. They came up with a geometric pattern which they presumed was that of the model village described by Father Brébeuf to his brother in a letter recorded in *Les Relations*. The archaeologist was also looking for remains of the site of the martyrization, but was unsuccessful.

Father Mackey was posted to Midland to help out with the influx of pilgrims who came to Martyrs' Shrine each summer. Once or twice a week a boat would come across Lake Huron from the United States. It would dock at Midland about nine o'clock in the morning. The visitors would flock off the boat and rush by taxi or bus to the Shrine, a forty-five minute drive from the town. According to the rules in those days, those wishing to attend Mass and take communion would have been fasting since midnight, and they wanted to have Mass so they could eat. Then they could spend some more leisurely time at the Shrine. There would be five or six Jesuits on hand to accommodate the sixty to a hundred tourists from the boat, plus the hundreds who arrived by bus.

On one occasion, Father Mackey and his colleagues were having lunch when an ambulance arrived at the Shrine carrying a teenaged girl from Toronto. She was in the final stages of tuberculosis. The x-rays and other diagnoses showed she was beyond hope. She was taken into the chapel on a stretcher and Father Lally blessed her with the relics — bones of the Martyrs — and said prayers over her. When he was finished, she said, "Leave me here. I want to pray."

He returned to his lunch.

Suddenly there was a tremendous commotion outside the church. The girl had stood up and walked out. Father Mackey later learned that she had x-rays when she returned to Toronto and was pronounced clear of tuberculosis. There was no medical explanation. This miracle formed part of the basis for the canonizing of the martyrs.

For Father Mackey it was a profound experience. Reflecting on it later, he asked himself if the suffering and death of the martyrs served any purpose, or was just a waste. By way of an answer, he interprets the broader phenomenon of the Martyrs' Shrine as being the work of the martyred Fathers coming alive in the spiritual work done there today. He believes that this shrine, which is unlike the commercialized Lourdes, is particular in the way the grace of God touches the pilgrims.

While still at Martyrs' Shrine in early September, Father Mackey learned that he had been accepted for the Darjeeling Mission and would depart in the fall. He next got a call from Toronto telling him to come and give a retreat to Sisters(nuns) in Kingston. Taken aback, he protested that he'd never given a retreat in his life.

In what was often the Jesuit style, the caller said, "Well, it's about time you gave one."

And promptly hung up.

The retreat went well and, in the years to come, Father Mackey would become sought after for his ability to give retreats. He had an attentive and sensitive ear, and early on learned the great value of simply listening. In many instances, his natural insight also enabled him to put his finger on an unspoken problem.

During the next few months, Father Mackey handled a variety of assignments. He gave several retreats, taught briefly at Loyola College and spoke at parishes and schools. These talks were supposed to be on the new mission. Unfortunately, Father Mackey didn't know much about it. He had read about it, but he drew most of his material from his imagination. Later, when he saw the reality of the Darjeeling District and his work there, Father Mackey realized with chagrin that most of what he had said was completely erroneous.

Finally, early in December of 1946, he returned to Montreal and packed his things. He would be leaving in a week or so — one of five Jesuits going to Darjeeling, all of whom had been connected with Loyola high school and college. Father Maurice Stanford and Father Bill Daly had graduated from both. Father John Prendergast had gone to high school at Loyola with Father Mackey. The fifth member of the group was a French Canadian Jesuit, Brother Paul Robin. He had not studied at Loyola, but worked there — in charge of both the health of the boarders and the boy's kitchen, looking after the food, the cooks, cleanliness and so on.

The departure ceremony, held in the chapel at Loyola on December 9th, 1946, was a major event for the five men, their families and friends, and the Society. The five received their mission mandate from Father John Swain, S.J., Provincial of the Upper Canada Province. The guest preacher was Father Mackey's old parish priest, Father Reid, who had told him many years before, "Billy, go right ahead. . . . You'll do well no matter where you go."

After the benediction came a reception.

The next day, at Windsor Station, Father Mackey said goodbye to his family, friends and several priests from Loyola, and with his companions boarded the train for Halifax. They left with the idea that they would not be returning. That was the commitment of Jesuit missionaries at the time. From Halifax, on December 15th, they sailed for England on a small freighter called the Bayano. After a rough crossing of the Atlantic they landed at Liverpool on Christmas Eve.

They would not be leaving for India for almost two weeks, and Father Mackey took advantage of the break to visit relatives in Ireland, managing to get to his mother's old family home late on Christmas day. He was surprised to find the attitude of awe and intimidation that the people felt in the presence of clergy. At one point someone asked him if he were a Jesuit. When he said he was, the person remarked: "Funny, you're not like the Irish Jesuits. You seem to be human."

Father Mackey joined his companions in London and they proceeded to Southampton. On the 5th of January, 1947, they boarded a P&O liner called the Strathmore and sailed for India.

4/

Darjeeling District encompasses the part of West Bengal that lies in the Himalayan foothills. Even by 1947, when Father Mackey arrived, the combination of terrain and climate had made it a world-famous tea-growing area. At its heart was the town of Darjeeling, with its spectacular views, particularly of the magnificent mountain, Kanchenjunga.

The British called Darjeeling the "Queen of the Hill Stations," the place most favoured as an escape from the summer heat of the plains, mainly in May and June, before the monsoon began. For the same reasons, various missionary organizations considered the town, and to some extent the hill area as a whole, a good place to locate schools. Towns like Kurseong and Kalimpong had an educational importance out of proportion to their size. But Darjeeling town had the best schools.

Darjeeling sits at an elevation of 2,130 metres on a crescent-shaped ridge whose concave side faces west. The main part of town lies in the middle of the crescent. At the ridge's north end (called, not surprisingly, North Point), some distance from the heart of town, was St. Joseph's College, established in 1888 by Belgian Jesuit Fathers. The College, often referred to as "North Point," also had a very posh school section.

In the centre of town was another Jesuit institution, St. Robert's High School, formerly a grand hotel. It lay below the Chowrasta (Darjeeling's version of a central square or plaza), above the Deputy Commissioner's Office, and just north of the busy Chowk Bazaar. Loreto Convent school, run by the Loreto Sisters from Ireland, was further down the hill. There was also a very posh Anglican high school called St. Paul's, and another Protestant school, Mount Hermon, run by Australian missionaries.

These were all English-language institutions.

Primary schools in Darjeeling tended to function in Nepali, reflecting the majority position of ethnic Nepali people in the District's population. Students switched to English for secondary and tertiary levels, in which the "better" schools were dominated by the elite and had been strongly under the British influence. Indeed, most of the best schools in India had been set up by the British for their own children or upper-class Indians. Most of the other good schools in the district followed the same pattern of local language primary schools and English high schools.

* * *

The trip to Darjeeling from Bombay, where Father Mackey disembarked, took ten days. First came a long train trip to Calcutta. The five men and all their baggage travelled to the station by truck. The Canadians were dumbfounded to see station coolies hoist the heavy steamer trunks onto their heads and carry them that way to the platform. Nor had they ever seen a train station like this one, with so many people rushing, ambling, lounging, sleeping.

By some miracle, however, when they reached the platform they found a sheet of paper on a bulletin board listing their names and giving the number of their carriage, or "bogie" as locals called it. At the bogie itself, they discovered another sheet listing the names of the occupants, including themselves.

The five Jesuits found the trip to Calcutta enthralling. What a panorama. Everything was foreign — the train carriage itself (simplified British style), the passing country-side, the food, the amazing variety of people. The newcomers, as Father Mackey put it decades later, were "gaga" at every station.

The bigger stations were the most exciting. The platforms were crowded with men wearing turbans of wild colours and strange pants of filmy white cotton, other men in common-looking business suits, women in graceful if sometimes soiled saris, other women in brightly coloured skirts and tops, still other women in full trouser-like bottoms and long shirt-like tops. There were hawkers selling all kinds of fruit and unfamiliar foods and sometimes trinkets. Beggars sat by the doorways, dogs dozed as flies buzzed around them and even cows wandered aimlessly around the platform.

The Jesuits were struck by the novelty of the tea service, especially at brief stops, when the *cha-walla* poured tea into small unfired clay cups and handed them through the train window. After drinking the tea, usually as the train proceeded down the track, the traveller would toss the cup through the window onto the roadbed, where it would smash and quickly degrade naturally.

The Jesuits found breakfast somewhat familiar, as usually they could get an egg and a piece of bread along with their tea. But the other meals consisted of various curries and rice. They found the curried food hot, but having no alternative, they tried to get used to it.

Arriving in Calcutta, after two nights and a day on the train, the priests found the chaos and crowds at Howrah station overwhelming. Again, fortunately, as in Bombay, Jesuit colleagues met the five and guided them. Coolies carried the trunks on their heads out to the front of the station. The Canadians could see no trucks around, but one of the Calcutta Fathers was negotiating with a fellow who had a long, simple, two-wheeled, flat-bed cart which he pulled through the streets of Calcutta. Coolies loaded the trunks onto the cart. The local Jesuit turned and said, "Okay, let's go."

Father Mackey pointed at the trunks: "Who the hang's going to stay with those?"

His guide said, "Don't worry, they'll be delivered. Let's get a taxi."

The Canadians threw a dubious last glance at their trunks before following. Three hours later, they received the consignment, completely intact.

The Jesuits spent four days in Calcutta, staying at St. Xavier's College. They met the Bishop, toured the city and were struck by the great respect shown to white people. India's independence would come later that year, but in early 1947 it was still the Raj, and "Europeans" were treated with almost exaggerated courtesy. As the Canadian Jesuits walked the streets everyone stepped out of their way, often nodding deferentially. Father Mackey would notice a change in the years to come.

The Jesuits travelled by train to a small mission outside Calcutta, their first rural experience in India. They visited another mission that could only be reached by boat. At one point in their country travels they were delighted to drink fresh coconut milk. The coconuts did not look like any they had seen before. These were green and much larger, as they still had the thick outer covering on them. After the top had been sliced off with a sharp machete, the trick was to drink the tasty liquid from the awkward vessel without having it spill all over your face.

In Calcutta, ever a chaotic city, Father Daly suggested a bicycle tour. Father Mackey agreed immediately. The priests borrowed two of the college's bicycles and pedalled out the main gate onto Park Street, a busy thoroughfare. They quickly pulled over. After a moment, they realized that traffic ran opposite to the way it did in Canada. But at first, as Father Mackey put it, they thought: "What in heck's happening here? All the cars are on the wrong side of the road."

* * *

Father Mackey had been posted to a school in the small town of Kurseong, located in the Himalayan foothills south of Darjeeling. His four colleagues were still travelling in the same direction, and with them, having survived Calcutta, he boarded the Darjeeling Mail heading north.

At Siliguri, a large drab town near the edge of the foothills, a local Jesuit helped the five get a taxi to Darjeeling, eighty kilometres north and 2,000 metres higher. Kurseong lay fifty kilometres up the road at an elevation of 1,475 metres. It was headquarters for the DHR, the Darjeeling Himalayan Railway, which operated the scaled-down "toy train" that ran between Siliguri and Darjeeling.

For its size, Kurseong boasted a surprising number of large educational institutions. St. Mary's Theologate was located above the town on St. Mary's Hill, and St. Alphonsus High School was in the town itself. Both were Jesuit institutions. Then there was St. Helen's Convent and school run by the Sisters of the Cross, a Belgian-Irish order. And nearby were Gauthals High School (Irish Christian Brothers), Victoria School for boys and Dowhill for girls (both Protestant) and Puspharani (a private Hindi-medium school).

The taxi, filled by the five Jesuits, climbed up into the foothills of the Himalayas along the narrow, winding road lined by forests and tea estates. This was mid-winter, yet the coolness seemed to come more from the vegetation than the season. The road went right by St. Alphonsus and Father Mackey got out there with a single bag. The rest of his luggage would follow on the train. He waved goodbye to his colleagues as they shouted wishes of good luck and proceeded on up to Darjeeling.

Father Mackey's first posting was St. Paul's Parish, Kurseong. He'd been sent to eventually take over from a middle-aged Belgian Jesuit, Father Michael Wery, who was in charge of both the school and parish. Father Mackey expected to say Mass and spend a month learning the routines. But as they walked to the church the first Sunday he was shocked to hear Father Wery say, "You hear confessions."

"I can't hear confessions! I don't know the language."

"That doesn't matter. It'll be a long time before you understand what they mumble in your ear. Just get in there and give an absolution."

Father Mackey memorized the formula in Nepali — "for your penance, say one Hail Mary" — then heard confessions and gave blessings. He later decided that the older man had been right. Months would pass before Father Mackey could be sure he understood what his parishioners were saying. Yet he became fluent in Nepali before any of his Canadian colleagues, and this he credited to Father Wery, who'd forced him immediately "into the deep end."

In that first month before Father Mackey was fully employed he got to know some of the other institutions nearby. He was impressed by St. Mary's Theologate, perhaps the oldest such institution in India, with its remarkable library collections on Indian culture and religion. The theologate, now over one hundred years old, has since been moved to Delhi. But its presence in Kurseong, with large numbers of Jesuits training and passing through, had great influence in the district, particularly in the development of schools.

St. Alphonsus had begun as a primary school in 1890 but had grown into a high school with an industrial school and orphanage attached. Among the tribal peoples of northern India, as in many rural parts of the world, and others not adulterated by modern development, orphans did not exist. If parents died, other family members or, in their absence, people of the village or community took care of the orphaned children.

But as change came to these societies, including conversion to Christianity, the old ways weakened. Those who abandoned a traditional religion could be removed from the other societal traditions. So, when Christian parents died, the children might not be taken in by their extended families or neighbours. Hence, in some ways the Christian missionaries created the need for the orphanages they began to establish.

St. Alphonsus High School had about 450 students, seventy of them boarders. The enrolment at the Industrial School was over 150 and included seventy Catholic orphans, and seventy-five veterans. The combined enrolment grew over the following years. Father Wery ran the entire operation on a shoestring, especially the Industrial School, which he had started five years before. He had found that Christian high school graduates and dropouts had particular difficulty finding jobs and undertook to give the young people more practical options. The government stipend he received for training ex-servicemen after the Second World War helped financially, but as long as the Industrial School remained part of St. Alphonsus, money was a problem.

Even though the high school did not need material and equipment as the Industrial School did, it ran marginally as well. It served poor people and so Father Wery kept school fees as low as possible. The classrooms were small, with whitewashed walls and home-made benches, and a few simple pictures on the walls. The dormitory was a bare room with three windows, a tin roof and some low tables that served as beds. There were no mattresses, and boys were lucky to have a blanket or two. They would hang their few items of clothing not in closets but on a piece of string.

The high school had eleven grades or class levels — infant or pre-primary, and then classes one through ten. Most lower class levels had two sections of about thirty students each. The higher classes tended to have fewer students. The three main subjects at the lower levels were Nepali, English and mathematics. Other subjects, like science, history and geography, were incorporated into the teaching of the languages. Class six marked the beginning of high school and more formal subject categories (like science and history) were specified.

Father Wery had been instrumental in changing the language of the school from Hindi to Nepali, at least for the lower classes, infant to class five. The majority of the people in the area were ethnic Nepalis and these people, often the poorest, were the ones Father Wery wanted to work with. Previously, many missionaries were content to carry on in their own languages or those of the establishment, necessarily avoiding close involvement with the masses.

But Father Wery had taken Christ's teachings on this matter to heart and made it his business to become completely fluent in spoken and written Nepali. He then wrote Nepali readers or *sahityas* and was able to set up instruction in Nepali. Until his death he strove to improve his language and teaching skills.

Father Mackey learned to speak Nepali reasonably well, and was able to teach and preach in the vernacular. He could read written Nepali but never became proficient at writing the language. If he needed to write a letter in Nepali, he would have someone else do it. And as English was a main subject at the school and the medium beyond class five, he functioned in a combination of the two languages, doing much of his teaching in English.

Yet he developed a speciality and even today he will challenge a native speaker of ordinary Nepali, "Do you know the meaning of *sab dui bahu tribuj*? No? How about *sama khon*?" And when the unwary victim admits he doesn't know these terms, "Pshaw, I know more Nepali than you!" Then he explains that he's talking about isosceles triangles, right angles and other geometric terms. Relatively few Nepali people know them as they were not native to Nepali but were brought in from the somewhat similar Hindi. Even a Hindi speaker has to be well-educated to know these school-book phrases.

St. Alphonsus school was primarily a day school. The limited number of boarders were orphans and sometimes a few students who had no relatives nearby, like the small number of students who came from the neighbouring kingdom of Bhutan. Father Mackey stayed in the boarding section, located upstairs in the old building, with the orphans, to keep an eye on them.

While Nepali was the medium in the lower classes, English was also stressed so that when students switched to English in class six they would have the language skills required. The other main emphasis was on mathematics — one of Father Mackey's strengths. And he had already taught for three years at Brébeuf. So he went ahead in his vibrant way. For about five months.

Then he realized that he wasn't getting his subject across to the students. Upon reflection, he realized that he was still trying to teach Canadian students, not Nepalis. He himself had been struggling with learning the Nepali language. But he had assumed that kids were kids and he could teach these students the same way he had taught those back home. It wasn't true. Kids were kids, yet they approached life and learning differently.

Father Mackey adjusted. He took time to find the knowledge base that his new students had so he could use it and build on it. He tried to get a sense of the religious and philosophic base that shaped their thinking. Just using local examples, he discovered, went a long way in enabling students to solve problems. This was a simple lesson to learn once his eyes were open, but it had been easy simply to project his experience of Canadian children onto his new students.

Outside the classroom, Father Mackey learned different lessons. From Canada, he had brought two baseball bats and a few softballs. The people of Kurseong were totally unfamiliar with this game. Some educated Indians had heard of the American game of baseball, but it remained foreign. Its nearest relative was cricket, but as any cricket or baseball fan will tell you, the two are worlds apart. Father Mackey had never played cricket. But he had played various types of baseball and introduced softball to St. Alphonsus.

The kids took to the game with enthusiasm. Soon they were hitting the ball into the brush and bushes that surrounded the field. The kids playing in the outfield knew what they were supposed to do: if they couldn't catch the ball when it was hit, then they had to chase it and retrieve it. However, often they were hesitant about going into the bushes, and once they refused to retrieve the ball. Father Mackey couldn't figure it out. "What's the matter with you people? Get the ball!"

In exasperation, he went to fetch it himself. In the rough area beyond the playing field he found what the local people called *sisnu*. Just another wild plant as far as he was concerned. He put his hand in, then let out a yelp. From then on he, too, refused to pick a ball out of the *sisnu*. Not only did these nasty nettles sting fiercely, but they caused his hand to swell up something awful.

Softball did not survive in Kurseong. It wasn't just the *sisnu*. You could poke around with a stick and get the ball out. But the boys soon learned how to place the ball when they hit it. A well-hit ball would go beyond the playing field, across the road and into the neighbouring tea estate. The small supply of balls soon ran out.

Another lesson Father Mackey learned among the boys concerned the question of equality. Every Sunday morning he was assigned to give the orphan boarders their allowance for the week. Of course it was meagre: four annas, or twenty-five paise in today's system — a quarter of a rupee. So Father Mackey would dole out four annas to each boy (about seven cents). But within ten minutes, he found, practically all the money would be in the hands of perhaps three boys. The rest would have nothing.

Those who came out ahead were money lenders. The boys had discovered that, by adding a couple more annas to their allowance, they might be able to buy something they really wanted. They'd borrow the difference — but the interest was astronomical. Bigger deals would place a borrower in debt for weeks or months, or theoretically forever, given how little they were receiving. A few sharp orphan boys had learned, at a very young age, a practice that has been a scourge of millions of working poor. And Father Mackey learned that not all boys had equal talents — certainly not when it came to business.

* * *

Father Mackey spent 1947 in Kurseong, working at St. Alphonsus school and St. Paul's Parish. But he still had Tertianship, the last part of his Jesuit training, to complete, and he spent most of 1948 in Ranchi, in the state of Bihar. Here, at Manresa House, along with Father Daly and Father Stanford, he took his last major programme of concentrated spiritual training, including his second, all important thirty-day retreat.

The entire programme featured a very strict routine, with the Jesuits under training confined to the Tertian House, as it was also called. They were not even permitted to read newspapers and magazines. Many of the trainees found it maddening to spend months without knowing what was going on in the outside world, and they would resort to just about anything to get information.

Within their strict timetable, a short part of the morning would find them in the toilets taking care of their daily bodily functions. There was no such thing as soft white toilet paper. Instead, and even this was a luxury for many, there was newspaper. But in keeping with the restriction against outside reading material, the newspaper sheets were torn into strips and pieces rendering most articles incomplete. Each trainee read whatever he found on his paper, and when the men congregated for lunch they exchanged pieces of information, each hoping that one of his colleagues could help fill out the story. It gave a whole new twist to the common tradition of reading in the bathroom.

Father Mackey took what rare opportunities he could find to escape the confines of Tertian House. Not far from Ranchi, in a place called Mundar, was Holy Family Hospital, a large hospital run by medical Sisters from America. They were in constant need of blood. So as often as he could, which was only three times during his stay in Ranchi, Father Mackey went to Holy Family. Each time it was an elderly Jesuit Father who needed the blood, and, unfortunately, Father Mackey's blood was not enough. All three of them died after the transfusion.

Father Mackey also got short breaks from Tertian House to give retreats. At the neighbouring St. Albert Seminary he gave an ordination retreat to seminarians about to be ordained. He also got back to the hills for four weeks. He was called up to Darjeeling to give retreats to the college and high school students at North Point. He did some preaching and generally enjoyed looking around the College. But he learned that his replacement at St. Alphonsus had not fared well.

Father Kevin Scott had come out from Canada just before Christmas in 1947 and was sent to St. Alphonsus to replace Father Mackey while he was away on Tertianship. This meant taking over Father Mackey's accommodation in the orphanage — a very small room, actually just part of the corridor which had been blocked off. The place was infested with bedbugs and fleas, but Father Mackey had got used to them quickly and took no notice.

Unfortunately, Father Scott could not ignore the conditions. He broke out in a rash all over his body and had to be sent to a doctor, a specialist in Calcutta. The doctor's reaction was, "Get this man back to Canada as quickly as possible." Father Scott had spent only a couple of months in the missions.

* * *

When Father Mackey returned to Kurseong in November of 1948, he became Headmaster of St. Alphonsus and assistant parish priest. He took up residence again in the orphanage hostel.

About 1954, however, Father Mackey and Brother Robin, who'd travelled with him from Canada, moved into the "cats' bungalow" just up the hill behind the school. This was a comfortable eight-room bungalow with good bathrooms, including hot water heaters and nice big bathtubs. It had belonged to an elderly spinster who lived there with her numerous cats. She was a friend of Father Wery and an admirer of his work, and when she returned to England, she gave the bungalow to him.

When Father Mackey and Brother Robin moved into the place, they had plenty of extra room by their standards. Previously, a few students from the neighbouring kingdom of Bhutan had boarded in the orphans' hostel, while others boarded with teachers. But the tough, semi-criminal milieu of the hostel was not really suitable for boys from good Bhutanese families, so when space opened up in the "cats' bunga-low," the Bhutanese boarders came there. A connecting sitting room and sun room were turned into a "boarding" for these paying boarders, who numbered about thirty.

Their presence at St. Alphonsus was quite logical. Bhutan had no high schools, so parents who wanted their children to get a secondary education had to send them outside the country. Virtually all of them went to India and most into the Darjeeling District. This happened for two reasons.

First, Darjeeling was nearby, and part of the district had even been within Bhutan's borders at the end of the 18th Century when the

Bhutanese occupied Sikkim, which then included much of this area. Bhutan House in Kalimpong was a headquarters for the Bhutanese Trade Commissioner in the first half of the 20th Century and later became the all-important Indian base — Bhutan's unofficial embassy in India — for the Bhutanese Prime Minister.

The second reason related to a large section of Bhutanese students, including those at St. Alphonsus. These boys were of Nepali ethnic origin and lived mostly along the southern border of Bhutan. Their parents wanted them educated in their own language, Nepali, rather than Bengali or Hindi. Because Nepali-medium schools were available in Darjeeling District, they would usually take all their schooling there.

St. Alphonsus, which followed the exam system set by the West Bengal Board of Secondary Education, was a good middle-of-the-road option for Nepali-speaking students, as it started from a Nepali-language base and moved into English. Students who by class or preparation could not enter the posh Cambridge system schools (before Indian independence it had been very difficult for Bhutanese to get into the posh schools in Darjeeling unless they were of royal descent) could start in their native language and wind up with a fairly decent English-language education.

As Father Mackey got to know the Bhutanese boys boarding at St. Alphonsus, especially those from the large extended Gurung family of Samtse — he remembers all the "Raj" Gurungs: Meghraj, Sibiraj, Nirparaj, Gajraj Gurung — he had no idea of the close connections he would have with them many years later.

*   *   *

As Headmaster, Father Mackey came up against some of the less obvious aspects of the school and community. One problem that was visible but not readily understood by the untrained eye afflicted a great many students. Roughly forty per cent of them came from tea estates. And some of those boys, like those from the Margaret Hope Tea Estate, had a three-hour walk up the hill to the school in the morning, and perhaps a two-hour run down again in the afternoon. During this long day, which included five hours of walking, they had no lunch. Their parents could not afford to provide them with a packed lunch.

Father Mackey became aware of this when a doctor came to the school to do a general check-up of the students. Seeing his interest, the doctor said, "Father Mackey, I don't think you realize the effects that this walking has on these kids. Now, the next ten kids, I'll tell you which kid comes from where and how far he has to walk."

Then, as the children came to him, aged between ten and thirteen, he judged them by their swollen stomachs. He said: "These kids get up. They take breakfast. As soon as breakfast is finished they have to walk, walk, walk. Walk up, maybe two or three hours. At lunch they have nothing. After school they go down. They take a big meal, maybe do a bit of homework or something and then go to bed." He looked at Father Mackey and said, "Constipation."

Father Mackey could do little to correct the situation. If the children were to be educated they had to come to the schools, which were already stretched to the limit financially and so couldn't provide food and lodging. Later, when schools were established on the tea estates, the health of the children improved and they became bigger and stronger.

Father Mackey became aware of the tensions between Nepalis and Bengalis when he was invited to a public meeting not long after he became Headmaster. School examination results had been very bad among the majority Nepali students in the area. The parents blamed the Bengali authorities and looked to Father Mackey for a comment, presumably confirmation.

He admitted that there might be some truth in their claim, but said he also didn't think the Nepali kids were working. The parents looked at him in surprise. What did he mean? He explained that often he'd take an evening walk through the bazaar. He'd look in at his barber's shop. The Muslim had a small shop with just two chairs. The barber would be cutting hair and in the corner of the shop his son would be sitting with his books, memorizing tracts he had been assigned.

Father Mackey would walk past a Bengali house. The children would be inside doing their homework, with their father helping out. At a shop owned by a Marwari (Marwaris, who originated in Rajasthan, have spread throughout India and acquired a reputation, sometimes unflattering, for business acumen), two or three kids were in the corner studying, helping each other. But passing a Nepali house, he said, "every darned kid is out in the street running around all night." This was not the kind of response the Nepalis wanted to hear, and it's doubtful that many took it to heart. It was easier to blame the Bengalis.

Father Mackey faced a particular set of problems among the boarders. Most of the high school students were normal kids from decent, though poor, families, and would go on to lead normal lives.

There were many who would go on through class ten and even beyond, into college. Father Mackey remained in contact with many of them long after he left the area, and saw their children growing up.

But the large student body included many boarder-orphans who had experienced very tough times, and among these were a number of difficult cases. Father Mackey calls them the "wild gang." A couple of times a week, he or Father Wery would be down at the police station trying to bail one or more of them out. The police knew they were St. Alphonsus boys and would call the school. Sometimes they kept the boys in jail overnight. Actual bail did not have to be paid. The police knew Father Wery, Father Mackey and the others, and appreciated what they were trying to do, including trying to handle the problems themselves.

The trouble these boys got into was not entirely of their own making, but derived from what Father Mackey perceived as Kurseong's normal growing pains. The medium-gauge railway was being extended to Assam and many outsiders came to the area to work. As Kurseong was a railway headquarters, the community experienced the adjustments and problems associated with any influx of outsiders.

At least the railway centre, and its ticket press, provided jobs for some students leaving the high school. The railway workshop nearby at Tindharia also offered job opportunities. As well, quite a few students chose education as their career. The Jesuit community gave them a lot of support as they sought higher education, and the graduates often found jobs at the same institutions where they had started school. Some forty or fifty families of the St. Alphonsus orphans became associated with the school and constituted a small community which flourished over the years.

* * *

On the fifteenth of August, 1949, seventeen years after joining the Jesuits, Father Mackey pronounced his final vows, and was completely accepted as a Jesuit. A year and a half later, he was made District Jesuit Superior, Dean of Darjeeling District, parish priest of Kurseong's St. Paul's Parish, Minister of the Jesuit House and head of the Mission. When the Canadians came out in 1947, Jesuit authorities had intended them gradually to take over, and now they saw Father Mackey taking a leading role in that process.

Father Mackey's Superiorship did not make him a full-fledged Superior in the usual sense of controlling a region. But the Jesuit authorities wanted at least a quasi-Superior for their growing community in Darjeeling district. This district fell under the jurisdiction of Calcutta on both the ecclesiastical side, under the Archbishop of Calcutta, and the Jesuit side, under the Provincial. The latter was a Belgian whose linguistic specialization was Bengali.

But the Jesuits and the Church recognized the need for specialization in Nepali for Darjeeling. Some years later, the Church would appoint its first Bishop of Darjeeling and he would be an ethnic Nepali. For now, Father Mackey was not the Nepali expert Father Wery was, but he was no doubt seen as more appropriate for a number of reasons — age, health, the Canadian take-over, administrative aptitude (at least compared with Father Wery), and perhaps Father Wery's less-than-popular immersion in the poverty of Kurseong.

Father Wery became assistant parish priest and maintained a few other responsibilities, such as censoring Nepali books. Brother Robin was named Director of the Industrial School, though in fact Father Wery still acted as its head. He was also still parish priest to most of the people. Father Mackey took care of the parish paper work — baptismal records, marriage records, accounts and so on — and parish work concerning the Anglo-Indians and the Sisters. He helped Father Wery with the Nepalis, but he knew Father Wery was adored by the people and could run the parish better than he could.

Father Mackey was content to let Father Wery and Brother Robin carry on with the Industrial School as best they could, even though their efforts kept the coffers of the combined schools absolutely bare. There are tales of the pair of them running to the office when they learned that someone had come in to pay school fees and then proceeding to ravage the cash box for the few rupees that had been deposited. Besides making the ongoing administration of finance extremely difficult for Father Mackey, Father Wery and Brother Robin's financial raids would have significant results a little later.

Father Mackey got along well with Father Wery. The younger Canadian did not have any of the repugnance that some Jesuits showed regarding the "dirty work" that Father Wery involved himself in. Father Mackey felt more at home working with the primary and high school kids, but did not shy away from the Industrial School orphans, and even shared their atrocious dormitory. He, too, grew close to the people of the community.

The majority of his students were Hindus, as were many of his teachers. He soon came to see Hindus, Buddhists and Muslims as people who were God's children no less than he was, and who could be as devout in their worship and daily lives as he was. For him, they just had a different approach to the Supreme Reality. And after only a couple of uneasy moments at his first temple visit and cremation, he grew to not only feel comfortable, but to enter into the spirit of the people and the events. He participated in their festivals — he especially liked Diwali, which is celebrated with lights — went to the homes of students when they were sick, and attended cremations. Some of this he felt was his duty as head of the school.

He found his spiritual attitudes broadening, as well, under the influence of Father Wery. The Belgian priest was much more concerned with the practicalities of helping the poor than forcing dogma on them. And he was not troubled to see aspects of Nepali culture incorporated into Christian feast days and celebrations. Father Mackey considered the older Jesuit "a fantastic missionary."

Their partnership extended to sports. Father Wery was not the robust athlete Father Mackey was, but he had promoted sports and, through his teachers, had trained good student teams, especially in field hockey and football. In fact, as if to add injury to the insult that the existence of his rag-tag school seemed to inflict on the North Point Jesuits, he took a team of scruffy field-hockey players to Darjeeling and beat St. Joseph's in the district finals.

Although Father Mackey had never played field hockey or soccer, the international brand of football, his school's teams always did well and often won district championships. When he tried to play football himself, he couldn't keep his hands off the ball and had to confine himself to playing goalkeeper. As a veteran ice-hockey player, he could never get used to the field hockey stick and the restrictive rules on how it could be used. But his enthusiasm and the coaching of some of his teachers built up good teams. And Father Mackey had an notable ability to organize tournaments and sports days.

His first primary school football tournament attracted well over thirty teams. Just about every primary school in the district had a team and some had two. Father Mackey had noticed that using the standard height limit, four-foot-ten-inches, meant short but full-grown men with strong legs could squeeze into the game. Father Mackey set his limit at four-foot-two inches, a height virtually no adult could sneak under.

The teams in the tournament did not look fancy. A proper uniform was rare and football shoes, or any shoes at all, were also scarce. But the event was a tremendous success. People came from miles around to watch. Never mind that it was the rainy season and everyone got drenched — and just as well that most of the kids playing in the mud had practically nothing on.

St. Alphonsus had only a small playing field, roughly the size of five tennis courts. But on a sports day, such was Father Mackey's organization, teachers could run off a hundred events in a couple of hours. Besides the standard athletic events of running, jumping and throwing, there were drill teams and gymnastics. Father Wery was a musician and he had a band made up of his orphans (one shudders to think what they sounded like) to play for the drill teams as they marched and did their patterns.

Gymnastics were part of school sports when Father Mackey arrived, but he added horse work. The gymnastics on the horse and the tumbling and pyramid building were an important part of the "circus sports" which made such sports days and entertainment programmes so popular in the community. And the school was a real centre for the community. It was large, the combined numbers growing to some 800 students through the 1950s, and showed good school spirit.

The school's reputation, built largely on sports and entertainment, attracted students. This is not to say that the school was not academically sound — it was. But little public entertainment existed except for what the school offered by way of sports events and concerts. So when the school staged an event, people would come from all around. Many parents in such rural settings knew little of academics and education, so they were not much interested in sending their children to school. Better to keep them at home or send them out to find some small job. But when they and their children saw the public activities of the school, the kids wanted to be part of the fun and activity and the parents were impressed enough that often the kids wound up at school.

Father Mackey managed to augment the meagre stock of gymnastic gear he inherited at St. Alphonsus when a British regiment was leaving the Darjeeling district. It was a regiment consisting largely of Irish Catholic soldiers. One day, a major came to the school with a group of children. He told Father Mackey that some of his men had fathered these boys, but now they were leaving and could the orphanage take them?

Father Mackey said yes — but remembered some fine gymnastics displays the army had put on and asked: "What are you doing with your gymnastic equipment?"

The major said they were selling a very good set — horse, spring board, mats, the works — for five hundred rupees. This was a lot of money. Father Mackey looked the soldier in the eye meaningfully, and the man stammered, "Father, I'd love to give it to you but it's already passed the audit and we have to put in five hundred rupees."

"Okay. Will you hold it for me, for five or six days?"

"Yes, of course, Father."

Some of the Darjeeling schools were interested in the equipment and better able to pay for it, but holding it for a few days was the least the army could do, having just received a favour from Father Mackey.

There was rarely five rupees to spare in the St. Alphonsus bank account, let alone five hundred. Father Mackey went to North Point where Father Maurice Stanford, one of the men who had come from Canada with him, was rector. He said, "Mo, I need 500 rupees."

St. Alphonsus needing money was nothing new. Father Stanford said he was sorry, but he'd just given a donation to another school and had no money left. Father Mackey knew the part about the donation was probably true. For all the posh school's elitism and airs, the Jesuits at North Point did a lot of charitable work in the district. But he also knew they weren't out of money.

"Mo, I need it bad, very, very bad."

"Ah, Bill, no. No, I really can't."

Father Mackey reached into his cassock and pulled out a photograph. Sitting across from him, Father Stanford, Rector of St. Joseph's College, looked very dignified. But in the snapshot, wearing nothing but a pair of shorts on board the Strathmore, he looked anything but dignified. Father Mackey said: "You see this picture, Mo? Five hundred or you know where it's going to go."

Father Stanford could imagine the boys at the College going wild at the sight of their Rector practically naked. He'd never live it down. "You wouldn't!"

"I would."

Father Stanford left the office for a few moments and returned with the money. Father Mackey took it and handed over the picture. Saying thanks, he stuffed the cash into his cassock and got up to leave. He was going straight to the army camp at Lebong. But as he walked out the door, he turned and said, "Oh, and Mo, I'll be back. I've still got the negative."

*   *   *

When Father Mackey and the others had left Canada in 1946 they had no idea when, if ever, they would return. As of 1951, none of the five had gone home, not even for a visit. Someone pointed out to Father Mackey that it was normal for a Superior to return to the home province from time to time to discuss mission affairs. At the suggestion that he go, he thought, "Why not?" While fund-raising and recruiting for the Mission, he could also see his family. He would go late in the year and try to make it home for Christmas.

Father Mackey decided to travel by air, which would still take almost a week. He took the train to Calcutta, then BOAC from there. The propeller-driven airplanes of the time could not make a non-stop flight to London, but had to make a number of refuelling stops. Trans-Atlantic flights stopped at Shannon, Ireland, and there he got stalled. An Atlantic storm delayed his departure, and he was stuck in Shannon airport the morning of Christmas Eve. He went into the restaurant and sat down for breakfast. The poor waitress was very upset. She looked at the Roman collar he wore with his dark suit and said, "But, this is a day of fast and abstinence. You can't eat."

Father Mackey looked up at her and said, "Well, where I come from I don't get meals like this. Besides, there's only one fast day in the Indian Church and that's Good Friday. Any other day we can eat, because we don't have meat most of the time anyway." And he explained how the Friday fish rule didn't make much sense where he lived and so it wasn't followed strictly either. He concluded by saying, "I'm an Indian missionary and I'm sticking to my privilege. I'm having my breakfast."

The young waitress was scandalized. But she went away and brought Father Mackey some eggs and toast for his breakfast. But there was no bacon coming out of that Catholic Irish kitchen that day.

Once across the Atlantic, the plane landed at Gander, Newfoundland for refueling at two in the morning. Father Mackey said to the older priest who was sitting beside him, "Look, let's say Mass."

The priest, on his way from Rome to Montreal, looked shocked. The rules of the day prevented such a thing. "No, I can't. You can't say Mass at this time of day unless you're a parish priest."

"Well, I'm parish priest, dean and superior. I'm saying Mass. Do you want to join me?"

Although the other priest refrained, he did serve Mass for Father Mackey. But as a man twenty years his senior, and working under the rigid constraints of Rome, he couldn't understand how someone as young as Father Mackey could hold any of his three jobs, let alone all of them.

Father Mackey arrived in Montreal mid-morning on Christmas Day and spent the afternoon with his father and two sisters. Later on his tour he visited his brother, Jim, who now lived near London, Ontario with his wife and two little girls. Jim had himself joined the Jesuits, a year after his younger brother Bill, but had left the order before being ordained.

When Father Mackey had decided to visit Canada, the Canadians in Darjeeling district had set about making a tape recording of each Jesuit speaking to his parents. In Canada, Father Mackey would turn these tapes into records that could be played on a phonograph, and then deliver the records to the parents. In Canada, after a lot of difficulties due to tape speed, Father Mackey had each missionary's voice dubbed onto a 78 r.p.m. disc. The quality was not great but the voices were understandable, and the parents who received these records were thrilled to hear the voices of their sons.

While he had time for family and friends, and even to take in a hockey game at the Forum, Father Mackey spent most of his four-month visit travelling within Canada, talking about the Mission. Now, of course, he not only knew what he was talking about, but had artifacts and photographs to show.

When he went to speak at the Jesuit seminary in Toronto, Father West, the Mission Director, said he'd first like to show the movie Father Mackey had previously sent from Darjeeling. This was a silent movie made when Father Mackey visited the school in a village called Mani Bhanjan on the border between West Bengal and Nepal. The movie showed a sports day and the various people from the area who had come to attend.

Father Mackey told Father West to go ahead. So, as an introduction to Father Mackey's talk, the Director proceeded to run the short film and, so as not to overwork his guest speaker, give explanations of what was on the screen. He had done this before. As Father Mackey listened to the commentary, he didn't know whether to laugh or cry. The explanations were usually wrong, and sometimes bizarre.

When a man in Western dress and a figure in a strange hat and a long red dress appeared on the screen, the Director described the couple as the school headmaster (which was correct) and his wife. The "wife" was, in fact, a Tibetan lama. Father Mackey squirmed in his seat for a few minutes and finally whispered to his host, "Look, can you stop it? Let's start again, and let me do the commentary."

When Father West heard the correct interpretation of the pictures on the screen, he was aghast: "My God, what I've been telling people!"

Travelling around Canada, Father Mackey could speak comfortably and appeal to any group. At the end of one sermon, he was chatting with people of the congregation, one of whom introduced himself as a farmer. He and Father Mackey talked for a while about the Mission. Then the man said he'd recently sold some land. "But, you know, Father," he said, "I don't really need that money."

He wrote Father Mackey a cheque for $5,000.

* * *

While donations in Canada had been generous, Father Mackey faced a major financial problem when he returned to Kurseong — one much bigger and more serious than usual. He was accustomed to an empty cash box and school bank account. It was a constant struggle to somehow deal with the perennial net deficit at St. Alphonsus.

The money Father Mackey had raised in Canada went into the Mission account in Toronto. Some was spent immediately to buy things like a lathe and tools, which he brought back for the Industrial School. Within the regular school budget there were no funds for extra science and sports equipment, library books and so on. Money for such items had to come from special, outside sources, usually through the Mission office.

There was money in the Mass stipend fund, but that came under the parish and was strictly controlled. Catholics have traditionally paid to have Masses said for personal reasons or "intentions" as they are called. A person might want Mass said for a departed loved one, or someone who is sick, or for a variety of reasons. In the early 1950s the cost of such a Mass was one or two dollars.

People could make the request and donation directly to the Mission, or else the Church — which usually received far more requests than could be filled by priests in countries like Canada — would allocate the extra Masses and their revenues to the missions. Only one intention could be accommodated per Mass, and a priest could say no more than six stipend Masses per week.

Money received by a parish or mission could be used only after the Masses were said. Use of the funds without saying the Masses is absolutely forbidden. Before Father Mackey left for Canada, he had roughly five thousand dollars in the Mass stipend account, each dollar representing one Mass that had to be said. He would pay out the stipends as the Masses were said by priests in the district.

When he returned from Canada, however, he found that the Mass stipend account was empty. Obviously, thousands of Masses had not been said while Father Mackey was away. This was a serious problem. Father Wery and his partner, Brother Robin, had not meant to steal the money or cheat anyone out of a Mass that had been paid for. But, as usual, they needed money, and rationalized that Father Mackey would be returning with lots of money, and would be able to take care of it. Unfortunately, Father Mackey brought back equipment and supplies, not cash.

The priests did what they could to work off the Masses, but the undertaking was hopeless. When Father Henrichs, Father Mackey's superior in Calcutta, next audited the Mass stipend account, he discovered the situation and Father Mackey was in trouble. Father Janssens, the Father General in Rome, wrote a letter of reprimand and stripped Father Mackey of his Jesuit Superiorship. The Archbishop in Calcutta relieved him of his ecclesiastical position of Dean.

Father Mackey and Father Wery would have to take a share in fulfilling the obligation, a kind of penance. The Society would arrange for the rest of the obligation to be fulfilled by Jesuits elsewhere. Every Jesuit in the world says one Mass a month for the General of the Society, and five thousand of these Masses were allotted to cover Father Mackey's intentions. Father Mackey and Father Wery each had to say twenty-five "free" Masses.

Many Jesuit Fathers in the hierarchy up to the General were not amused, especially Father Mackey's immediate superiors, who would have had their knuckles rapped as well. When he pointed out that he hadn't taken the money himself, Father Mackey was told he should have had more sense — that he should have known Father Wery and Brother Robin well enough not to leave them with the money.

While the episode constituted a serious breach of Church law, the Kurseong Jesuits did not lose their sense of humour over it. Father Wery did a quick calculation of the dollar value of their punishment, compared with the money they had taken from the account. He reckoned that the fifty Masses they had to say were worth about 100 dollars each. He said, "God bless us, let's try it again!"

As for losing his job as Superior, Father Mackey was just as happy. He said it was a headache trying to guide "a bunch of headstrong Canadians."

5/

Father Michael Wery died in 1957 from a heart attack, and his funeral was probably the largest Kurseong had every seen. The wailing, tear-streamed mourners in bare feet and shabby clothes overflowed the church. The crowd following the coffin from the church, in the words of one of Father Wery's friends, "swelled like a river in the monsoon. The graveyard was a sea of the sorrowing poor."

Less than two years later, Father Mackey moved to Darjeeling town as headmaster of St. Robert's High School. This was the result of a bizarre campaign that extended back ten years, to when Father Mackey was requested to act as a polling officer in a local by-election. He had not been much interested and didn't have time to spare. He responded by saying, "Look, I can't be a polling officer here, I'm a Canadian."

The district commissioner countered that he had to do it: "You're the only man we can trust."

Father Mackey realized this might be true, even though the commissioner didn't really know him. He reluctantly agreed. His main jobs were to oversee the voting, making sure only registered voters cast ballots, and then to count the votes. He was provided with the list of eligible voters, which he consulted each time a prospective voter came into the dak-bungalow, the government rest-house, where he sat in the front room.

It was a straightforward procedure: he just checked names on the list. At the time, Father Mackey was barely aware of the fierce political struggle between the ethnic Nepalis and the Bengalis in Darjeeling District. But as people arrived to cast their ballots, he realized that there were few if any Bengali names on the voters' list. Presumably, a Nepali clerk typing the list had omitted all the Bengali names. People whose names were not listed were understandably unhappy, but what could Father Mackey could do about it?

Most just grumbled and left. But then Doctor Guha arrived. He was the founder and head of the tuberculosis sanitarium in Kurseong, a well-known, respected and influential man and a personal friend of Prime Minister Nehru. Also a Bengali. Upon learning that his name was not on the voters' list, he grew livid. Father Mackey could only say, "Well, I'm sorry, your name's not on the list. Nothing I can do about it. The only rule I have, what I was told, is that a person's name has to be on this list in order to vote. Your name's not here so I can't let you vote."

This was an outrage. Doctor Guha, an intelligent and well-informed man, knew that Father Mackey had nothing to do with the situation, but many other people in the Bengali community blamed Father Mackey. He was accused of siding with the Nepalis against the Bengalis.

At four o'clock that afternoon, when voting ended, Father Mackey had to count the votes. Along with thirteen other men, he took the ballot box into a smaller, more private room. Each of the four parties was represented by three men — the candidate and two scrutineers — and there was an officer from the *katchari*, the district civic administration office. It was hot and soon grew dark.

The men finished the vote count by the light of a Petromax pressurized kerosene lamp. The two leading candidates stood for the Gurkha League and the Communist party. At seven o'clock in the evening, the count gave the Gurkha League a narrow win, by seven votes. Maila Badze, the Darjeeling Communist leader, was one of his party's scrutineers. When his candidate lost, he said, "Recount!"

Father Mackey had spent his entire day, from nine o'clock that morning, on this exercise, which was obviously flawed, when he could have been doing his own work. Now, in this hot, uncomfortable room, he would have to help count all the votes again. He uttered a caustic remark about the Communist call. The men proceeded with the recount. At eleven that night, the recount again gave the Gurkhas a seven-vote win. Maila Badze could do nothing more — not that night.

But the following week, Father Mackey heard a funny story from Darjeeling. Apparently, Maila Badze had stood on his platform in Chowk Bazaar at a public rally on the intervening Sunday and denounced Father Mackey. He accused him of putting butter on the railway track and stopping the "toy train" that ran between Siliguri and Darjeeling. He also accused Father Mackey of beating up Bengalis, or at least encouraging his Nepali boys to do so.

The charges were ludicrous and everybody at St. Alphonsus laughed, including Father Mackey. The idea of him inciting physical violence on Bengali people was ridiculous. As for butter on the tracks, the toy train got stuck often enough without it. A heavy rain, which was quite common, was enough to do the trick. When the monsoon rains came, two men sat at the front and threw sand on the tracks for traction.

While everyone around Father Mackey laughed at Maila Badze's accusations, the Communist Party was not without influence. Allegations of anti-Bengali attitude and actions were made periodically against Father Mackey. It was no doubt true that from time to time Nepali boys from the school beat up Bengali boys, but Father Mackey would not condone this activity, let alone encourage it.

Nevertheless, false allegations built up and anti-Father Mackey sentiment grew over the years. Negative reports were registered in the *katchari*. Bengalis in Kurseong wanted him removed. By the late 1950s this pressure reached the point where a couple of Catholics working in the *katchari* went to the Monsignor, the senior Catholic in the district, and told him Father Mackey was in serious trouble, and should be moved out of Kurseong. The Monsignor and the Jesuit Superior deliberated. They decided to switch Father Mackey and Father Prendergast.

Father Mackey became headmaster of St. Robert's High School at the beginning of 1959, the year of its Silver Jubilee. Father Prendergast took over at St. Alphonsus. This was treated as a normal change. Father Mackey had been at St. Alphonsus for over ten years. The idea of a move, to give both the institutions and the individuals involved a revitalizing change, seemed reasonable to him.

He learned the reasons behind the move only later.

At the time, Father Mackey was sorry to leave the people and the place he had come to know so well. But the people showed their gratitude. He had played a big role in the Kurseong community, not just in his own school and sports (for which it was once reported that he came ih for "a lot of hero worship"). He had been involved with activities like the Boy Scouts, and sat on or chaired many boards and committees — the Kurseong Municipal Education Committee, the managing committees of many schools, the Cemetery Board. There was a big farewell function and a gift, and the obvious sentiment behind these made him feel good about the job he was leaving, and ready for the challenge ahead.

Father Mackey stepped into a well-run, well-funded and well-respected high school, for which he credits Father Prendergast. Father Mackey was especially impressed with the staff, most of whom were old boys from the school. They were good, qualified, dedicated teachers and Father Prendergast had pulled them together into a team that was not only organized but also had a family spirit. He had also fostered sports, concerts and other entertainment programmes.

St. Robert's was not rich but well set. The building had been the world famous Park Hotel before an archbishop bought it in 1934. The taxes were paid by the Archdiocese. The fees (which were still only six rupees per month, just over one dollar) were sufficient to pay the teachers and run the school — electricity, maintenance, even the regular purchase of books and lab and sports equipment. Here, Father Mackey did not have to worry constantly about whether he would have the money required for the next month's expenses. He even had a reserve fund and the flexibility to plan future purchases. Quite a change from the days when Father Wery and Brother Robin would rob the St. Alphonsus cash box of its last rupee.

St. Robert's had the same number of students as the high school section of St. Alphonsus, about 550. It also had a boarding facility, a planter's house that held thirty to forty boarders, most of whom came from Bhutan. The hostel, opened in Father Prendergast's time, was called Bellarmine Hall, so St. Robert's doubly honoured Roberto Bellarmine, the Italian Jesuit saint. Father Mackey's capital addition to the school was a science laboratory. He raised the funds by soliciting donations from Canada and also received money from the Archbishop in Calcutta.

Darjeeling offered more opportunities for activities and mixing with other schools. Although he continued with community-interest activities like concerts and school science exhibitions, Father Mackey remained most keenly interested in sports. St. Robert's was better equipped than St. Alphonsus, although expensive sports like field hockey were still a stretch. Being right in Darjeeling gave him the opportunity of visiting North Point at the end of the school year and approaching the man in charge of sports. This request for aging equipment became standard. Father Mackey would drop by and say, "What have you got for me?"

St. Robert's had a strong sports programme when Father Mackey took over, but he pushed it even further. Being in the town where so many district sports finals were held, he made sure St. Robert's participated at every opportunity. One major coup was getting St. Robert's into tournaments with the posh schools. There had been a barrier to this previously, and at first his students were treated like second-class citizens.

On one early occasion, St. Paul's — the Anglican high school considered the best school in the district — invited the St. Robert's Boy Scouts to take part in some joint practice. Both troops were preparing for the upcoming Jamboree, and they thought practising together could help everyone. But while the joint activity went ahead, the St. Robert's boys were not accorded the hospitality that would have been extended to, say, St. Joseph's, the posh Jesuit school.

Father Mackey was offered a cup of tea but his boys were not. He was furious and refused to take their tea. Fuming at the slight, he took his boys down into the bazaar and treated them to a feast of *momos* (the tasty Tibetan meat-filled snack, a little like a wonton or ravioli). Unfortunately, he had no money in his pocket and had to borrow from a friend in the bazaar to pay for the treat.

Father Mackey's involvement with the St. Robert's Boy Scouts proved to be very successful. Each year, Darjeeling scout troops vied for the Jackson Shield, a trophy offered for a competition that included athletic events. Schools like St. Joseph's and St. Paul's lent their excellent facilities and equipment to their scout troops, but North Point's "poor cousins" at St. Robert's managed to capture the Jackson Shield three years in a row under Father Mackey's coaching.

His forte was gymnastics. Father Mackey had led the boys to victory one year with gymnastic horse work, and the next year he decided to go with human pyramids. St. Paul's also made this choice. At the competition, St. Robert's went first. When the St. Paul's scouts saw Father Mackey's boys build their elaborate human pyramids, they decided not to present theirs. They didn't want to embarrass themselves.

For many years the better schools established under the British Raj maintained an air of superiority over the less well-endowed schools of the district, as the latter were finding their way. This included girls' schools as well as boys'. And while their academic records were impressive, partly due to selection of students and students arriving better prepared, on the sports fields the posh schools had a fight on their hands.

Father Mackey had little time to attend competitions his own school was not involved in, but when the posh Loreto Convent School, which counted a number of princesses among its girls, was pitted against the poorer Nepali girls at St. Teresa's school, he would make a special effort. He'd take a bunch of boys from Bellarmine Hall, the St. Robert's hostel, along to cheer with him. A field hockey match would see the Loreto girls in their smart uniform skirts and blouses, shoes and stockings, while the St. Teresa's team was rather tatty, a bit mis-matched and usually in bare feet. Father Mackey and his boys cheered wildly for St. Teresa's, much to the displeasure of the Loreto Sisters, as the scruffy-looking, barefooted Nepali girls overcame their well-dressed, well-heeled opponents.

* * *

All the while Father Mackey was in India, his older sister Tess was his contact person back home. Instead of sending individual letters to each of the family members, he'd send one to Tess. She'd re-type the letter and send copies to the others. Tess was also the one who would do favours and send whatever "Father Bill" needed.

In October of 1959, Tess came to India to visit him. She was an intelligent, vibrant woman who made the most of the trip. And once past her surprise at the grass airstrip (it had iron grating over the grass) and small shack that served as Bagdogra airport, near Siliguri, she took most of the sights in stride. She wallowed in a mass of colourful cloth in the sari shop, visited a tea estate and rode on an elephant, and shared brandy with Mother Carmel at Loreto Convent where she stayed for most of her visit. Father Mackey's friends and colleagues were lavish in their hospitality, and made her visit a memorable one.

Another woman came to visit Father Mackey one day at St. Robert's — one he thought he'd left behind long ago in Kurseong. Early in his stay there, he'd received a letter written in Nepali and signed Narbada. At the time, his understanding of the written language was not very good, so he took it to Father Wery for translation. Father Wery took the letter and read it to himself. He glanced up at Father Mackey with an inscrutable look and said, "Ohhhhh."

Father Mackey was intrigued by the older man's reaction: "So what does it say?"

Narbada was a woman in the parish. "She says every time she sees you she gets bad thoughts. She wants to come and discuss them with you."

Narbada was an attractive woman in her mid- or late-twenties. Father Mackey had taught her husband a few years before, and oddly enough, the letter was delivered by her husband's younger brother. Her husband was in the army and they lived in the nearby Dowhill community. But apparently the husband was away a lot and she got lonely.

Father Mackey did not have the looks of a movie star, but something made him attractive to her. As the years went by and it became evident that she might be slightly unwell mentally, he felt some compassion for her situation. But he was not about to discuss her "bad thoughts" with her. The matter became something of a joke among the Jesuits. As there was little he could do about it, Father Mackey shrugged it off.

It was about seven years later that Narbada appeared at St. Robert's, looking, apparently, for Father Mackey. The occasion was the high-school fete, and she came across Father Murray Abraham who vaguely resembled Father Mackey — fair skinned, red hair and glasses. He was in charge of the fete money and was upstairs in the school counting cash. Father Abe knew the story and recognized Narbada when she came into the headmaster's office. And from the look in her eye, he realized that she thought he was Father Mackey. He wanted nothing to do with her bad thoughts. He stuttered out, "B, b, b, but I'm not Father Mackey. He, he, he's downstairs," and sent her off in a direction he was pretty sure was wrong.

The following January, when Father Mackey was alone in Bishop's House, preparing a sermon on a cold Darjeeling Saturday night, the door bell rang. When he opened the door, there stood Narbada. Despite the years of this standing joke, he had never really prepared himself to handle such a confrontation. He wasn't prepared now, and could only say, *"Hunde na!"* (Nothing doing!) and slam the door. That was the last time he saw her.

* * *

Father Mackey got his first scooter while at St. Robert's. It was a Bajaj, the most common make in India. While he had never had a scooter of his own, he had learned to drive one and was quite proficient. He'd had the new machine a month when Bishop Eric Benjamin asked Father Mackey to teach him to drive it.

Bishop Eric was the first Nepali in India to be ordained into the Catholic priesthood. He was consecrated Bishop in 1962 at the age of forty-two, and it was the following winter, on a Saturday afternoon, that he approached Father Mackey with his request.

Father Mackey put the Bishop on the scooter behind him and drove him over to North Point's large football field. Bishop Eric had great difficulty getting the power and balance coordinated so he could move forward, but after an hour or more, he managed that. From the end of the field near the College buildings, Father Mackey and a North Point colleague sent him down the centre of the football field. All was well.

Bishop Eric sailed along, crossing centre field and continuing on, heading in the direction of Mount Hermon School. By the time he reached the far goal posts, his coaches were shouting, "Turn, turn!" But Bishop Eric hadn't mastered turning or braking. He just kept going straight until he hit the cement wall at the end of the football field.

Fortunately, he wasn't hurt and the scooter suffered only a bent fork. Father Mackey managed to get them back to Bishop's House on the damaged vehicle, and had it repaired the following week. Bishop Eric never did learn to drive a scooter.

* * *

At St. Robert's, Bhutanese students made up almost eighty per cent of the boarders. The key person for these boys — and for Father Mackey's future, as it turned out — was the prime minister of Bhutan, Jigmie Dorji. He took great interest in all aspects of student activities. And not just those of his brothers and son, or other highly-placed children studying in Darjeeling, but also the thirty or forty boys who were not from Bhutan's elite.

While in Darjeeling, Jigmie Dorji would visit the schools and, if he found achievements to acknowledge, would host modest celebrations. If the achievements were particularly good, he would provide dinner at *the* restaurant in town — Glenary's. If he were less pleased with student performance, he might take the boys for afternoon tea.

Besides the Bhutanese students at St. Alphonsus and then St. Robert's, Father Mackey also met some of the boys at St. Joseph's. In particular, he got to know the Dorjis — Lhendup, Jigmie Dorji's youngest brother, and the Prime Minister's son, Paljor. Less well, he knew Jigmie Dorji's other younger brother, Ugyen, or "Rimp."

Ugyen had been recognized at an early age as a reincarnated lama and hence was referred to by the honorific "Rinpoche" (or "Rimpoche") later informally shortened to Rimp. He had been sent to a monastery for the religious education befitting a high lama, but he decided that such a life was not for him. He went on to be educated at St. Joseph's and then to become his country's wealthiest businessman.

Father Mackey got to know Lhendup, or "Lumpy" as he was called by family and friends, when he was asked to train a gymnastics team at North Point. Lhendup was a superior athlete and practiced tumbling with Father Mackey. And though younger and smaller, Paljor or "Benji" also joined Father Mackey's gymnastics team.

Father Mackey admired the ability and fearlessness of these boys. They would try anything and usually succeed. Lhendup Dorji had no fear in most areas. He had a reputation as quite a "boy about town," and a flamboyance that would extend his reputation far beyond Bhutan in future, when he gained a place in Shirley MacLaine's *Don't Fall Off The Mountain*.

* * *

Father Mackey's trouble with Bengali authorities did not end with his move to Darjeeling. He was removed from the heat of Bengali sentiments in Kurseong, but he was more prominent in Darjeeling and his enemies ranged beyond the small town of Kurseong. He was not without friends, even among Bengalis and authorities like the police. In fact, he was very popular: most people liked him and appreciated his work. But it didn't take many voices murmuring in the right places to continue eroding his position.

Father Mackey may have been pro-Nepali, but he was certainly not anti-Bengali. Yet every situation that could possibly be twisted into showing bias was distorted in this direction. One of the first such occasions in Darjeeling concerned a man referred to as DOPE because he was Director of Physical Education (Indians have a great propensity for referring to things by their initials, abbreviations or acronyms).

This man's job was to organize sports activities in and around Darjeeling. But when Father Mackey arrived at St. Robert's, he learned that DOPE had not organized any activities for a couple of years. Apparently the man had encountered a problem at some point and simply chose to do nothing after that. The combination of Father Mackey's interest in sports and his action-oriented personality led him to get involved. He soon had inter-school sports leagues and tournaments going: first volleyball, then football and finally sports days.

To the first sports day, Father Mackey invited the Chief Inspector of Schools as Chief Guest. The Inspector came and brought a visiting high official from the West Bengal Board of Secondary Education. During the sports day, this gentleman asked where DOPE was. Father Mackey said, "Well, he was invited, but he's not here."

"Is this not his work?"

Father Mackey said no: "I've been here a couple of years and he hasn't organized any sports."

The official followed up and took DOPE to task. DOPE defended himself by accusing Father Mackey of interfering with his office. His word was taken over Father Mackey's simple statement of fact and another black mark went against his name within government circles.

Father Mackey's enemies were not without subtlety, as evidenced by harassment over his credentials. The government of West Bengal had a policy of upgrading less qualified teachers to the Bachelor of Teaching (BT) degree level. Every year a number of them went to an authorized institution for this upgrading. The Canadian Jesuits in the area were all well educated, and their qualifications had never been questioned by the government until Father Mackey went to St. Robert's.

When he wanted to raise the high school to higher secondary, meaning class 11 instead of class 10, the government insisted that he have a BT. The West Bengal Board of Secondary Education required him to enter the BT programme at the Darjeeling Shree Rama Krishnan B.T. College, an extension of the University of Calcutta. As the government was paying he had no argument to make. Yet it seemed most odd to the College staff that Father Mackey had to attend the College as a student. He was a member of their managing committee and sometimes taught mathematics there.

The BT programme was a two-year programme, but Father Mackey joined it three months before final examinations and completed it in that period. At the same time, he maintained most of his workload at St. Robert's. Besides running the school, he usually taught mathematics, concentrating on classes 10 and 9. On College class days he would teach a maths class before leaving St. Robert's in the morning and then teach another after returning in the afternoon.

Even at the College, Father Mackey managed to get into trouble. He was taking educational measurement from a young Bengali professor, Miss Bose. On this day she was at the chalk board working out a problem. Father Mackey had already worked out all the problems in the book and was sitting at the back of the class studying the history of Indian education, which he found complicated. He heard her say of the problem she was working on, "The answer in the book is wrong."

Knowing this to be untrue, he looked up and said, "Miss, if you use the other formula, you might get the right answer."

Miss Bose stood up, slammed her book closed, walked out and refused to the teach the class as long as Father Mackey was in it. (Eventually, she gave him a failing grade — not enough to prevent him from getting his BT with a second-class mark.)

The BT programme included an evaluation of teaching ability in the classroom. By this time Father Mackey was an old hand at teaching in general, and the West Bengal syllabus in particular. Besides knowing how to teach the syllabus so that the students really understood the material, he knew the exam system completely. He could predict ninety per cent of any government maths exam. This was a sign of a good teacher.

While it was important to teach well beyond the expected exam material, failing to stress exam questions would leave one's students behind in a highly competitive system. And while some teachers focused only on the exams, a really good teacher mastered both approaches.

Knowing that he was under particular scrutiny, Father Mackey didn't want to leave the judgment of his practicum to chance. Neither did he want his real teaching programme interfered with. On the first day the practical examiners were expected, he put a maths problem on the chalk board and told his students, "We're going to carry on with our regular work. But if that door opens, I'm teaching this problem."

One of the boys said: "Don't worry. We've got lots of teachers through. We'll get you through."

The next morning, three Bengali professors from Calcutta University came into the classroom and sat down. Father Mackey and his students slipped easily into the problem on the chalk board. It was an interesting, rather complicated problem about time which required an algebraic solution. But it could be simplified somewhat by having the hands of a clock represent two runners in a race.

The hour hand represented a "short, fat, lazy Nepali," while the minute hand represented a "long-legged, fleet-footed Bengali." Father Mackey thought this would flatter the Bengalis. However, as he commonly did, he used a few Nepali words and phrases. And when Father Mackey referred to the faster Bengali runner by using the Nepali word *lamkhute*, which means "long-legged," it didn't occur to him that the same word also means "mosquito." The Bengalis took offence and duly noted that Father Mackey was ridiculing Bengalis.

Language in a more serious, official context created further problems for Father Mackey. India is home to scores of languages, and possibly hundreds. The government recognizes many of them, although the most important and supposedly "national" language is Hindi. In West Bengal, the state language is Bengali. But the majority of people in the hills of Darjeeling speak Nepali and have long fought for official recognition of their language.

Occasionally, this campaign has become fierce and even violent. So when Father Mackey tried to have the school language policy changed, he was venturing into a very dicey area. At the time, five languages were taught in classes 7 and 8 in Darjeeling high schools. There was Nepali, the mother tongue of the great majority of students; Bengali, the language of West Bengal; Hindi, the national language; Sanskrit, the classical language; and English.

This heavy load of languages was simply not sound pedagogically, so Father Mackey went to see the inspector of schools to see what could be done. This was the head man for the West Bengal Board of Secondary Education in the Darjeeling District. Father Mackey said, "Could we have a meeting of the school heads and try to send a petition to the Board, asking that we not have five languages?"

The inspector said, "I wouldn't advise it. It's a very political move."

"Well," Father Mackey said, "can I try?"

Reluctantly, the inspector agreed and a meeting of the local school heads was convened. There were about a dozen of them, and seven were Bengalis. They all agreed that the language load was too heavy. The next obvious question was, "Which languages do you want?"

Father Mackey said, "Well, looking at St. Robert's, where practically every student is Nepali, number one I would take Nepali. And English we have to have. So English and Nepali. Then I'd say let's take one more." Most agreed that a three-language system was reasonable. That left a choice among Sanskrit, Bengali and Hindi. Father Mackey made the mistake of volunteering his choice. "Let's take the national language." The choice of Hindi left Bengali out, leading the majority of headmasters, staunch Bengalis, to accuse Father Mackey of being anti-Bengali.

But even more serious charges were to come.

St. Robert's was very strong in sports, particularly volleyball. The school even had two staff volleyball teams, an A team and a B team. In a 1962 volleyball tournament, St. Robert's wound up in the finals in three classes: staff (Father Mackey himself was on the Staff A team), senior students and junior students. They won all three. This was great cause for celebration. They won on a Saturday, and Father Mackey declared the following Monday a holiday. On the intervening Sunday there was a large language procession: Nepalis were demonstrating against the government, demanding the acceptance of the Nepali language.

This procession may have closed the noose around Father Mackey's neck. Staff and students from St. Robert's were going to take part and Bishop Eric asked Father Mackey if he would head the contingent. Father Mackey refused, saying, "My name is bad enough with the Bengali authorities. I don't want to make it worse."

But on the day of the procession, the Bishop called Father Mackey and said, "Please go and warn the teachers and students to behave themselves and keep the protest peaceful."

Father Mackey went to the demonstration and gathered the St. Robert's group around him and said, "Now behave yourselves and don't cause any trouble." At that moment a police photographer caught the scene with his camera.

Earlier that year, 1962, the Chinese invaded north-eastern India and war broke out. Darjeeling was declared a sensitive area and remained under a kind of special rule for quite some time. This meant the authorities, including the military and the police, could do almost anything they wanted in the name of security. Following the language demonstration, a young policeman named Lakpa came to see Father Mackey.

The Jesuit had no reason to be surprised. Lakpa, of Tibetan origin, had been one of his students and then one of his teachers before joining the police. They had always been friends. They chatted casually and in the course of the conversation Lakpa asked, "Who changes you people? In your postings, I mean."

"Well," Father Mackey said, "the Provincial or the Superior: the Darjeeling Superior or the Provincial of Calcutta."

Lakpa nodded and went no further in that direction.

This was late in 1962 and the Jesuit Superior, Father Jim McCabe, was visiting Canada for a few months. Father Mackey knew that the tide was running against him, but he didn't know how badly until Father McCabe returned to India the following spring. One March morning

Father Mackey got a phone call from the Superior: "What are you doing down there? The police are after you!"

"Well, I don't know. What am I doing?"

"I'm coming to see you."

Father McCabe had received an order from the police that Father Mackey would have to leave the District. When the Jesuits tried to negotiate and get the order reversed, the police allegations came out more clearly. A photograph was produced, showing Father Mackey, according to the police, "haranguing and stirring up and inciting the students to go against the Bengalis." Father Mackey's explanation of what he had really said was ignored. A further allegation was made: "You closed your school after the language procession, to go against the government."

This caught Father Mackey by surprise. He couldn't remember anything about a language procession and a school holiday. He had to consult his school diary. Coinciding with the date of the language procession, he found the school's victorious record at the volleyball tournament. He took the diary to the Superintendent of Police and said: "Look, this is the school diary. Volleyball final Saturday: junior team, senior team, staff A team — we won all three championships. Monday's declared a holiday."

"No! You closed it for the language procession."

"Look, I didn't know anything about these accusations, but here's the document."

"No." The police were determined to get rid of Father Mackey. At one point when Father Mackey was defending himself against specific charges, the senior police officer said, "Whether they are true or false, Father — it doesn't make much difference. Every time there is trouble, your name comes up."

The Jesuits, the Bishop, many local people and even a member of parliament, Mrs. Chhetri, fought the expulsion order. Those who had connections in New Delhi tried to pull strings. But it was all to no avail. The security restrictions left no room to manoeuvre. Public meetings were suspect and people had to be careful not to get themselves in trouble with the authorities. Even the Bishop and the Jesuits knew they could push only so far. In the end, Father Mackey had to go.

Numerous goodbye parties showed the tremendous support of the people and his colleagues, and the Bishop spoke in particularly strong terms at the teachers' farewell. He had received information that some of the reports against Father Mackey had come from teachers at St.

Robert's. Whether this was true or not, he denounced such false charges and those who would fabricate them. He went on to praise Father Mackey and his work.

Nor was Father Mackey alone in leaving the District. Others were forced out for a variety of reasons. Anyone who happened to be on the authorities' "black list" stood no chance of fighting an expulsion order. There were stories of local Chinese who were Indian citizens being picked up in the middle of the night and taken away. At least Father Mackey fared better than that.

Yet when the day came to leave, this thought, the farewell parties and the kind words were little consolation. In his seventeen years in the Darjeeling District he had got to know the people. He had gained a good understanding of their culture. He spoke their language. They had accepted him as one of their own. He had been influential educationally, having headed two large schools, and socially, especially through sports and his religious work.

"When I had to leave Darjeeling as being unwanted after seventeen years," he said later, "well, that was the hardest thing I ever had to do in my life: to get on that bus and go down to catch a train and leave behind me seventeen years of my life. To leave all that behind, humanly speaking, was mighty hard. And I had to call on the better part of my spiritual training to accept it."

6/

While waiting for his permit to enter Bhutan, Father Mackey was exiled to Jamshedpur in Bihar state. He left Darjeeling at the end of June 1963, and took up a temporary position as Secretary to Bishop Picachy of Jamshedpur. The Bishop was having trouble with Rome — especially the benevolent organization, the Holy Childhood — because his records were never straight and his books never balanced.

Father Mackey and the parish priest were asked to put the books and files in order. They saw immediately that the Bishop was not administratively minded. His office was a terrible mess. He didn't file letters and statements properly, and just stuffed records into old shoe boxes.

There was only one thing to do. They asked the Bishop to make himself scarce for a weekend so they could concentrate on the job. The few useful and recent papers they found, they filed, but they burned ninety per cent of the letters and old material. As a token gesture, they took a few letters, put them in boxes and carried them up to the attic. When Bishop Picachy returned, they told him the files were all organized and they'd established a system so he didn't have to shove everything in shoe boxes any more.

They told him: "All your mail is in the attic. We've separated all the different letters — to Rome, the Holy Childhood, bishops, on priests, on schools, on religious orders, Sisters' convents, everything." The Bishop cast a concerned glance towards the attic, but never climbed the ladder to check.

While at Jamshedpur, Father Mackey worked with Mother Teresa of Calcutta. He had met her a number of times, both "officially" and informally, in Darjeeling, where she had set up a convent and initiated work with the poor. She was originally of the Loreto order (before founding her own order), and in Darjeeling the priest from St. Robert's took care of Loreto Convent matters that required a priest — Mass, confessions, and so on.

In Jamshedpur, Bishop Picachy asked Father Mackey to act as a liaison officer in the work Mother Teresa was undertaking with TELCO, a huge, multi-faceted industrial enterprise. She wanted to set up a small convent and facilities to help the poorer workers at TELCO, as well as local leprosy patients and destitute people. The Bishop's office served as her base and communications centre when she visited.

Father Mackey handled the related correspondence, assisted Mother Teresa when she visited, and helped obtain the space for the convent and facilities. TELCO handed over the property to Father Mackey. It included two sets of officers' quarters close to the area where Mother Teresa would work.

She visited to see the accommodation and check on progress. She always travelled by train, third class, and Father Mackey met her at the station with Bishop Picachy's car and driver. This was an old black Packard, a gas-guzzling American monstrosity few people could drive and almost impossible to park. Father Mackey took Mother Teresa to the quarters allotted by TELCO. After a quick look around, she asked, "What kind of quarters are these?"

"They're company officers' quarters."

"No, that's no good. I want ordinary workers' quarters for my Sisters. They will live as the poor people live."

TELCO wasn't pleased with her decision, but provided three smaller sets of workers' quarters in the poor section of Jamshedpur.

Father Mackey could see Mother Teresa's point. She realized that if her Sisters lived near the officers, the poor would feel intimidated, and the officers would object to large numbers of poor invading their area. In these and other ways, the Sisters could better serve the poor by being among them.

Father Mackey observed that Mother Teresa seemed to gain strength and vitality from working directly with the poor. However tired she might be, in the presence of the sick and the troubled she would come alive and pour forth "a sanctity, a holiness, a love of the poor." For Mother Teresa, he said, the lowest of the low are close to God. And involving her Sisters with the absolutely destitute was her version of what you do to your neighbour, you do to God.

Mother Teresa was not alone in experiencing this uplifting effect — her Sisters also exhibited "tremendous cheerfulness" and were the happiest group of Sisters Father Mackey ever knew. As he put it: "Mother Teresa is a very strange phenomenon in that sense. I would say she's a saint and a very holy person. She is a person very, very close to God."

* * *

The rulers of Bhutan have always maintained a low profile in the outside world. From the end of the 19th Century until 1964, relations even with neighbouring India were delegated to a very high-ranking government officer and trusted friend of the kings. This official maintained a major presence at Bhutan House, the quasi-embassy located in Kalimpong. From 1952 this person was Jigmie Dorji, who also served as Loenchen, or "Prime Minister."

During his seventeen years in Darjeeling, Father Mackey never saw the King of Bhutan — but he did know the entire Dorji family. Besides the boys at school, he'd met the prime minister's sister, Ashi Tashi, who frequently visited Loreto Convent school and St. Joseph's. ("Ashi" is an honorific title, roughly equivalent to "Princess.")

When Father Mackey arrived in Paro from Darjeeling, Ashi Tashi was the one who decided he should build the new high school in Eastern Bhutan. Ten years before, she had spent time in Tashigang, helping to administer the large eastern district. The area was heavily populated (for Bhutan) and relatively poor, although it was made up of farmers with small land holdings, just like the rest of the country. Ashi Tashi told Father Mackey that most development had taken place in Western Bhutan, and now it was time to build something significant in the East. Some have said that, since this was an uncertain venture, it was safer to embark on it there, rather than in the more visible West.

Because no roads crossed the country, and given the north-south configuration of mountains and rivers, Eastern Bhutan was much farther away than a map would suggest. All traffic between West and East had to go via India. That was the way Father Mackey would go, as he left Paro, bound for Tashigang.

Father Mackey had already spent a good many years in the mountains. But still he found Bhutan's landscape and roads astounding. It was rougher, more virgin — and the sheer "mountain-ness" was more impressive than anything he'd seen. Also, he marvelled at the variety of climate and vegetation. As he travelled from the plains of Assam, still warm and humid in mid-October, through dense, damp, tropical forest and over high, cool mountain ridges, he found the vegetation could change dramatically as you rounded a sharp curve in the road.

The area around Tashigang is hot and dry. At 1,120 metres, the town has the lowest altitude of any population centre in Bhutan's interior. Monsoon rains arrive as elsewhere, but the surrounding mountains and other factors, like slope, soil type and deforestation, make this one of the most arid regions in the country. In October, however, shortly after the monsoons, and with the sun receding southward, the weather would have been very pleasant. The rains would have left the hillsides green, and temperatures would have hovered in the mid-twenties, Celsius.

Today, Tashigang is a thriving community, and though the hillsides upon which it is built are occupied to capacity, it is not overcrowded. The bazaar area is nestled in a small valley formed by a large stream. This stream and the irregular layout of the bazaar give the community more of a sense of a compact "downtown" commercial centre than is found elsewhere in Bhutan.

But in 1963, when Father Mackey arrived, the place was very different. Although the Dzong and a few important institutions existed, making it a significant place, Tashigang could hardly be called a town. It was, essentially, the Dzong, which Father Mackey calls "a fort-cum-monastery."

The name Tashigang means "auspicious mountain." Built in 1656, the Dzong sits at the end of a mountain spur, some 300 metres above the river below, and dominates the valley around it. At the main entrance level, the outer section rises only three storeys, but inside, parts of the monastery rise higher, and on the down-mountain side it measures five stories in height. Made of whitewashed stone, the structure stands out majestically on the mountainside.

Its fortress role had long since faded away, but its work as administrative centre of the district — Tashigang Dzongkhag — was growing. And its importance as home to the district's complement of monks from the government monk body remained. Much of the space and activity within the Dzong was devoted to the monastery, which housed about seventy monks. The Dzong was held to be a sacred place and as such should be set apart from the ordinary aspects of a community. The major government institutions that existed outside the Dzong — the school, hospital and army cantonment — were located on the next spur, some distance away.

When Father Mackey arrived, the main administrative officers were the *thrimpoen,* the *nyerchen* and their *rabjams.* Technically, *thrimpoen* means "Master or Lord of the Law," and the Thrimpoen of Tashigang did administer the law. But he was also the de facto governor or chief administrator of the district. His duties, however, were not onerous in those simpler times. The *nyerchen* was like a chief quartermaster, responsible for the collection of taxes, which were paid in kind. Both officials had a *rabjam* or assistant, which was quite an important position.

All of these individuals would have been known by the honorific title "Dasho," first by virtue of the positions they held and then, at some point, because of having been officially designated Dasho by the King. The awarding of a long, broad, dark red scarf (called a *kabney*), a sword and the title of Dasho is akin to a knighthood and is usually a recognition of service to the King. The scarves are worn, draped around the body in a particular way, in *dzongs* and religious places and on official occasions. For ordinary men they are white, and for women they are of a different style — short, narrow, usually hand-woven and colourful, and just laid over the left shoulder. The women's *kabney* is also called a *rachung.*

The main garment worn by men is called a *go.* It is a very wide, ankle-length robe that is first folded across itself in front of the body to produce two thicknesses of material in front and one in the back. It is then gathered at the sides and hiked up so the bottom edge is at the knees, and the voluminous top half blouses around the abdomen. The two sides are then folded around behind the back, where they almost meet, making deep pleats on either side of the back. A long hand-woven belt is wrapped round and round the waist very, very tightly to hold the heavy pleats in place. It is an extremely difficult garment to put on.

A loose, white shirt called a *toego* is usually worn under the *go,* with fifteen centimetre cuffs formed by folding back the overly long arms of the *go* and *toego.* Well-dressed men wear long stockings and shoes with the outfit. Villagers (as Bhutanese peasants are called), especially when Father Mackey arrived in Tashigang, would wear neither, and probably no *toego.*

The women's garment is called a *kira.* It is a large rectangle of cloth, the width of which is the distance from a woman's shoulder to her ankles. The *kira* is wrapped around the body in a particular way, such that it wraps around under the arms, but so that the front and back can be hooked together at the shoulders. A belt is wrapped very tightly around the waist. A long-sleeved shirt, called an *onju*, is worn under the *kira*, and a light jacket, the women's *toego*, is worn on top. Cuffs are formed by folding the long arms of the *toego* and *onju* back. It is not an easy garment to put on either.

The Dzong stood apart from the rest of the community, and no ordinary residences were allowed nearby, but a few buildings were located on the up-mountain side. Outside the front courtyard — the *nyerchen's* residence was actually inside this courtyard — were the residences of the *thrimpoen* (this building still serves as the Dzongdag's residence) and the *rabjams*, and also the wireless station. A small police station was built in the same area a little later. The police detachment was small, just an officer and a couple of policemen. They lived in the same little complex. On the other side of the Dzong, down behind it, was a small prison.

There was virtually nothing in Mithidrang, the present day bazaar area, except a small, water-driven mill on the stream that runs down between the two main mountain spurs. There were no shops. In fact, no shops existed north of Samdrup Jongkhar, except for the occasional canteen run by Dantak, the Indian para-military organization building the road to Tashigang.

Some of Dantak's larger camps had canteens where anyone could shop. The selection was limited, and included items like soap, liquor, blankets and towels, some clothing and basic rations like salt and sugar. The monks had once tried to start a shop inside the Dzong but it didn't work out.

The first real store, the "community shop," would come later at Phomshing, about a kilometre west of the Dzong. Other district centres in the eastern interior, like Mongar and Lhuntse, were further from the road head and had no stores. Travellers had to carry supplies and might occasionally be able to trade with a farmer for local produce.

In the mid-1960s, shops began to appear along the Samdrup Jongkhar-Tashigang road. Tibetan immigrants, who had more of an aptitude for business than the native Bhutanese, often started them. In the more central interior — district centres like Wangdue Phodrang, Tongsa, Jakar (Bumthang) and Mongar — shops emerged even later, in the 1970s, as the "lateral road" gradually crossed the country. Restaurants, of course, were unheard of, and even in government guest houses travellers were expected to bring their own food.

In October of 1963, the road north from Samdrup Jongkhar extended only as far the village of Rongtong, about seventeen kilometres short of Tashigang. Father Mackey and Father McCabe absorbed the scene as they hiked these last kilometres along the hot, dusty trail. As they rounded the last big bend in the trail, their fatigue vanished at the exhilarating sight of Tashigang Dzong.

Father McCabe, the Jesuit Superior, stayed in Tashigang only a day or so — just long enough to see the set-up. Then he returned to Darjeeling, and Father Mackey was alone with his work.

* * *

The Tashigang elementary school was located where the junior high school stands today, near the top of a hillside that is actually the north-west slope of a spur of the mountain on which Tashigang is built. The ridge of the spur slopes down gently, behind and parallel to the original U-shaped building which remains part of the school today.

At the end of the spur, where the hill falls off abruptly, was the site of an old Bhutanese fort, where workers were using stone blocks from the ruins to build a guest house. On the other side of the spur, a shallow cirque lies between the spur and the mountainside, a hollow broad enough to provide a bit of flat space. The hospital was, and still is, located there, and further down in the hollow were three large bamboo sheds housing some 350 leprosy patients. The doctor's house was nearby.

About midway between the hospital and the school, but higher up, near the point where the spur joins the mountainside, was the small army cantonment called Wing 4. Its presence was not imposing. Wing 4 was supposed to protect the area north of Tashigang, but across the northern border was Tibet, and relations with the Chinese government that now controlled the area were good. There were two houses for officers (now teachers' quarters), the barracks (now the boy's hostel for the school) and the small parade ground which also served as a helicopter landing pad.

The school's classrooms and office were located in a one-storey, U-shaped building that was standard design for Bhutanese schools. There were three sets of teachers' quarters, each having two or three one-room "apartments." The senior Bhutanese teacher had his own house, and another building served as the school kitchen.

The school had about 200 students at seven class levels: LKG (Lower Kindergarten), UKG (Upper Kindergarten) and classes one through five. About two-thirds of the students were from the surrounding area, or boarded with local families. The other third, boys from farther away, stayed in huts of woven split bamboo near the school. Each hut housed boys from a particular village and had a kind of matron from the village who looked after them.

An Indian woman named Miss Pant ran the school. She was in her late fifties, and the sister of Appa Pant who had been the Indian Political Officer for Sikkim and Bhutan. By all accounts, this man had been a real friend to Bhutan, dedicated to its development and progress. His sister, who apparently never married, must have been very dedicated to the cause of education in Bhutan.

For an Indian woman of her position to work in a place like Tashigang was remarkable. She lived in one room with no glass in the windows, no electricity, no inside water and only cold water outside — conditions that would be considered extremely primitive by Indians of her class.

The school boys told many stories about her. Her bathroom was a simple wooden affair outside her quarters. It doubled as a toilet, for which there was just a hole in the wooden floor. When she wanted to bathe, Miss Pant would take a bucket of water into the small structure. Outside, boys would creep up and watch her through the cracks in the wall.

Miss Pant had run the school for two years and had earned the respect of the teachers, the Dzong administration and the children. She was not much of a disciplinarian, but her womanly touch probably balanced the harsh discipline of some of the *lopens* — the Bhutanese language teachers.

Mr. Kharpa, who was in effect the Bhutanese head of the school, was not so bad, but one of the *lopens* was called Lopen Tak — Lopen "Tiger." He was excessive in his punishments and the boys lived in terror of his wrath, which could be invoked by the slightest infraction — perhaps just a movement, a slight noise, or less than perfect work. The lightest punishment might be a swift blow to the head with a stick.

The *lopens* considered Miss Pant too gentle. When a boy called "Radi" Jigme was caught one night in a hut with a girl, he was brought for punishment at next morning's assembly. Miss Pant said, "You won't do it again, will you, Jigme?" She had a little stick and gave him tap.

Mr. Kharpa thought this inadequate. The following morning he called Jigme up at his private assembly. He had a piece of twisted bamboo rope soaking in some water. He lifted up the boy's *go* — as was common, the boy wore no underpants — and gave him half a dozen stinging cracks on his behind with the wet bamboo rope.

Miss Pant was very kind and helpful to Father Mackey. But he felt she was disappointed that he would be taking over "her" school. When she left in early December, there was no farewell party for her. Perhaps it was not the practice at that time. She walked to Rongtong as everybody did. From there, considering her brother's position, she was probably well taken care of by Dantak.

* * *

Tashigang school had been started by one of Bhutan's few trained veterinarians, Doctor Karchung, during a period when he was chief administrator of the district. He was a strong-minded man who was known to ride roughshod over people. On one occasion, some time after getting established in Tashigang, even Father Mackey wound up at odds with him when he somehow interfered in school matters.

Father Mackey got very angry and made up his mind to confront Doctor Karchung. Father Mackey's close friend, the resident medical officer, Doctor Anayat, tried to cool the Jesuit down, saying, "No, no, don't fight with him. He's an important man."

Doctor Karchung came from the village of Ramjar, a half-day walk from Tashigang. As a child he had been chosen by the government administration to attend school in India. His mother was told to bring the boy to the district administrator — the Dzongpoen, in those days. She didn't see the point of education. The important thing was the farm: that's where the boy was needed. Before going to the Dzongpoen, she told Karchung: "You pretend you're deaf and dumb. If anybody speaks to you, just say 'aagh.'"

The two went to the Dzongpoen and Karchung's mother made the traditional gestures of deference to this great authority, keeping her eyes down and covering her mouth with her hand as she spoke. She had brought her *chanjey*, the gift offered by a person to another person of higher rank — some produce from the farm or a piece of hand-woven cloth. She said, "I don't know why you're picking my son. He's deaf and dumb."

She turned and spoke to the boy.

His reply was vague and unintelligible: "Aaaagh?"

The Dzongpoen shook his head and sympathized: "I'm very sorry. But if he's deaf and dumb, I guess we can't take him."

He dismissed Karchung's mother and she backed away, still keeping her head down. She led her son to the door. But as the boy was going through it, the Dzongpoen called after him, *"Kota, naga ming hang?"* (Son, what's your name?)

The boy turned and said, *"Janga ming Karchung gila."*

His mother was furious. The Dzongpoen suppressed a smile and admonished the woman. Karchung went first to Scottish Universities Mission Institution (SUMI) in Kalimpong, and then earned a degree in veterinary science at Calcutta University.

Doctor Karchung, also known as Babu Karchung, became a legendary figure in Bhutan not so much because of these accomplishments, but because of his strong personality and a couple of less official "accomplishments." Rumour has it that he had a hand in the murder of a lama, and while the killing itself was shocking enough, this lama was no less than a reincarnation of the great Shabdrung, the founding father of Bhutan. The deed was supposed to have brought a curse upon Doctor Karchung's family.

Doctor Karchung's virility had inspired other stories. The King called him "The Stud of Bhutan," and he was reputed to have a wife in every district and children in every town.

In response to Doctor Anayat's caution, Father Mackey said, "I don't care who he is, he's not getting away with this!"

And off he went to give Doctor Karchung a blast.

A few days later, Father Mackey was passing by the man's house. Doctor Karchung called the priest in and served him tea. The larger-than-life character was big enough to make amends.

*   *   *

Father Mackey was eager to get on with establishing a first-rate high school. Given that the few scattered schools existing in Bhutan were primary schools with little or no common direction, he had to start from scratch. This suited him fine.

The government had asked Dantak to suggest possible sites for the new school. The Indian road construction organization had as good a sense as anyone of where a school might be built. The Indian officers had been educated at reasonably good schools in India, had experience in construction, and had become familiar with the land while building the road from Samdrup Jongkhar to Tashigang.

They presented their ideas to Father Mackey. A number of factors, including his own personality, probably contributed to their willingness to help, but the major one was probably the knowledge that the prime minister and the King were strongly behind the Jesuit.

Father Mackey investigated several sights near Tashigang but nothing suited him. He had clear ideas of what he needed for the school. Space, especially level space, was first among the requisites. From his experience as student, teacher and headmaster with an orientation towards sports, he knew the value of good playing fields. And he wanted a spacious campus with room to grow. He didn't forget the aesthetics either. In a place like Bhutan, an impressive view should be an easy requirement to fill.

Looking beyond the immediate area, Father Mackey decided to go farther north. He wanted to visit the schools at Tashi Yangtse, Lhuntse and Mongar. He could judge those sites, look for others along the way, and make an informal assessment of the existing schools at the same time. Early in November, he set out.

He brought with him a Bhutanese supply officer and his assistant, who enlisted local porters from the "towns" they visited, who would guide, carry and cook. Supplies included bedrolls and simple food — rice, dhal and a bag of salt. Dhal is a type of pulse or lentil used to make a spicy stew, also called dhal. This is an Indian dish not traditional in the interior of Bhutan, but was part of school diets. The men would trade the salt as they travelled, exchanging it for accommodation and meals as well as eggs, vegetables (mostly chillies) and sometimes meat.

They had ponies, acquired in the same way as porters, though Father Mackey preferred to walk. The wooden Bhutanese saddle, really a pack saddle, was small and uncomfortable, and on the narrow mountain trails, up and down steep inclines, he felt safer walking.

The first day's hike took the party down to Chagzam, the suspension bridge crossing the Drangmechhu below Tashigang Dzong. Two chains made of huge elongated iron links supported the bridge footway, which was covered with woven bamboo matting. Two more chains on the sides added support and provided something to hold on to. People and animals could cross, if nervously, the fast-flowing river below on this swaying, bouncing, flexing contraption.

The day's destination was a monastery named Gomkora, up the Drangmechhu twenty-four kilometres north-east of Tashigang. The river valley sloped gently. At an altitude of 750 metres, the walking was hot. Gomkora lay amid paddy fields where the river valley widens and provides some space for farming on the valley floor. It was something of an oasis surrounded by relatively bare, arid hillsides.

It was dark when the party arrived. They ate dinner seated around a campfire. Then their hosts picked up Father Mackey's bedroll and, by lantern-light, led him inside a building and settled him for the night. He crawled into his bedroll and fell asleep almost instantly. Next morning, as light came through cracks around shuttered windows, he awoke. The first thing he saw was a pair of huge statues looking down at him — Guru Rinpoche and Avalokiteshvara. They surprised him, but looked benevolent enough and he said: "Very good, statues or no statues, I'm saying Mass."

The following day, the party travelled up the Kulongchhu towards Tashi Yangtse Dzong. The river valley, higher and steeper, featured dramatic gorges. Father Mackey was struck by the mass of colour and beauty of the flowers as they hiked up the valley.

The small *dzong* was the administrative and religious centre of a sub-district called a *dungkhag*. The *dungpa*, chief administrator of the *dungkhag*, had arranged an elaborate reception. But as the *dzong* was some distance off the main trail, he brought the reception to Father Mackey and his party — on the trail. All the important people and monks of Tashi Yangtse attended, and tea, the ceremonial dish of sweet yellow rice, and traditional snacks were served.

Tashi Yangtse school was four kilometres further up the valley, where it broadens out on the east side of the river to form a large, flat cirque, creating a sizeable area for farming. Most impressive was Chorten Kora, the gigantic monument near the river at the opening of the valley. Its square base measures thirty metres on a side. Chorten Kora is built in the style of Nepalese stupas and is one of a very few such structures in Bhutan.

Father Mackey enjoyed meeting the children and teachers at the school. But he was looking for a site and had heard of an attractive spot farther up the valley. The next day he hiked a few hours up the Kulongchhu to the place called Bumdeling. A beautiful spot, located on the river, with plenty of flat land, it had everything Father Mackey needed.

He returned to Tashi Yangtse school the same day.

The next part of the tour involved hiking over a range of mountains between the Kulongchhu and the Kurichhu to the west. The party stopped for the night before crossing the pass that would take them to the other side. The high altitude made it very cold, and Father Mackey found his bedroll inadequate. He was happy to get on the move again the next morning.

Crossing the 4,080 metre pass, Dongla, the men tramped through snow more than half a metre deep. Father Mackey rode a pony part of the way, as his guides thought this was safer. He marvelled at the porters carrying the bedrolls and supplies, as they wore no shoes yet remained unaffected by the snow and cold.

The party slept that night at an old school on the western slope, then carried on down to the river, the Kurichhu. They crossed a suspension bridge, then hiked upwards to Lhuntse Dzong. There, having slept in a room in the *dzong*, Father Mackey woke before five o'clock to the chanting of monks.

Besides looking for a school site, Father Mackey was charged with doing an informal inspection. He found the headmaster at Lhuntse, an Indian named Krishnan, running "a fine little school." Measured in terms of access from the southern border, it was the most remote school in Bhutan. To get there before the Tashigang road was built, teachers like Krishnan would walk two weeks or more from India. Then they would face feelings of remoteness, cultural differences and a complete lack of amenities like entertainment and electricity, as well as difficulties in getting supplies.

Physically, though it is now a junior high school, Lhuntse has changed little since then. The school perched above the Dzong on a small patch of level ground on a narrow mountain spur. Always happy in a school setting, Father Mackey went into the classrooms to see how teachers were teaching and what students were learning.

Most students wore no shoes, not even cheap rubber *chappals* from India. Their dress consisted of a simple *go* — the students were all boys — and, in some cases, a simple shirt of coarse, hand-woven cloth, under the *go*. There was no underwear. These clothes also served as their bedclothes as very few had blankets.

Krishnan led Father Mackey a couple of kilometres along the trail beyond the school to a small leprosy colony. More than one hundred patients lived there, in thirty or so small huts scattered around the mountainside. A lone Bhutanese compounder, or simple paramedic, ran a small dispensary and ministered to the patients as best he could.

At the dispensary Father Mackey noticed a microscope. Next day, he brought the senior students — the school went up to class four, though the boys were well into their teens — back to the dispensary and taught them about the microscope. The boys were amazed at what they could see through it.

Seeing their interest, Father Mackey recalled some simple science tricks he'd learned long ago. One involved using a glass full of water with a piece of paper on top. He held it up, turned it upside down — and the water stayed inside, astonishing the boys. The Jesuit lit a candle, put it into a bowl of water, placed an upside down jar over the candle. When the oxygen was consumed, the candle went out and the water rose. The students were awe-struck. His simple science demonstration made him a magician.

Next stop was Mongar, a three-day hike south of Lhuntse, most of it along the Kurichhu. The ponies carried supplies along this leg of the tour, and halfway to Mongar, a section of flood plain provided an opportunity for a bit of sport. The men decided to have a pony race. After removing their loads, Father Mackey got on one pony and one of his companions got on another. They raced up and down the level stretch shouting and laughing. Father Mackey was judged the winner as he fell off less often than his opponent.

At Mongar, Father Mackey found a school even better than Lhuntse, with the Indian headmaster, Sivadasan, doing an excellent job. This was the only school he found that attempted a syllabus. While there, Father Mackey had the pleasure of riding a horse with a real saddle, and he took the opportunity to ride to Lingmethang, a rich farming area west of Mongar.

The low altitude gave it a tropical climate that was very pleasant at this time of year. The army had a small detachment at Lingmethang, and Father Mackey spoke to the *drimpoen*, or sergeant-major, in charge. It looked like a good school site, with plenty of flat land and a river. But the *drimpoen* told him no: "Father, don't come here. There's malaria. The kids will get sick, you'll get sick. We've had a lot of trouble here and you just can't control the mosquitoes."

Father Mackey didn't mention the place in his report.

He rode further west, up the mountainside, two days up and two days back. The scenery was beautiful but, except at Sengor, which was distant from the nearest road, far from flat. A large farm occupied the only other place with any possibilities, and he'd been asked not to disturb farms if he could help it.

Father Mackey decided to leave Sengor to the yaks and Lingmethang to the mosquitoes and rode back to Mongar. He spent a day teaching maths and science, repeating his Lhuntse performance. Having found a bottle of the right size, he added another demonstration. He slipped a lighted candle into the bottle and then, in the mouth of the bottle, placed a peeled hard-boiled egg. It sat part way down in the mouth, making an air-tight seal. Fifteen students in the senior class sat watching, and broke into shouts of surprise when the egg wiggled down into the bottle as the burning candle produced a vacuum inside.

From Mongar, Father Mackey headed home to Tashigang, travelling east, up and over Korila, then down to the Sherichhu where they camped for a night. They crossed another mountain range and camped again before descending to the Drangmechhu and following it upstream to Tashigang.

The tour had taken four weeks. Father Mackey was no closer to choosing a school site, but he knew a lot more about Eastern Bhutan. He later noted that in all the time he spent wandering the country, people were never surprised to see him. They offered him hospitality and accepted him as a person, regardless of the fact that he was the first European most of them had ever seen.

* * *

When he first arrived at Tashigang, Father Mackey put up temporarily in a room at the hospital and took his meals with Doctor Anayat and his wife Lingshay. After Miss Pant left, Father Mackey moved into his quarters near the school. One of three rooms built of wood, together in a row, his new home measured about four metres across and five metres deep. At the front he had a door and a window, at the back another window and, as he had an end "suite," on one side he had two more windows. Instead of glass, the windows had sliding wooden shutters.

All surfaces were unpainted wood, hewn or planed by hand. Father Mackey erected a partition, establishing a space for his bed in one corner, another small area for a chapel and the rest for a work room. Of the other two rooms in the row, one was occupied by a teacher and the other set aside for another Jesuit expected in the new year. Father Mackey's quarters had no kitchen — usually such quarters included a small separate kitchen built just behind — so he continued to take his meals with the Anayats.

There was a water tap outside, between Father Mackey's row and a row of four rooms opposite, where other teachers lived. Everybody shared the one stand pipe and the toilet, the same one Miss Pant had used.

Father Mackey had no radio and no books, except a few Father McCabe sent from Darjeeling. He wrote to his sister Tess and asked her to send books, but that would take months. There was no electricity. For light at night, there were candles and Petromax pressure kerosene lamps. These lamps created a bright light, but were notoriously temperamental and could be dangerous. Father Mackey became expert at fixing them.

When Father Mackey joined the Bhutanese government service, he did not become a salaried employee. The government felt that the traditional approach to civil servants could extend to him. This meant that he received no money, but had everything provided. This was not the case for the Indian teachers, who were essentially contract workers.

Father Mackey had no objection to the arrangement in principle. The Dzong supplied rations for his meals to Doctor Anayat, and also things like candles, kerosene for the Petromax and so on. In the odd circumstances when he might need cash, for example to buy something in Samdrup Jongkhar, Father Mackey could obtain that, too, if he produced proper justification.

In practice, Father Mackey found it a nuisance to be applying continually to the Dzong for supplies or cash. And after a few months, the Director of Education, Dawa Tshering, sent an order saying he was to be paid an honorarium of 700 rupees per month, about 150 dollars. The order also said he could draw his rations from the Dzong, debited to the education account. This may have marked the beginning of the government's cash payment system to its civil servants. In any case, Father Mackey's honorarium made him the best-paid person in Tashigang, even though Doctor Anayat also received a salary.

In January, Father Mackey got a permit to travel to Darjeeling, and Dantak organized transportation. For himself, he hoped to bring back clothes, bedding, books, religious vestments and paraphernalia for his chapel. For the school, he sought books and science equipment. Of the existing books, most were in Hindi. The exceptions were English readers and grammars, and a few maths textbooks. Father Mackey had already sent home asking for books. But he had a particular objective in mind regarding science equipment.

In Darjeeling, he went to North Point to see Father Hayden, who was in charge of the physics laboratory at St. Joseph's College. Father Mackey had known him for many years. He told him, "Look, if I could get some equipment . . ., see, this little school we're building up, it's going to turn into a high school."

Father Hayden replied that he was a scrupulous man: "If I gave you equipment, I'd have worries and trouble with my conscience — scruples. Here's the key. You go in there and take what you need and don't tell me."

He gave the key to the wrong man. Father Mackey departed with a microscope, a telescope, magnets, two boxes of lenses and many more small items. He took them back to Tashigang.

*   *   *

Early in 1964, the prime minister came to open the new Royal Guest House in Tashigang, and to select the new school site. Father Mackey had sent him a report on his survey of sites, but had not yet fixed on any single location. He had visited Yonphula a number of times. It was south of Tashigang and had been suggested by Dantak. During his first visit, on a clear fall day, he had been impressed with the space and magnificent view. But thereafter, every time he'd visited, the site (at 2,500 metres) was shrouded in cloud. And cold.

From his northern tour, the only place that stood out in his mind was Bumdeling, north of Tashi Yangtse. Close to the high mountains along the Tibetan border, it was a beautiful spot with magnificent scenery, a good stream and lots of level space. Father Mackey loved it. But realistically, it was too far away. To reach even Tashigang would take three days, and there were no plans to extend the road farther north.

Father Mackey narrowed his choices to two. The first was Thragom, a site near the village of Kanglung, about twenty-two kilometres from Tashigang, down the Samdrup Jongkhar road still under construction. It had good flat land, a *chorten* (of modest size, not like Chorten Kora), and a view extending many miles, from the Mongar area on the left to Tashigang Dzong on the right. If you climbed higher you could even see down to the river. Only trouble was, this was good, cultivated farmland, and half a dozen families would have to be moved.

Father Mackey's second choice was also at Kanglung, downhill a bit from his first. It had good flat land and, although you couldn't see Tashigang Dzong, still had a great view. Moving to this site would not disturb any active farms — there were two unused farm houses — but this property had been designated as a new base for the Royal Bhutan Army. Wing 4, perched on the hillside at Tashigang, needed a better spot.

Father Mackey had ruled out another attractive spot nearby because of lack of space. Further south, there was a place called Dewung, which he hadn't yet seen. And Yonphula, despite his assessment — "it's too darned cold and misty" — could not be ruled out entirely if there was nothing else.

Father Mackey wore traditional Bhutanese dress to meet the prime minister's helicopter as it landed on the army parade ground. This was the first time he had worn a *go* and its accessories, and he lost a bit of decorum as the helicopter touched down. The problem was the large white *kabney* or scarf draped around his body. When the helicopter came in, the wash from the rotor sent the *kabney* flying. Father Mackey was trying to pull it back into order as the prime minister stepped from the helicopter. Walking towards Father Mackey, he asked, "What are you doing, Father?"

"I'm chasing my *kabney*, which you blew off."

When they had a chance to talk, the prime minister solicited Father Mackey's thoughts on the school site. It was time to make a final choice. Father Mackey summarized the possibilities and said the best ones were at Kanglung. The prime minister wanted to see the sites himself and had the helicopter take them to Rongtong. After lunch, they hiked the few kilometres up to Kanglung.

Father Mackey explained his preferences. The prime minister rejected the first choice as expected: too many families would have to be moved. The Jesuit moved to his second choice, the lower of the two Kanglung sites. He said he liked the site, but understood the army was going to get it. The prime minister said, "Father, it's yours. The army can find another site."

It was as simple as that. The two men sat on a big rock at the site and drew tentative plans on the ground. A boys' hostel could go here, a playing field there . . .

The army ended up at Yonphula.

7/

L anguage could be a problem in a place like Eastern Bhutan. Often, just moving from one valley to the next could mean a significant change in language. However, four larger groupings existed in the country. The first was the national language, Dzongkha ("the language of the Dzong"), which was dominant in Western Bhutan.

In Eastern Bhutan, Tsangla dominated. It was commonly called Sharchopkha, sometimes shortened to Sharchop. Given the area's population, far more people spoke it than spoke Dzongkha. The southern border regions of Bhutan were heavily populated as well, largely by people of Nepali extraction. They, of course, spoke Nepali, another major language.

Besides these three, there was a major language grouping in Central Bhutan, plus a number of other languages or dialects spoken by smaller populations scattered around the country.

These languages, apart from Nepali, were not written. The written language used for religious, scientific and official documents was Choekey, Classical Tibetan. Except for a small number of well-educated officials and members of the monk body, however, few people could read Choekey. A rough parallel might be drawn with Latin in the Western World, or Sanskrit in India.

This lack of a popular written language had led to the earlier decision to conduct primary education in Hindi. With no widely used written language of their own, presumably the Bhutanese felt the next best thing was the main language of India, with whom Bhutan had the greatest contact and which offered an abundant supply of teachers.

Around the time Father Mackey arrived, two major changes occurred regarding language. For now, we will look only at the decision to make English the medium of instruction in Bhutanese schools. One can only guess at the reasons, but to start with, Bhutan had no completely indigenous written language. Choekey was a "foreign" classical language used mostly within the Buddhist religion, and for government documents.

Hindi was little spoken in Bhutan; its use in the schools had been purely pragmatic. And it was, after all, the language of a neighbouring country. Nepali was a written language, but its use was more or less limited to the Lhotsampa, or Southern Bhutanese. And it, too, was the language of a nearby neighbour.

English, while also foreign, was an international language. Even India recognized English as one of its languages, and used it officially and quite generally. As well, English had already been taught as a subject in Bhutan's schools. Adopting English would not involve any perceived threat of cultural influence from a neighbouring country. And finally, the better schools that Bhutanese leaders had seen were English-language institutions. The choice of Father Mackey to start the country's first quality school fit well with the adoption of the English language for schools.

For communicating on a day-to-day basis, Father Mackey was not badly served by his Nepali. In Eastern Bhutan, it was probably the best language to have after Sharchopkha. And as roads opened up Bhutan, Nepali became a kind of lingua franca, except in rural areas. Father Mackey could speak English with most of his staff and others in the education system.

Mr. Kharpa, his second-in-command, was fluent in English. Many Bhutanese officials, and not just those from Southern Bhutan, spoke Nepali. Many others spoke Hindi, having been educated in that language, and Hindi and Nepali are close enough to allow reasonable communication. This was the case with Thrimpoen Tamji Jagar. He spoke Hindi and Father Mackey spoke Nepali; they understood each other and got along very well.

Some people in Tashigang, however, spoke no English, Nepali or Hindi. These included two of Father Mackey's best friends. One was Phongmey Dungpa, who came from a village in Bumthang district. He spoke Bumthangkha as a first language, but used Sharchopkha in Eastern Bhutan. Father Mackey began picking up Sharchopkha, mostly from Phongmey Dungpa. And this unschooled but intelligent man could usually decipher Father Mackey's jumble of Sharchopkha and Nepali.

Another person whose closest language was Sharchopkha was the Umdze of Tashigang Dzong. Normally the head of the monk body at a *dzong* was called Lam Neten, the Abbot of the monastery. But for some reason, Tashigang did not have a Lam Neten when Father Mackey arrived, and the Umdze or "Master of the Choir" was head of the monk body.

Father Mackey was interested in Buddhism, especially as taught and practiced in Bhutan, and he and the Umdze became good friends. The Jesuit would visit the Umdze at least once a month. As his Sharchopkha was not good enough to conduct an involved conversation on religion, he'd take an interpreter along, usually one of his best students, the naughty but clever Radi Jigme.

Radi Jigme would have been about fourteen years old when Father Mackey took him to the Dzong for visits with the Umdze. To translate theological discourse at that age is quite impressive. But Jigme was not privy to everything shared between the Umdze and Father Mackey. A case in point arose after Father Mackey had visited the Umdze a number of times.

The Jesuit had understood that no liquor was allowed inside the Dzong, and certainly not around the monastery. On this occasion he and Jigme came in, greeted the venerated religious leader and expected their usual dialogue to be accompanied by *suja*, or "butter tea." But the Umdze told Jigme to leave the room and wait outside. Father Mackey wondered but said nothing.

The Umdze sat behind an ornately decorated *choedrom* — a small, low Bhutanese "table" with three sides closed and a shelf within. He reached over to a trunk-like wooden box, unlocked and opened it, and withdrew a bottle. The bottle contained an almost clear liquid. Just the faintest hint of pink indicated high quality *ara*.

The Umdze took two glasses from the *choedrom* and filled them with this smooth but potent liquor. Wordlessly, though Father Mackey managed to express his pleasure, the two men enjoyed their drinks. Then the Umdze returned the bottle to the box and set the glasses aside. He had young Radi Jigme summoned and the two men resumed their theological dialogue, perhaps a little more enthusiastically than on previous occasions.

* * *

Father Mackey had always been known for his energy and sense of humour, and during his first months in Tashigang he became friends with two men who enjoyed a joke as much as he did. The first was Doctor Anayat Yaganegi — known only as Doctor Anayat, or just Anayat. They came together in Father Mackey's first days, when he had no place to cook meals and ate with the doctor and his wife Lingshay, paying them, of course.

This arrangement continued for three years, even after Father Mackey got his own quarters and was joined by Brother Quinn and Father Coffey. The friendship remains strong even today, and Father Mackey speaks of the "charming" couple and the "tremendous amount they did for the country."

Doctor Anayat's parents had emigrated from Iran to India, where they became Baha'is. When Anayat began working in Bhutan, he ran into a lot of trouble with the Indian police and immigration officials because he couldn't prove, to their satisfaction, that he was an Indian citizen. He had a record saying he was born in Pune, India, but Father Mackey always believed he was born in Iran.

Never one to care much for bureaucracy, Doctor Anayat would say, "I'm universal!" His problems with the Indian authorities came to an end in the 1970s, when he was granted Bhutanese citizenship. This was a rare honour and recognized the valuable work he was doing for the Bhutanese government. Doctor Anayat speaks several languages, including Persian, and follows the Baha'i faith.

His wife, Lingshay, was teaching at Tashigang school when Father Mackey arrived. She was a Lepcha from Kalimpong where her father, A.R. Foning, was a teacher and head of the Lepcha community. In the 1987, his book, *Lepcha, My Vanishing Tribe* would be published. Lingshay, a clever young woman with good English, was invited into Bhutan by the prime minister as a secretary.

The prime minister had also recruited Doctor Anayat, who worked as a doctor on the road being built between Phuntsholing and Paro. In the course of his work and visits to Paro, Anayat met Lingshay and they fell in love. A little lax as a practicing Baha'i, he was noted for his drinking — but Lingshay put an end to that. Finding him drunk once too often, she dragged him under a stand pipe and turned on the ice-cold water until he sobered up. That marked the end of his drinking.

As for the relationship between the pioneering doctor and the Jesuit educator, even today, despite their advancing years, one of them is apt to dump a dish of ice cream on the other's head. Such foolishness dates back to the early days in Tashigang, as with high jinks on the suspension bridge.

This was the same bridge Father Mackey had to cross when he set out on his tour of school sites. It was sound enough, but didn't feel secure and would jiggle and swing. Father Mackey did not fear heights and had no qualms. But poor Doctor Anayat. Father Mackey learned that he was nervous about crossing suspension bridges, and would play on this at any opportunity.

It was not unusual for the two men to find themselves crossing the bridge below Tashigang, as they sometimes picnicked by the river. When Doctor Anayat was crossing, Father Mackey would get behind him and jump up and down, making the bridge swing as much as possible. Terrified, Doctor Anayat would get down on his hands and knees and hold on, yelling, "You bloody fool, Mackey! Wait'll I get hold of you!"

Father Mackey's second great friend, Phongmey Dungpa, came from Promrong, a village in the Tang Valley of Bumthang district. His given name was Drolma Sithub, though nobody called him that. The appellation "Phongmey Dungpa" was actually a title. The village of Phongmey, a day's walk east of Tashigang, was the headquarters of the sub-district, or *dungkhag*, of Phongmey. The head of a *dungkhag* was a *dungpa*.

Father Mackey learned that Phongmey Dungpa owed his title, and so his name, to an archery match between Bhutan and Sikkim. As the tight contest neared completion, he was the last Bhutanese contestant up. With the contest riding on his last arrow, he hit the target and won the day for Bhutan. The King and prime minister were present, and as a reward made the archer Dungpa of Phongmey.

By the time Father Mackey arrived in Tashigang, Phongmey Dungpa no longer held this position, though he would carry this name until he died. He was related to the *thrimpoen*, Tamji Jagar, and worked for him. Father Mackey met Phongmey Dungpa when he was supervising the building of the Royal Guest House. This was built with the stones of a ruined fort on the site, which was very near the school.

Father Mackey got to know Phongmey Dungpa through Doctor Anayat, who was a mutual friend. During the prime minister's visit in January of 1964, Father Mackey realized that, besides having a great sense of humour, Phongmey Dungpa was also a very capable man. He not only handled the extensive arrangements for the official visit, but through it all kept everyone laughing.

When Doctor Anayat and Phongmey Dungpa got together, anything could happen — as Father Mackey witnessed in an incident involving some attractive Brogpa women. The people commonly referred to as Brogpas are semi-nomadic herdsmen of Eastern Bhutan. They are often seen in Tashigang, and in 1963-64 some of them were helping construct the Royal Guest House. On this particular day, Doctor Anayat came home from the hospital for the noon meal. Father Mackey was already seated. But the Doctor barely got through the door when Lingshay attacked him with a stick. He put up his arms to protect himself and cried: "Hey, what are you doing?"

Lingshay answered: "What were you doing with those lovely Brogpa girls in the hospital? You locked the door! What were you doing with those girls?"

"Who told you about that?"

"Dungpa."

Doctor Anayat couldn't let this go unanswered. After lunch, he visited Dungpa's wife. He called her outside and pointed to the construction site. "Ama, look at that guest house over there. Look who Dungpa's with, all those beautiful Brogpa girls. What's he doing with those girls?"

When Dungpa came home for dinner, "Ama" — Madam or Mrs. or Missus, as well as Mother — gave him a beating. But that same evening, Father Mackey saw the two couples going for a walk together.

As for the Jesuit, being with such irrepressible characters as Dungpa and Anayat brought out the best — or the worst — in him, and together the three of them achieved national notoriety as the three *guluphulus.*

The expression " *guluphulu*" means "rascal," and also suggests a bit of a fool. Given the wild sense of humour the three men shared, it is not surprising that they got to calling each other " *guluphulu.*" Nobody knows who started it, but before long everybody in the area knew Father Guluphulu, Doctor Guluphulu and Dungpa Guluphulu. Such entertaining stuff doesn't take long to travel in Bhutan, and it reached the very top.

During a visit to Tashigang, the King looked out the window of his chamber in the Dzong and saw three of his *dungpas* standing together in the courtyard below, among them Phongmey Dungpa (who was technically no longer a *dungpa*). He went downstairs, outside into the courtyard and walked quietly up behind the men as they chatted. His first words were, "Which one of you is Dungpa Guluphulu?"

The three nearly jumped out of their skins. Then the other two pointed at Phongmey Dungpa: "Not me! He's Dungpa Guluphulu!"

Phongmey Dungpa went after Father Mackey. In mock rage, he chased him around with a stick. He figured Father Mackey was the only person who would mention something like that to the King.

But His Majesty was no fool. From his own assessment of Phongmey Dungpa, and from talking with people like Tamji Jagar and others at the Dzong, he realized that this was a capable, valuable man. That, however, didn't prevent him from calling him Guluphulu ever after — though he used the term in a positive way, almost a term of endearment.

* * *

With the new school site chosen, Father Mackey worked at improving his staff, partly by recruiting teachers he had known, or even taught, in Darjeeling District. Most of the teachers in Bhutan came from the Indian state of Kerala, which has a highly educated populace and has long exported teachers to other parts of India and the world.

Indian teachers had made up the bulk of the teaching staff in Bhutan since the beginning. Many of them came to Bhutan for the money. Bhutan offered jobs and, on average, better pay than teachers could find in India. Although they took advantage of this, many of them maintained a superior attitude over the people and culture of Bhutan. But whether they brought arrogant or open and accepting attitudes, conditions for them in the early days were not easy.

Father Mackey had a lot of respect for most Indian teachers. He had, of course, worked with many in Kurseong and Darjeeling. He could see the dedication it took to do a good job in the remote areas of Bhutan, such as he had seen in Tashi Yangtse, Lhuntse and Mongar. Before the road arrived, these teachers would have to walk from the Indian border, sometimes for weeks, to reach their schools. And as any outside supplies had to come the same way, they were extremely limited and expensive.

The life-style was very basic. There was no electricity, so most activity stopped at sunset (between six o'clock and seven) and local people went to bed early. There was no entertainment — no cinema, nightclubs, television or videos, not even shops or restaurants: you had to create your own entertainment. For most Indian teachers, the culture, the climate and the terrain were completely different from anything they'd known.

Some could not take it. Father Mackey says a new teacher stood a fifty-fifty chance of winding up a good teacher or a drunk. You had to go one way or the other, it seemed, to preserve your sanity, although the second choice didn't guarantee that. Getting fully involved with the school, the kids and the community provided an outlet for one's energy and creativity. If you didn't relate in that way, cheap booze was always available — either locally-made *ara* or commercial liquors like the popular Apsoo rum.

Mr. Kharpa, who was Bhutanese, taught English. But most of the few Bhutanese teachers were Bhutanese Language Teachers, who taught rudimentary Choekey and then Dzongkha when it came into the schools. They were also known as BLTs, Dzongkha Lopens or just Lopens. *Lopen* (*lopoen*) is the Bhutanese word for "master," and is used to mean "teacher" or educated person.

Apart from the Dzongkha *lopens*, most of whom had been monks, Bhutanese teachers were rare. To teach, one required some education, and nearly every educated Bhutanese was taken into another profession. While the King and the prime minister recognized the importance of education, the government in general regarded education as a second-class occupation.

The developing country desperately needed educated people for virtually every profession. The civil service and, to a lesser extent, business could absorb just about anyone who reached the class eight level. The lower end got ordinary administrative or clerical positions in the government, or similar status in the army, while the top end went for studies in medicine and engineering, some as army officers. Even the odd person who had a personal inclination towards education would be recruited for a more "urgent" need.

Besides upgrading the teaching staff, Father Mackey gave priority to obtaining science equipment and books for the library. He discovered the enthusiasm for science in 1964, when he demonstrated the apparatus he'd brought from Darjeeling to his senior students, the newly established class 6.

Interest was so great that Father Mackey organized a Saturday afternoon science exhibition open to the public. In proper Bhutanese fashion, he invited a Chief Guest. This was the Thrimpoen, who brought his wife. It seems that, contrary to the present-day practice of wives staying away from official or quasi-official functions, wives commonly joined in on such occasions.

Father Mackey escorted the couple through the exhibits, pointing out the main features of each. At one exhibit, he picked up two bar magnets. He held them so that a north end and a south end faced each other, and showed how they pulled together and stuck. Then Father Mackey offered the magnets to the Thrimpoen's wife. "Here, Ama, you try them."

She hesitated a moment, then accepted. As he handed the magnets to the lady, Father Mackey turned one of them around. When she tried to duplicate what he had done, the magnets, instead of pulling together, pushed apart. Thinking there were devils at work, she dropped the magnets and fled, right out of the room. Father Mackey then tried the trick on the Thrimpoen. He, too, was uneasy about this business, but tried the magnets different ways and discovered how they worked.

The Thrimpoen showed interest, as well, in an exhibit involving a small piece of paper, some water and a kerosene-fired Bunsen burner. The students showed how they could make a little cup out of paper so it would hold water. Then if they held it over the flame of the Bunsen burner, they could bring the water to a boil. The wet paper, placed at the right distance from the flame, did not burn. But the heat went through and heated the water. As the students carried this out, the Thrimpoen watched with great interest. Then he turned to his wife and said, "Ama, I'm not going to buy you any more *dekshis*. From now on you're going to have to cook your rice in paper."

Visitors enjoyed seeing how a lens could concentrate sunlight into burning heat, and watching electrical experiments that used batteries. But the telescope stole the show. People marvelled over its magnification, which brought distant objects much closer. But they were equally amazed at the phenomenon of this very basic telescope inverting the image.

Father Mackey focused the telescope on the trail below the Dzong and let the people look through it. They saw ponies moving along the trail upside down! This confounded everyone. A pony walking upside down along the trail — how could this be done? For months after the show, local people and monks would visit the school and ask to see this amazing machine that made a horse walk upside down.

The students benefitted hugely from seeing science experiments for themselves. Those written up in the books began to make more sense to them. And, though their resources were limited, under Father Mackey's guidance they began using local materials like pieces of wood and stones to study basic machines — levers, inclined planes and so forth.

This approach had lasting benefits. Students who furthered their education in India often did exceptionally well in science. And a high proportion of students from this, Bhutan's first class 6, later became key people in professions like education and civil engineering.

When Father Mackey saw how science caught on, he tried to enhance it still further. He usually visited Calcutta each year, sometimes for a month during the winter holiday, and he would bring back as much science apparatus as he could. Especially popular were a series of mirrors, both convex and concave, which could make things fatter and thinner and turn them upside down.

Father Mackey also addressed the desperate need for books. There were few books at the school when he arrived, and his budget limited what he could buy in Calcutta. He wrote his father and asked him to try to find some used books and send them for the Tashigang school library. His father took on the project with a vengeance. He solicited all his friends and neighbours, asking them to collect any useful books they could find, perhaps children's books that now gathered dust in the attic. Would they please pack them, five books to a parcel, and send them to Bhutan? The response was phenomenal. Father Mackey started receiving two or three large Canadian postal bags at a time, each filled with five-book parcels.

Regular mail service did not yet exist in Eastern Bhutan. Father Mackey's mail went to a tea estate near Kumarikata, just south of Samdrup Jongkhar, and from there came to Tashigang via Dantak. The postal bags always arrived intact, never having been opened.

This was not the case with Father Mackey's *National Geographic* magazines. His old Scout master sent him the magazine faithfully every month. When it arrived, he could see that it had been opened. Next time he was at the tea estate, he asked the Bengali gentleman who ran the post office if he knew what was happening.

The man begged him not be angry. He explained that he loved the magazine, and that he had been opening it and reading it. He always made sure not to soil or damage it. Father Mackey was touched. He told the postal agent to carry on as before, and they became good friends.

Father Mackey added the *National Geographic* magazines to the school library, along with the books from Canada. He managed to get more money for books, and eventually created the best school library in the country. When he moved to the new school, he left both the library and the science equipment in the hands of two Indian teachers who took over from him. After they left the school, Father Mackey discovered that every book and piece of science equipment had disappeared.

8/

The most important man in Tashigang when Father Mackey arrived was Tamji Jagar, the Thrimpoen or chief administrator of this large and heavily populated *dzongkhag*, or district. Born in Bumthang Dzongkhag, he had joined the civil service (actually the service of the king) as a teenager and worked his way up. He was about five years older than Father Mackey, and would go on to become Bhutan's first minister of home affairs, or Kidug Lyonpo.

Tamji Jagar was well known for his deep understanding of people, rural people in particular. As Thrimpoen he often had to judge disputes, and here he exhibited wisdom and compassion, if also a certain unorthodoxy. Father Mackey had the chance to watch at least one case unfold, as it involved the school in a small way.

Two groups claimed ownership of a piece of land. Both were adamant and vociferous. But instead of trying to calm the claimants, the Thrimpoen did the opposite. The first morning, he goaded one group into a rage, got them ranting and raving, letting the other side sit and listen and even enjoy the vexation of the first group. Then he rose and said, "Okay, cup of tea, come back in the afternoon."

That afternoon, he provoked the anger of the other side, while the first group regained their composure and felt their reputation was restored. He continued this pattern for three days, exhausting the anger of both groups. It was cathartic. Now the Thrimpoen could make his judgment knowing that both groups had derived some satisfaction from the exercise. Even those on the losing side had vented their spleen, and could boast to friends that, "It was a very important case. Dasho Thrimpoen spent three days on it."

Father Mackey appreciated the supportiveness of the Thrimpoen, which showed itself early on in regard to accommodation. When he arrived in 1963, students from outside Tashigang village lived in small huts of woven split bamboo. He preferred to see them together in conditions over which he had more control, not just to prevent incidents like Radi Jigme's "night hunting" (as it is called in Eastern Bhutan), but also for considerations of dining, health, discipline and study.

In seeking alternatives, and realizing that building a new boarding facility was out of the question, Father Mackey analyzed the existing school building. He invited Dasho Thrimpoen over and pointed to the roof: "If we can lift the darned roof of the school we can make a 'boarding' and put the kids there. Then we'll have more control over things."

The Thrimpoen saw the wisdom and practicality of the suggestion. He nodded and said, "Ah yes, very good idea." The two of them planned the project and charged Phongmey Dungpa with getting the job done. Tamji Jagar maintained his interest in the project, checking frequently on progress until it was complete.

Tamji Jagar might have been expected to resist the move from Hindi to English in the schools. As a boy he had studied Choekey, and he spoke Hindi and Sharchopkha, as well as his own first language and probably Dzongkha, but no English. While others objected to the change, however, or were unsupportive at best, he endorsed it and assisted whenever possible.

Father Mackey also noticed Tamji Jagar's compassion, as exemplified in his treatment of a boy named Nima Wangdi. His father, Bachha Bumthang Sangye, had been implicated in the most infamous crime in Bhutan's modern history (of which we will learn more later). Later he would be exonerated, but now he was put under a kind of house arrest and sent to Tamji Jagar. He arrived under a cloud of suspicion and disgrace, and he brought his son, Nima Wangdi.

Other people might have left the boy to his own devises. But Tamji Jagar took some interest and recognized that the boy was intelligent. The Thrimpoen spoke to Father Mackey and explained the situation. He said he'd like to see the boy in school, but didn't want his name to appear on the register. Father Mackey had no objection.

Then came a period in 1964 when the school was short of food. About thirty students, especially from distant Khyeng, were unable to provide their rations, largely because of travel difficulties involving swollen rivers. Father Mackey went to the Thrimpoen, whose reaction was direct: he provided rice and corn from his own stores. This was kept quiet, with deliveries arriving about ten o'clock at night, when everyone was in bed.

On another occasion, the authorities were trying to discourage farmers from making distilled alcohol from grain, and confiscated many large copper pots. Always looking for ways to help the school, the Thrimpoen asked Father Mackey if he could use them. The Jesuit took them for storage containers.

Holding the elevated position of Thrimpoen never prevented Tamji Jagar from dropping in on Father Mackey like any ordinary neighbour. Father Mackey often ate dinner at the Thrimpoen's home, and enjoyed the older man's subtle sense of humour. One evening, his Indian dinner guests included some who did not eat bovine meat. One of them eyed the meat suspiciously and asked if it was beef.

The Thrimpoen maintained the dignified bearing he assumed when appropriate, but those who knew him discerned a faint smile on his face as he replied, "No, it's yak meat." Now, to Father Mackey a yak is simply a "glorified cow," but the Thrimpoen's guests, who had never seen a yak, could now enjoy the delicious meal with a clear conscience.

* * *

The second most important man at the Dzong was the Nyerchen. His name was Tashi Tshering, but he was known as Babu Tashi. He was in charge of all accounts and payments, plus the collection of taxes. Rather than being primarily a banking task, in addition to the accounting part, this was a stores-man's job, as payments came in the form of produce, like corn or rice, and woven cloth. Each household was also obliged to provide a certain amount of labour, called *ula*, to the Dzong, roughly one person-month each year.

While today many Indians use the term "Babu" in a sarcastic way to suggest a glorified clerk or an Anglicized Hindu, the word (from Hindi and Urdu) originally denoted respect. And that is how people used it in referring to Babu Tashi, who came from Pemagatshel, in south-east Bhutan.

He had been selected in 1914, under the first king, Ugyen Wangchuck, to go to school in India, at the same time as Karchung and Kharpa. He took teacher training at the University of Calcutta, and so he and Mr.

Kharpa were the first two trained Bhutanese educators. Babu Tashi started some of Bhutan's first schools, under the second king, and tutored the third king. He spoke Sharchopkha (his first language), Dzongkha, Nepali, Hindi and English.

Babu Tashi was a strict disciplinarian. If Father Mackey let it slip that his son, Sonam Tobgye (who has since gone on to very high government offices), had misbehaved at school, the boy got a severe beating at home. He seems not to have been a warm person and most people feared him. He was also very religious, but Father Mackey thinks "overly so."

Father Mackey recognized Babu Tashi for his abilities, which were significant, and his work for education, but felt that he exhibited neither the wisdom nor the vision of Tamji Jagar.

One day in conversation with Babu Tashi, Father Mackey suggested the possibility of a newspaper appearing in Bhutan. The man responded sternly: "We'll never have a newspaper."

Two months later, it appeared: the first edition of *Kuensel*, Bhutan's national newspaper.

* * *

Father Mackey did not know the Thrimpoen's *rabjam* well. He was a monk who had been recruited for the job and lived in the Dzong. He was not part of the regular "gang." However, Father Mackey became good friends with the Nyerchen's *rabjam*, or right-hand man, Tenzin Dorje, commonly called Ten Dorje. His forte was finance and accounts, which he undertook with great care and diligence. At one point Ten Dorje taught Father Mackey the old Bhutanese system of calculation, which used an abacus-like principle but with stones, and without a frame.

Although Bhutan had its own currency system, Indian money was widely used, even by the government. And when India switched its currency from the complicated rupee, anna, paisa system, Ten Dorje was responsible for converting the system in the Dzong. Having used the old system all his life, Ten Dorje went to Father Mackey to learn how to do the conversion. The Jesuit taught him the decimal system.

Every amount of money recorded in the accounting system and pertinent at the time, had to be converted — no small task in those days before micro-chip calculators. But Ten Dorje undertook it with patience and conscientiousness. He might have been excused for a reasonable degree of "rounding off" but, according to Father Mackey, he was scrupulously meticulous in doing every conversion exactly.

It would be many years before the term *"ngultrum,"* the basic unit of Bhutanese currency, would be commonly used. The *ngultrum* is tied at par to the Indian rupee, and Father Mackey continued to use the term "rupee" on into the 1980s.

Ten Dorje had three daughters who attended the school as day scholars. (In fact, all girl students were day scholars, as the school had no boarding facilities for girls. Those few who came from villages outside Tashigang stayed with relatives or other families.) Father Mackey referred to Ten Dorje's daughters as "the dumb one, the clever one and the beautiful one."

Apparently, though, they all had a lot on the ball. The so-called dumb one, Kiba, could beat up any boy in the school. She had been known to mete out after-school retribution on more than one lad. Kiba went on to become an excellent teacher, in Father Mackey's estimation, and to run her own school in Thimphu.

The eldest daughter, Sangye, was clearly very intelligent. She wrote the Bhutan matriculation (class ten) examination in 1969 and came fourth, excelling in every subject. She followed in her father's footsteps and became an officer in the finance department. She married an officer in the Royal Body Guard and they raised a large family.

Deki was the daughter Father Mackey thought of as the beautiful one. And apparently her good looks attracted suitors at an early age. She was in class seven, along with one of Doctor Karchung's sons, Lhendup, when she came to Father Mackey one day and said, "Father, the boys are writing love letters."

"Oh, that's very, very bad," he replied. "Who's writing them?"

"Lhendup."

"May I see the letter?"

"No!"

"Oh, very good." Father Mackey nodded his head sagely. "Yes, I'll talk to him."

Father Mackey never mentioned it to the boy.

Later, Lhendup went to Australia for engineering studies and specialized in motor mechanics. After returning to Bhutan he ran the government automotive workshop in Samdrup Jongkhar for several years. Stopping at Samdrup Jongkhar one day, Father Mackey ran into Lhendup and his old student invited him for dinner. Father Mackey accepted and went to the young man's residence that evening.

Who should be serving the dinner? The beautiful Deki.

The scene brought out the tease in Father Mackey.

Over dinner, he said, "Deki, do you remember the time in class seven you complained about a certain boy writing love letters?"

"Shuuush!"

"Well, you loved him, didn't you? So what were you upset about?"

*   *   *

The crime rate in Bhutan was very low. Violence was extremely rare when Father Mackey arrived, and arose mostly out of drunken arguments. Even so, Tashigang had a police station near the front of the Dzong, and a prison behind and down below the back. It was really just a few bamboo huts, with not much security and never more than a dozen prisoners.

Serious criminals might have suffered real punishment within the Dzong. Some aspects of life were still rather medieval, after all, and Bhutanese authorities no doubt meted out some harsh punishments.The prisoners Father Mackey saw, however, were not hard done by. They were kept in leg irons, but that was the only security measure used to keep them from running away (although Father Mackey occasionally saw prisoners wearing collars of wood — two boards about a metre long, bolted together).

Prisoners were required to work all day but free to walk around the village afterwards and on Sunday, when the Dzong was closed. They would visit and chat with friends and then return to their quarters Sunday evening. Certain crimes brought imprisonment but no shame. One was the traditional practice of shifting cultivation, which involved burning forest for agricultural use (and sometimes the fire would get out of control). Villagers — the peasant farmers — needed fresh land, and if caught, shared the blame in turn.

Theft was unknown. Father Mackey found that he could leave his door open with no fear. In those early days, most people didn't even know the value of the Indian paper money. If a boy saw a ten-rupee note on Father Mackey's table, he might pick it up and examine it out of idle curiosity, but he'd have no real interest in it.

Disputes did arise over extramarital sex. The Sharchopas, down-to-earth and uninhibited people, condoned premarital sex — but adultery could lead to trouble. If a case was deemed injurious, the guilty party, usually a man, might be beaten. He might also be required to pay compensation to the woman's husband. If a baby were born from such a problematic liaison, the child was taken care of.

Divorce was usually straight-forward, settled by mutual agreement. Father Mackey saw very few cases of divorce. On the other hand, a man could acquire a second or even a third wife (usually sisters of his first wife) without any problem. A woman having more than one husband (always brothers) was less common, but was also accepted by the community. Multiple spouses usually created a division of labour within the family, with individuals devoting themselves to cattle, cultivation, the home, or in some cases a business in town. On the farm an extra person committed to helping with the hard work was nearly always a boon.

Sexual attraction was one reason, but often not the main reason for taking another spouse. It might be noted, as well, that because many men became celibate monks, eligible women outnumbered their counterparts. Sexual attraction usually played a greater role in premarital sex and the choice of one's first partner.

Eastern Bhutan has been notorious for its apparently liberal approach to sex and the practice of "night hunting." But Father Mackey found the open approach to sex — no mystery, no taboo — to be very sane. For Sharchopas, sex is a normal, healthy aspect of life, and the source of much joking. Married women, especially, enjoy making sexual jokes.

At his schools, Father Mackey encountered very few problems related to sexual behaviour among the students, largely because of his overall approach to supervision and activity. And from what he learned about kids' lives at home, he knew there was a lot of sexual activity that stopped short of intercourse, a lot of "horsing around."

The community saw "night hunting" as a natural way for young people to enter into sexual adulthood. The practice often led to marriage. If a pregnancy occurred in a case where marriage was not wanted, the baby would be absorbed into the family.

Part of the boys' "roaming" was like a competition to see how many houses they could get thrown out of. Once past puberty, the boys were free to be outside at night. They might even stay together in a hut separate from the main house. So they had the opportunity to wander around the village at night, joking and seeing what they could get up to.

Nobody had inside plumbing, and so a boy might try to sneak into a house while a girl's mother and father made a final trip outside. More often than not, giggling from the girl's bed would alert the parents when they returned. They'd discover the boy and out he'd go. Then he'd try another house and maybe another until he was successful, or more likely, tired. Next day he could brag or joke about his exploits, successful or not.

Most disputes arose, however, not over sex but land, which was the source of livelihood. People needed land for cultivation, for pasture, for water and for wood. Boundaries were often not well-established or marked and absentee landlords were common. If a farmer noticed that a bit of land adjacent to his was not being used, he wouldn't miss an opportunity to encroach. If and when the original owner noticed, a confrontation would ensue that could end up in front of the *thrimpoen.*

Further problems arose when powerful people, land owners like members of the royal family, who might live in Thimphu, gave land to servants. Often such transactions were verbal and so invited disputes. The boundaries of the land may not have been clearly specified. More than one party might claim the land. Sometimes the original land owner would forget that he'd given away the land, or to whom. Such a case would be complicated by the claimants' relative positions in society in a country where "little" people did not challenge "big" people and where big people were not supposed to take advantage of little people.

Father Mackey saw some of his students get involved in land disputes. If a parent died while an heir was at school, other relatives sometimes took over the property. The boy would have to hurry home to secure his rightful ownership. There were also cases where, in order to make sure his land was properly protected while he was at school, the boy would take a wife, perhaps a "good solid matron." She would run the farm and send him pocket money. Later, if he wanted a second wife, he might pick a younger woman and marry her.

* * *

For seventeen years before arriving in Tashigang, Father Mackey had lived surrounded by mainly Nepali people. Nepalis are more open and demonstrative than the Drukpas of Bhutan. The Bhutanese enjoy a good time as much as anyone, and one can have warm friendships with them on certain levels. But they have always been, and perhaps always will be, an insular and even secretive people that keeps private a large and important part of their social psyche. They are classic in the sense of "the inscrutable East."

This has never bothered Father Mackey. He is no amateur sociologist or anthropologist. He takes people as they come. He has learnt much about the Bhutanese, but he has never tried to pry into their souls. His modest, moderate approach is probably one of the traits that endeared him to the people. He has learned, he has been reasonably observant — but he has not stuck his nose where it wasn't wanted. His behaviour, on the contrary, has won him respect and love.

While a newcomer to a place like Bhutan can't learn much in six months, one might expect that he would sense trouble brewing. Father Mackey was totally unaware, however, that serious tensions were gripping the country. As with many periods of Bhutanese history, this one remains unclear to the outsider. We do not even know how much is clear to the Bhutanese.

Rather than speculate from an extremely limited base of knowledge, let us simply say this: In early 1964, serious political problems arose in Bhutan. They involved the Royal Family, the related Dorji family, the army and a number of individuals.

At the peak of the crisis, on April 5th, 1964, Prime Minister Jigmie Dorji was shot at the guest house in Phuntsholing. He died an hour later.

Three months before, when he had agreed on the Kanglung site for the school, he had given Father Mackey a battery-operated short-wave radio intended for someone else, and had subsequently sent him books. The news of the assassination shook Father Mackey profoundly. He regarded the prime minister, who had brought him into Bhutan, as something of a patron, and a friend.

Yet he found the shock of the assassination easier to handle than the reaction that followed. His own first response was to organize an appropriate function at the school. He went to the Dzong to invite senior officials to come and speak to the students about the late prime minister. As far as he was concerned, Jigmie Dorji was a great Bhutanese and should be remembered. He assumed that everyone would agree.

As it happened, not all officials were in Tashigang at the time and those who were apparently did not feel it appropriate to speak at Father Mackey's gathering, though they did attend.

Father Mackey alone talked to the students about the prime minister, his good works, and his service to the country and its people. He told them about his relationship with Jigmie Dorji, starting back in Darjeeling, about the prime minister's interest in education, development and modernization. The Bhutanese officials could have talked far more knowledgeably, but they were unwilling to take any chances.

This was Father Mackey's first major lesson in how little he knew Bhutan. Later, he pieced together the story, and got some sense of the trouble that had been brewing over recent years. He learned the basics from Indian newspapers. Then, from time to time, he'd hear a story relating to the assassination.

There was, of course, speculation of various sorts. There was a suggestion that the Prime Minister's wound need not have been fatal and that aspects of the medical attention may have been inadequate. Such talk was natural and there seemed to be no insinuation that any inadequacies were deliberate. More serious, however, was the suggestion that there was significant tension between the Dorji and Wangchuck families.

The speculations were never supported by evidence, or even by a credible explanation. However, the rumours and distrust created a cloud over Bhutanese politics for years, and many people were hurt and embittered. One man was judged responsible for the assassination and he paid the price.

Finally, Nari Rustomji, who had been an adviser to the King at the time, published a book, entitled *Bhutan: The Dragon Kingdom in Crisis*. It offered no clear-cut account of what had transpired, but many have accepted it as definitive.

The fallout from the assassination went far beyond the loss of one important man. As Father Mackey put it: "Who all was involved, what were the exact details — I wouldn't know, I don't think anyone knows. But there was a lot of unease. People didn't know which way to jump. Everybody was sitting back, waiting to find out what was going to happen, how things were going to turn out. But there was deep unease in the country. And a lot of sadness."

9/

G iven that Father Mackey had come to Bhutan directly through the offices of the prime minister, the man's dramatic demise might have been cause for personal concern. However, nothing changed. The King showed keen interest in Father Mackey's work, and asked the Jesuit to establish a made-in-Bhutan examination system.

Father Mackey knew the curriculum would include Bhutanese language, English, mathematics, science, history and geography, but recognized that the Bhutanese system had to fit into another system elsewhere so graduates could attend college or university. The logical choice was one that would fit with an Indian system, of which two were available nearby — the West Bengal Board of Secondary Education and the Cambridge system.

Father Mackey opted for the first model. Not only was he thoroughly familiar with it, but the King had found that many students returning from the more elitist Cambridge schools did not fit well into the country. Nari Rustomji — the Indian political officer and advisor to the King — assured the Bhutanese that their class ten graduates would be accepted into Indian colleges.

In 1964, Father Mackey started the Bhutan Matriculation system in Tashigang with his first class six. The students and system would grow together, progressing one year at a time until the students wrote their class ten examinations in 1968. A few schools followed Tashigang into the new system, the first being Mongar, Paro and Thimphu.

Through these early years, Father Mackey's chief partner in building the system was Dawa Tshering, whom he had met in Paro in October

1963. His father had been in service in the Dorji household. He'd been recognized as a bright boy, and educated in a style almost equal to that of the Dorji children. After graduating from university with a degree in economics, he joined government service, working with the Dorjis. His responsibilities included education, and he'd been involved in the earliest discussions with Father Mackey.

Dawa Tshering was already involved in recruiting teachers, mostly from South India, for the remote Bhutanese primary schools. He actually took the 1962 group to their posts himself. He gained a reputation among teachers as a caring man. Living conditions were difficult, but Dawa Tshering did what he could and made sure teachers got paid a decent salary.

He and Father Mackey liked and respected one another, and worked well together through these years of education development and the building of the showplace school in Eastern Bhutan. Even later, when he became Bhutan's first foreign minister, Dawa Tshering remained keenly interested in education, and helped Father Mackey any way he could.

Before Father Mackey arrived, Bhutan had little that could be described as an education policy. During his tour of Eastern Bhutan in 1963, he'd discovered that schools operated independently and shared no common syllabus. While discussing this with Dawa Tshering, the official suggested they "put something down on paper."

In early December, 1964, when the school year ended, Father Mackey travelled to Thimphu. He stayed for a week, while he and Dawa Tshering drafted Bhutan's first education policy. Later, drawing on ideas from education administrators recruited from India, and also other Jesuits, the two of them expanded this document into a second policy paper.

Later still, more government officials got involved, especially from the planning department, and the documents became more voluminous. These modern versions included history, planning, objectives and more detail, but according to Father Mackey, they said fundamentally the same things as the earlier ones.

* * *

While Father Mackey began receiving an honorarium only after several months, the great majority of teachers, from India, were already on the salary system. In receiving their salary, however, delays of two or three months were not uncommon. This was not a major problem, as people had nowhere to spend the money anyway.

Tashigang Dzong was the education paying office for all of the eastern interior, which included schools at Tashi Yangtse, Lhuntse, Mongar, Pemagatshel, Radi and Bidung. Someone would come from each of the schools every month to collect the money. For nearby schools, the trip, on foot, might take only a couple of days. But for the more distant schools, it could take a week or more.

There were often delays in Tashigang. Thimphu and Paro were far away, and road conditions, weather or administrative slip-ups could slow the arrival of funds. Then the visitor would have to walk back whence he'd come. A round trip could take three weeks — for one month's salary. If the Dzong had no money at all, a person might have to return empty-handed.

Obviously, the school head could not always collect the money. He would hardly ever be in the school. Teachers usually rotated the task, though even then, obviously, it was a terrible waste of time.

In Tashigang, Father Mackey served for a while as paying officer, and quickly realized the extent of the waste. He went to Ten Dorje and said, "Look, this is crazy. Why not appoint a man to take the money around?"

Ten Dorje gave the job to a trustworthy man.

If this fellow were lucky, he'd make the circuit in six weeks. He'd leave the Dzong with a bag of money, visit all the schools and get back to the Dzong barely in time to pick up another bag and leave again. The system worked. Only occasionally, in the worst of the monsoon season, when rivers were too swollen to cross, would the messenger be prevented from reaching some schools.

After a few years, the man got tired of constantly travelling. He approached Father Mackey, who arranged for him to become a language teacher.

Later, most large Dzongs had a Regional Education Officer who was responsible for paying teachers. So Father Mackey no longer had the responsibility of getting money to the teachers. Later still, when post offices were built, teachers were paid by postal money order.

* * *

Boarding students needed rations, and the government provided the basics: rice, salt and dhal. Dhal — the pulses or lentils that go to make

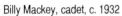

Billy Mackey, cadet, c. 1932

Young Billy Mackey.

Bill Mackey, probably at Muskoka, between 1936 and 1939.

Funeral procession for Father Michael Wery, Kurseong, 1957.

Sherubtse Public School, Kanglung, c. 1968.

Father Mackey looking out across Paro valley, October 1963.

Father Mackey on the road from Samdrup Jongkhar, first trip to Tashigang, October 1963.

Father Mackey leading children in the singing of "Old MacDonald had a farm;" man wearing *kabney* (long white scarf) is Ten Dorje; Tashigang, mid-1960s.

Left, wearing white *kabney*, Father Mackey; centre, bending, wearing sword, King Jigme Dorje Wangchuck; Tashigang, c. 1964.

Prime Minister Jigmie Dorji, near Kanglung on day of choosing site for Sherubtse, 1964.

Father Mackey and gymnast, Tashigang playing field, mid-1960s.

Rare photograph of Phongmey Dungpa, dressed on this occasion in borrowed Western clothes, with a puppy on his hat; he is wearing chappals on his feet. Tashigang, probably 1960s.

Second from left (standing behind), Doctor Anayat; third from left (with horn-rimmed glasses), Prime Minister Jigmie Dorji; right, Thrimpoen, Dasho Tamji Jagar; the two other men are visiting Jesuit Brothers from India. Tashigang, 1964.

King Jigme Singye Wangchuck pins Druk Zhung Thuksey medal on Father Mackey, Thimphu, 17 December 1973.

Father Mackey, Thimphu, late 1980s

up the spicy Indian stew of the same name — was not a traditional food in the interior of Bhutan, but it was nutritious and students accepted it well. The defining element of the traditional Bhutanese diet is hot chillies, fresh when in season and dried otherwise. The school would usually purchase these from local farmers, for whom chillies formed an occasional cash crop. Many children brought their own, and parents visiting the school were expected to bring chillies and *tegma* (crushed, lightly roasted corn which was usually eaten for breakfast or snacks).

In addition to the government rations, each student was required to bring fifteen seers, roughly fifteen kilograms, of food every month. They might bring corn (maize, the staple food in Eastern Bhutan), rice, potatoes, white radish or *tegma*. Of course, when times were tough on the farms, this couldn't be relied upon. And whether the government provided rations or, as later, money for rations, either could be delayed.

When Father Mackey began working in Tashigang school, rations came through the army. Deliveries weren't always on time, and when stocks were getting low, Father Mackey would send a wireless message to headquarters, saying: "No rations. Closing school." Often nothing happened and he would send another wireless: "No rations. Closing school in two day's time."

This usually drew a response: "Do not close. Rations arriving."

In a day or so the supplies would appear.

When government provision for school boarding changed to a money system, Father Mackey received ten rupees (about two dollars at the time) per student per month. As students usually brought corn and rice from home, he used the money to make up the balance of rations. This might include rice, but definitely cooking oil, dhal, salt, sugar and *chiyapati* (tea leaves), which were not produced locally.

This stipend sounds small now, but at the time it was usually sufficient, given that the rupee's buying power was much greater. Father Mackey purchased supplies from the Dzong, which usually stocked some of his requirements, or from Samdrup Jongkhar, where a man named Chabeldas Moth ran a general store called Moth & Co.

Father Mackey worked out an arrangement with Chabeldas, making him essentially general buyer for the school. In addition to standing orders, Father Mackey only had to send a note and whatever he asked for would arrive a week or ten days later, whether payment was made at the time or not. Chabeldas knew Father Mackey was a good, reliable customer and provided him with good service. He may have charged a bit more than other merchants, but Father Mackey felt he was getting his money's worth.

As long as the road ended at Rongtong, supplies coming from Samdrup Jongkhar by truck had to be carried from Rongtong to Tashigang by more primitive means. The simplest way was to take all the students to Rongtong and give each a share of the load to carry back to the school. Two to three hundred students (their numbers grew over time) could handle a substantial consignment of rice divided up into little bags, and the walk to Rongtong and back offered a break from the routine. The walking time was only about four or five hours, but the operation would take all day. Father Mackey found that using this method might result in a loss of up to ten per cent. But that was still cheaper than hiring porters to carry the load.

The rice went missing as boys hid it in their *gos*, a handful each, maybe more — hardly overpayment for the work they did. They liked having a bit of their own food on hand. Bhutanese children were, and to a great extent still are, very self-reliant, even from a young age. At home, many of them were *wadipas*, or cowboys, who took care of the cattle and of themselves as well. Besides tending cattle out on the mountainsides, some of the students had to walk many days to get to school, and had to cook at least some of their meals along the way.

Like most children, they liked camping out. At school, if they had some food, students could slip away, build a small fire and make themselves a meal. Besides any rations they could lay their hands on, they might snitch vegetables from the school garden, or have extra food brought by their parents when they visited. Many students had relatives or family friends in or around Tashigang, whom they could visit on a holiday. Bringing a bit of rice (a treat for villagers whose staple food was maize) or something else ensured that they would be invited again.

Father Mackey applied the food-collecting principle — many students, small loads — to the gathering of firewood to fuel the kitchen fires. Every Saturday afternoon, each student had to bring in a bundle of wood — the size depending on the size of the child — from the mountainside above the school.

The gathering started with ground wood or dead branches taken easily from trees. It progressed to live branches, then full limbs stripped from trees. Then small trees would be pulled or cut down. With three hundred or more students gathering wood every week, the forest shrank and the children had to go higher and higher up the mountainside to get their wood — as high as Rangchikhar and beyond by the time Father Mackey left Tashigang. Later, firewood would have to be purchased.

* * *

Before Father Mackey arrived in Tashigang, organized sports did not exist at schools. This is not to say that there were no sports in Bhutan. The national sport is archery, and the Bhutanese are masters of their traditional version, practised with simple, hand-made bamboo bows and arrows. The target is a wooden board thirty centimetres wide and just over a metre high. The accuracy of archers is truly remarkable, given the length of the "field" (usually about 130 metres) and the style of shooting used to project arrows such a distance.

Another common sport is *dego*, which involves the throwing, underhand, of stones. The stone is of a size that can be held in one hand, and the first thrower — usually an average thrower — establishes the distance. Father Mackey likens the sport to curling, as it includes placing stones and knocking out other players' stones. In Tashigang, *dego* was played by both school children and men, but especially by monks, as archery was forbidden to them. On a sunny day, when they went out to bathe and wash their robes in a nearby stream, they would play *dego* for hours while waiting for their robes to dry, draped over bushes or rocks.

For children, the most popular, traditional game was *kuru*. This is an outdoor game of large darts, the darts measuring about thirty centimetres long and the target placed at about twenty metres. The wooden body of the dart is best fitted with feathers to make it fly straight, but in the absence of feathers paper would serve. Major holidays like the three-day Tshechu — which honours Guru Rinpoche, the great saint of Tibetan Buddhism — and Losar, the Bhutanese new-year holiday, feature a lot of *kuru*. At these times, chickens were apt to lose a few feathers for schoolboys' darts.

Father Mackey introduced football (soccer) and volleyball to the school, and used the army's small parade ground above the school as football field and volleyball court. Over the years, mostly with boys doing the work, he expanded the playing field by cutting into the mountain on one side and building up on the other. Later, after Father Mackey left Tashigang, a bulldozer expanded the field to the reasonable dimensions it is today, probably twice its original size.

Father Mackey's forte, also played on this field, was gymnastics. When he arrived, the school had no gym equipment and he had to make do with whatever he could find. Many things, like complicated races and pyramids, did not require special equipment. For basic tumbling, he would lay a thick bed of *gos* on the ground. In time, using money donated from Canada, he had a gymnastics horse built in Samdrup Jongkhar. He also had Moth & Co. make up some mats and he designed a simple spring board. On his model, the gymnasts got their spring from hitting the middle of the board rather than the end.

The boys loved gymnastics and their displays on sports days were a great hit with the public. Father Mackey had a taste for spectacular crowd pleasers, which usually required a lot of skill and practice: elaborate pyramids, five-legged races with four kids tied together, chariot races involving seven boys per team. These events were fun to watch, but the most spectacular event saw gymnasts dive and somersault over the horse and through rings of fire.

At one of Father Mackey's sports days, the special guest was His Royal Highness Namgyal Wangchuck, half-brother of the King. When a boy named Tarpola went to do his diving somersault, he caught his foot in the *gos* which were serving as mats. Instead of landing on his feet he did a nose-dive into the hard rough ground of the playing field. He did not lose consciousness, but was pretty bashed up and had to be taken to the hospital.

His Royal Highness was very concerned about the boy and visited him at the hospital next morning. He gave the boy a gift of a new *go* and 150 rupees (a very large sum in those days). This cheered the boy immensely, but the other gymnasts protested: "If we knew His Royal Highness would do that, we could have all used our noses to plow up the ground."

* * *

During these early years, Father Mackey's right-hand man was Brother Michael Quinn. He was an ex-Mountie, over six foot tall, who'd worked with the Inuit in the Canadian North. This experience in a remote setting was one reason he was chosen to go to Bhutan. He was also suitably talented: he was a good teacher, handled children well, and had the aptitude and training to be of great use in medical matters.

He tended to be quiet and happily accepted the position of a Jesuit Brother in the partnership with a Jesuit Father. He also had a good sense of humour, albeit quieter than Father Mackey's.

When it came to entertainment, Brother Quinn's specialties were concerts and drama. Every year for six or seven years he staged a Shakespearean play adapted into simple English. The kids loved performing these. In later years, when he had higher classes, Father Mackey made sure he always had several copies of Lamb's *Tales from Shakespeare*, the most popular book in the library.

One of Brother Quinn's comic classics got Father Mackey into hot water. The children were staging Jerome K. Jerome's little account of "How the elderly family man puts up a picture" in *Three Men in a Boat*. In the Canadian school readers, the selection was called "Uncle Podger Hangs a Picture." Translating this into Sharchopkha, Father Mackey thought it appropriate to substitute Phongmey Dungpa for the hilariously bumbling Uncle Podger.

This was a natural for the students, who played it up. Phongmey Dungpa dropped in for rehearsals and got a great kick out it too. However, when Phongmey Dungpa's wife got wind of it, she grew indignant and went to see Father Mackey: "How dare they make fun of my husband!"

He tried to appease her. "No, Ama, we love Dungpa. We're not making fun of him."

Unmoved, she insisted that this was not right. Father Mackey said, "Okay, Ama, we'll change the name."

Perhaps to show the indignant lady that they were not scandalizing anyone, they named the main character Dasho Tshering. He was the Thrimpoen at the time, certainly an official no one would belittle in public. So it was "Dasho Tshering Hangs a Picture." But rehearsals had already gone on for ten days using the name Phongmey Dungpa. When the students came on stage, their first words were, "Phongmey Dungpa Hangs a Picture" — and Dungpa's wife was after Father Mackey again.

This didn't stop him from adapting any work he could to make it more meaningful to students. He used classic nursery rhymes in English class and concerts, but "Old King Cole" would become "Drubthob Wangchuk," with a boy dressed up for the part. In "Baa Baa Black Sheep," there would be "one for the *rabjam*, one for the *nyerchen* and one for the *thrimpoen* who lives in the Dzong."

Father Mackey also played up universal elements of song and story-telling like rhyme and dramatics. He was neither a singer nor much of a dramatist, but he was not shy about acting the fool to bring things alive for the students. When he said, "baa," in "Baa Baa Black Sheep," he did so in a funny, exaggerated voice. For "Humpty Dumpty," Father

Mackey had a boy squat on a table, and called him "Kota Jyakpo" (which, roughly translated, means "funny fat boy"). For his "great fall," Kota Jyakpo would somersault from the table, land on his feet, crumple to the floor and be laid out flat. Father Mackey would rest a foot on the boy to show he was truly dead.

His altering, even slaughtering, of classic nursery rhymes was often poorly received by visiting English experts. But the kids and their parents got a great kick out of this sort of thing. Many children's stories from the outside world were meaningless to those who had never seen a motor vehicle, a picture book or a magazine, much less listened to radio or watched television.

During Father Mackey's time, Tashigang school made tremendous progress in English. The language had only been adopted for education, and few spoke it in the community. Starting with nothing, Father Mackey and Brother Quinn worked hard at getting books, including simple reading books for the students. In addition to establishing a working level of language skills, they instilled an enjoyment of reading and writing.

The students' willingness to write, combined with their limited knowledge of the wider world, produced some surprising results. This was the case when the road was completed to Tashigang around 1964-65, stopping short of the Dzong by about three kilometres, at Khiri, where the petrol pump is located today. Everyone went to see the first vehicle arrive at the official opening of the new road. Afterwards, Brother Quinn told his students to write an essay on the opening of the road.

A boy named Tenzingla (who would go on to earn a master's degree and a government position in agriculture) went with Father Mackey to the opening. As they walked up the road, they saw the first official vehicle arrive — the Brigadier's Jonga, much like a jeep but larger and closed in, commonly used in the Indian military. The next thing Father Mackey knew, Tenzingla was running away up the hillside. The boy's version of events appeared in his essay for Brother Quinn:

"I was walking along the road. It looked like a football field. It was narrow, but it was very level. I was kicking a stone along. Then I heard a noise. I looked up. A strange animal was coming towards me. Two eyes were shining in the sun. Smoke was coming from its tail. In fear, I ran up the hillside. I slipped, rolled down, and closed my eyes. I expected to be bitten or kicked by the beast. Then the belly of this strange animal opened and a man got out. I could not believe my eyes. I went closer and looked inside. There was a nice little room with seats. In front, there was a smaller room with a wheel sticking up in the air and a new kind of clock. Then I went around in front and touched it with my hand. Never did a pony have such a hot nose."

* * *

Father Mackey rarely needed medical help and had little personal experience with local medicine. He did keep a tin of "black medicine" which he would bring from Darjeeling each year. It was a multi-purpose sticky paste used to draw poison or pus from a boil or similar affliction. Probably it was belladonna, which is still widely used in India. From time to time, he ran across another "black medicine" — opium.

Despite its reputation as a habit-forming scourge, it is an ancient medicine that many rural people on the Sub-Continent use. Usually they take it as tea for medicinal purposes, and never even dream of smoking away their lives in an opium den. Similarly, the marijuana that grows wild and abundantly in Bhutan has virtually never been used as a "recreational" drug. It's fed to pigs. No doubt it makes the pigs content and lethargic, encouraging the development of the thick layer of fat the Bhutanese so love to eat.

Whenever medical problems arose at the school, Brother Quinn would take charge. A tall, well-built man, he nevertheless had a gentle touch. This was useful when a student wondered whether to follow the advice of Western medicine or that of the lamas. Fortunately, both Brother Quinn and Doctor Anayat respected traditional medicine and tried to work with it rather than against it. Mild clashes between Western and traditional medicine would occur from time to time though, and Brother Quinn usually convinced the children to do it his way.

On one occasion, though, a rabid dog bit several children. To all but one, Doctor Anayat administered the injections that counter the fatal disease. But the other boy's father, who happened to be a *gomchen* (a layman who has some religious knowledge and often functions in the community as a religious practitioner), blessed the boy and gave him some local medicine. This boy refused to take Doctor Anayat's injections. One of the children who took the injections died, and the boy who'd had the blessing and local medicine lived.

For centuries, Bhutan had been known in Tibet for its wealth of medicinal vegetation. Father Mackey marvelled at the odd concoctions people used, and both Doctor Anayat and Brother Quinn tried to discover which medical problems were best approached by traditional medicine, and which were better tackled by their own Western science. They collected traditional remedies, kept their minds open and used whichever approach seemed best.

Ordinary diarrhoea, for example, would probably be treated traditionally, while evidence of bacterial infection like blood and pus would warrant a penicillin shot. As far as the school was concerned, the approach seemed to work, as student health tended to be very good.

Doctor Anayat was also influenced by his wife, Lingshay. As a Lepcha, she had grown up in a society that relied upon traditional medicine and, given a choice, would usually choose that over Western medicine. Whenever possible, Doctor Anayat would call in a lama before carrying out any major operation or treatment. He found that the presence of a lama and the lama's blessing of a patient could bring a peace that made the patient physically and mentally more responsive to treatment.

He would also use the hospital compounder, a man named Bhakte, in an unorthodox way. "Compounders" served as paramedics and basic pharmacists — hence the name — but also dealt with simple medical cases, gave injections and helped out in child birth. They could recognize serious medical problems and refer patients to a doctor. Their training and duties were probably similar to those of the Health Assistants posted at the Basic Health Units nowadays in rural Bhutan.

But it was often Bhakte's ethnic background and slightly theatrical bent that Doctor Anayat called upon, especially for hysterical or psychosomatic patients. Bhakte was Southern Bhutanese, that is, ethnic Nepali, and it was the part of a Nepali *jankri* that he might be asked to play. As a *jankri* (a kind of intercessor between human beings and the gods of nature) his act was to drive out evil spirits. Bhakte seemed to enjoy the performance himself, and would really play it up. He'd move in an exaggerated, dance-like way and wave a thin stick around, banging it on the bed or whatever was handy. But whether or not he was genuine, his movements and chanting were usually beneficial, and rendered patients more amenable to Doctor Anayat's treatment.

10/

I n July of 1965, a third Jesuit arrived in Tashigang and added another lively personality to the rich mix. Father John (Jack) Coffey was shorter than Father Mackey and Brother Quinn, and of medium build, with a round jolly face. He was cheerful and outgoing — more like Father Mackey than Brother Quinn.

He joined his fellow Jesuits in the small triplex above the school, where living arrangements reflected each man's special interests. Each partitioned off a corner of his room for a bed and used another corner for personal items and a work space with table and chair. Besides that, Father Mackey had a tiny chapel for the three Jesuits and the reading library. Brother Quinn had the school textbooks and medicine. Father Coffey had the food.

Each man specialized, as well, in his professional responsibilities: Father Coffey in English language and syllabi; Brother Quinn in history and geography, plus English drama; and Father Mackey in maths and science, sports and contact with the Dzong. He was the de facto "superior," but was never referred to as such.

The three continued to take their meals with Doctor Anayat and Lingshay, paying them for board. But while they appreciated these meals, overseen or cooked by Lingshay, the diet was limited. The Jesuits occasionally got fed up with the monotony, though they took it in good humour. They joked about having potatoes, dhal and rice for lunch and rice, dhal and potatoes for dinner. Breakfast was usually left-over rice, fried, sometimes with an egg. Meat was rare. What was available from time to time was often unacceptable — rotten or the product of an unknown disease.

Father Coffey took a much more active interest in food than his two colleagues, and a year or so after he arrived, largely through his insistence, the Jesuits built a kitchen — just a basic cooking place, behind their quarters. It was common for people like the Jesuit educators to have a cook. Given their heavy work load and the time it took to prepare food using the primitive available methods, this certainly made sense.

A most unlikely looking candidate appeared — an old Nepali mountain climber, a Sherpa called Kripa, who had worked with Phong-mey Dungpa. Brother Quinn got the fellow cleaned up, and he and Father Coffey trained him to cook something besides rice and dhal. Kripa was designated Father Mackey's orderly, paid a monthly salary, and stayed with the Jesuits for twelve years.

The other two Jesuits were delighted to have Father Coffey under-take to improve their diet. A small garden produced fresh vegetables through the summer. And the Jesuits received food parcels from family members in Canada, perhaps a package a month. These made for treats like tinned meats, easy-to-make pancakes and even cakes made from cake mixes. But mostly Father Coffey relied on what was available locally, and tried to produce proper meals, complete with dessert.

Father Coffey's food "portfolio" was based largely on his own real interest, but also on the simple fact that his colleagues were already totally occupied with other duties. Brother Quinn did, however, make a significant contribution to the diet when he started making bread. He built a simple oven of stones and mud outside the triplex and got some bread tins from Samdrup Jongkhar. His bread was very popular with Doctor Anayat, people at the hospital and other teachers, who all looked hopeful whenever he had bread in the oven. With only a few loaves, the warm and generous Brother Quinn was often at a loss.

Father Coffey also added to the social circle. He liked to play cards, as they all did (including Lingshay and some of the other teachers), and took a particular liking to the Keralan game "28." Father Mackey preferred bridge, and a foursome could be gathered from among Brother Quinn, Father Coffey, Doctor Anayat and Lingshay. Some of the Indian teachers played as well. On cold winter nights and during the holidays, a foursome played bridge almost every evening.

All three Jesuits enjoyed reading, and would share books and their opinions on them. Father Mackey enjoyed everything from religious philosophy through geography and historical novels to Perry Mason whodunnits. Brother Quinn read mostly non-fiction, especially history, and his intellectual bent often led to "theological breakfasts." For some reason, breakfast, more than any other meal, inspired the three to discuss theology, sitting and carrying on long after they finished their meal. Father Coffey was perhaps less intellectual than the other two, and had his own particular taste in novels.

Father Mackey received books from his father and sister and also his Jesuit colleagues in Darjeeling. If the Tashigang Jesuits wanted something in particular, they could usually get it by writing to their fellows in Darjeeling. And each year, when they returned from their winter break in Darjeeling or Calcutta, they'd bring a big box or trunk full of books.

Father Mackey read everything he could find about Tibetan Buddhism and built up a small library on the subject. He also tried to learn as much as he could from religious people around him, like the Umdze at Tashigang Dzong. He would also "have sessions," as he puts it, with the *lopens* at the school. He found that Babu Tashi, as well, knew a lot about Buddhism. At least once a month, he would make a point of visiting one of these Buddhist teachers and discussing religion.

These pursuits may not sound like much in the way of entertainment, but Father Mackey didn't have a great deal of spare time. During the school year, besides running the school as headmaster, he taught thirty-five periods a week, did his share of study supervision, supervised and coached sports and games, and helped organize concerts and other functions.

For many years he was also the paying officer and an education advisor. He gave teachers' courses and looked after education in Eastern Bhutan. He was also working on establishing the new school in Kanglung, and pioneering Bhutan's high school system, adding a chapter in its development each year. He was not only implementing a higher level of education each year, but introducing new approaches to education that were subtly different from those of India. This work not only occupied time, but provided much intellectual stimulation.

Father Mackey did believe in taking time on Sunday to read or go walking. He walked as much as he could, both for enjoyment and to clear his head, to think and solve a problem. Class days didn't allow much opportunity, though if he had a rough day he might go walking in the afternoon or early evening.

*   *   *

During his years in Tashigang, Father Mackey spent many evenings with Doctor Anayat and his wife, eating, talking and playing cards. But few could compare with the evening the doctor greeted Father Mackey and Brother Quinn at the door, announcing: "I've got some tiger cubs."

Proudly, he displayed two greyish-yellow, puppy-like felines, each about thirty centimetres long. A Bhutanese villager had found them on a nearby trail. He brought them to Doctor Anayat, who was a sucker for this kind of thing, and offered him the cubs for twenty rupees each. That was a lot of money, but Doctor Anayat agreed.

The three men played with the cubs and thought them marvellous until Father Mackey began asking questions: "Where did this guy pick them up?"

"Oh, just coming up from the river."

"Well, where in hang's the mother?"

Just then, they heard a low rumbling growl from outside the small Anayat home. They looked at each other. What now? They peeked out the door and saw nothing. Maybe the tiger had gone away? Lingshay, typically unconcerned, began feeding her baby girl. The tiger cubs, smelling the fresh mother's milk, started a commotion. They were hungry, too.

This brought a laugh and eased the tension, but then the men would hear the cubs' mother growling outside. Presumably, she sensed by smell that her cubs were in the house. Dinner time came and went. The Anayats' kitchen was about twenty metres from the house and the cook had dinner ready. The men went to the door and yelled to the cook, "Have everything ready! We're coming to get it, but we're going to run. Have it all ready, 'cause we're just going to grab it and run right back. If you see or hear anything, you tell us. We'll stop there, we won't come back. Okay?"

All in all, it was an exciting meal. When it was over, Father Mackey and Brother Quinn stood wondering about how to get home with a tiger lurking outside. And Doctor Anayat was mulling things over. He questioned the wisdom of keeping two wild cubs in his home while their mother was looking for them. He said to himself, "I don't want these damned cubs around here tonight when everybody's sleeping."

Doctor Anayat went out the front door and called to someone. A man came, and, after a few words from the doctor, took away the cubs.

Father Mackey and Brother Quinn decided to retire. They said goodnight and ran home. When they got to their quarters, there stood the man to whom Doctor Anayat had given the cubs. He handed them to Father Mackey.

"I don't want the darned things," he said. "Here, you keep them."

The man refused: "No, no, no, no!"

Father Mackey and Brother Quinn put the cubs in the school stores for the night. Next morning, the problem remained. What to do? Doctor Anayat no longer wanted the cubs. Father Mackey said, "Put them outside and maybe the mother will come and pick them up." They put them out and had someone watch from a distance. The mother did come, they were told, but she sniffed the cubs, then turned around and left them. Obviously, they were too tainted by human smell for her to take them back.

Doctor Anayat took the cubs back in. He didn't have to worry about the mother anymore. The cubs still ran around when Lingshay breast-fed her baby, but then they were given milk purchased from villagers. Soon they became very solid young cats. And Doctor Anayat again started to worry about what to do with them.

Eventually, he gave them to Brigadier T.V. Jaganathan, the chief engineer for Dantak, who took one look and said: "They're not tiger cubs, they're leopard cubs."

* * *

From time to time, Father Mackey would participate in archery competitions. These might be held in Tashigang, even on the school football field, with archers shooting diagonally from corner to corner, or else in nearby villages. Competition was fierce but good-natured. The meets would last all day, or even longer, and would involve eating and drinking and other entertainments — some, like dancing girls, designed to distract the opposing team. Participants would taunt the opposition, appeal to deities for assistance and celebrate good shots with ritual dance steps.

Initially, Father Mackey was very disturbed at the apparently cavalier way players treated on-coming arrows. After archers finished shooting, they would go down to the target to cheer their own team and distract the opposition. They would stand, even dance and play the fool, very near the target. They'd watch the arrow sail towards them and step aside at the last moment.

The traditional archery field was usually about 130 metres long, but this would vary depending on terrain. It wasn't easy to find a suitable stretch of ground that long. And it wasn't uncommon to have the "field" stretch across a ravine or a stream. Archers had to be able to adjust quickly to different conditions.

It takes years to become a proficient archer, and the better Bhutanese grew up with the sport. Father Mackey was not an outstanding archer — though he did not embarrass himself on the field.

Over the years, despite the apparent risk the archers took by standing next to the target, Father Mackey saw no more than half a dozen people hit by an arrow, and then never seriously hurt. Boys were very good at dancing and singing in front of the target, then dodging an arrow just before it hit them, perhaps just leaning their head aside. But at school, Father Mackey made sure they stayed a safe distance away.

Nowadays even more care has to be exercised as many Bhutanese have acquired powerful international competition and hunting bows. Arrows shot from these move much faster, with much more force, and do not take the traditional arcing trajectory.

At an archery contest, as at any large social gathering, an attendant hazard was *ara*, the locally made alcoholic drink. Often referred to as "wine," it is a spirit distilled from fermented grain. Run-of-the-mill *ara* has a nondescript taste and is not terribly strong, though a series of cups can take a toll.

Better-made, strongly distilled *ara* can be tasty and pack a punch. In Eastern Bhutan, it is a very common drink and a visitor could find himself invited to indulge at any hour of the day (from dawn!). Having given in to the first persistent invitation, he dare not refuse at other houses, as people would take great offence.

To survive required a strategy. One could politely refuse every offer (perhaps citing some illness); one might manage by drinking the minimum (carry your own small cup and take only small sips until the host has been able to fill the cup the requisite three times, at which time you can politely refuse more); or one could throw caution to the wind and take what comes. In the last case, one might not get very far down the trail.

Father Mackey had a reasonable capacity: two large tumbler-fulls. Beyond that he could be in trouble. But he knew the trick of never drinking the *ara* quickly, because the host would keep filling the cup to the brim. By sipping slowly, thereby allowing only minimal top-ups, he could keep his intake under control. Drunk reasonably like this, over time in conversation, the alcohol did not pose a problem.

In an awkward situation, he had been known to toss the *ara* out the window when no one was looking. He also had to judge what he was getting. With the variation in the alcoholic strength, one could be caught unawares, drinking too much of a particularly potent variety.

An archery competition was traditionally an occasion for a lot of drinking, and the rural hosts liked to get their guests feeling very happy. At every opportunity, they would fill a guest's cup. For such occasions, Father Mackey carried a small, hand-turned wooden *gorbu* in his *go*. It didn't hold much. And as the competition was held out of doors, with everybody moving around, he found it easy to spill more than he drank.

11/

After clambering up onto the back of the elephant in its resting position, Father Mackey took hold of the rope that passed around and under the animal. There was a piece of quilted padding on the animal's back and Father Mackey positioned himself on this. He was told not to sit, but to stay on his feet and crouch down, and hang on to the rope. This would give him more stability. His small travelling bag was passed to him and, as directed, he put this between his knees. He held the rope tightly as the grey, wrinkled beast got to its feet, tipping Father Mackey back and forth. As they lumbered down into the river, Father Mackey watched the brown muddy water rise around them.

This was at Samdrup Jongkhar, 180 kilometres south of Tashigang. The river bed of rounded rocks measured about thirty metres across at this point, but shallow water usually covered only a third of this. There was no bridge, but for most of the year trucks and jeeps could ford the river. During the monsoon, however, the water sometimes became too deep.

On either side of the river, some vehicle would nearly always be available to take the occasional traveller onward — but one had to get across the river to access it. And if the river was too high to drive across, probably it was too high and swift to walk or swim across. Enter the elephants. An important Bhutanese family kept them for logging, but when necessary, they let travellers ride them across the flood-swollen river.

The idea of climbing onto an elephant to ford a river sounds exotic and exciting, but the reality could be frightening. There was no howdah

144

or secure box to sit in. There was a mahout, and room on the elephant's back for as many as four passengers — two facing back, two front. But these had nothing solid to hang onto. And feelings of insecurity were not the only problem.

Father Mackey learned to trust the elephant, though the first few times he rode he felt uneasy. Often as he sat aboard the elephant in the middle of the stream, a huge tree would come speeding toward them. The animal seemed oblivious, but just before the tree hit, the elephant would snatch hold of it, swing it around and let it go down the river. Father Mackey made half a dozen monsoon crossings before the bridge was finally built.

* * *

The man who owned the elephants, J.P. Pradhan, was commissioner for south-east Bhutan. One of his sons was not doing well at school in Gauhati, Assam, the Indian state that borders Bhutan south of Samdrup Jongkhar. He was known as Janga, and had already been thrown out of schools in Darjeeling. Gauhati had just enough cinemas to keep the young teenager out of school most of the time.

Janga's older brother, a rising civil servant named Om Pradhan, told Father Mackey all this when he arrived in Tashigang with the boy. He said: "We want him to study under you."

"Well, there's no movies here," Father Mackey said, "so there's no danger as far as that's concerned. And he won't be running around outside the school because there's no place to go."

Om Pradhan had brought another man, and now he introduced him as Janga's cook. Father Mackey told him to take the cook back: "If he's here, he eats like everybody else and none of this business."

Neither brother cared much for this response, but next day, Om Pradhan left with the cook.

Classes were held on Saturday morning. After lunch, every student had to fetch a load of wood for the school kitchen. Father Mackey called Janga. Pointing, he said: "See that jungle up there? You get a rope. You get a *chowang* [large Bhutanese knife]. And you go up there with somebody who knows the way and you bring back one load of wood."

Father Mackey did some work in his office, then headed over to Doctor Anayat's house to eat his own lunch. On his way, he was surprised to see Janga walking towards the school kitchen with a load of wood on his back. To himself he said, "Wait a minute now. That was quick work."

After lunch he went to the school cook. "Where did this boy get the wood from?"

"Father, he's a *badmash*! He came in, picked up a load of wood from the pile, did one tour around the football field, came back, dumped the wood and disappeared."

Father Mackey called Janga to his quarters. "Now you may do that in Gauhati and other places," he said, "but not here. Now, over the bed."

The boy bent over and Father Mackey picked up the thin metre-long bamboo stick he kept for such occasions. He lifted the boy's *go* and gave him four or five good licks. The boy was shocked. He had never been punished like that in his life. Father Mackey said, "Don't let it happen again. Now, out!"

For a while, it seemed that Janga had learned his lesson. But a few weeks later, Brother Quinn found that his chickens had stopped laying eggs. The Jesuit was puzzled and annoyed. He couldn't understand it.

One day in class, Brother Quinn realized he'd left something behind in his quarters. He told his students to carry on for a few minutes and went to his room. While rummaging around at his desk, he heard noise from the small chicken coop just outside. The former Mountie quietly stepped outdoors and waited by the chicken coop. A few moments later, Janga emerged.

Brother Quinn reached inside the top of the boy's *go* and found four eggs. He'd solved the mystery of the lazy hens. Again Janga found himself facing Father Mackey, and again he received a dose of the cane. After that he straightened out and fitted in well. When he finished school he went to Australia and wound up staying there, working with handi-capped children.

* * *

As early as 1964-65, the road from Samdrup Jongkhar reached Khiri, just three kilometres short of Tashigang, but it was very unreliable. Around Rongtong, fourteen kilometres back, it seemed like the road was always blocked by sliding soil. In 1965, Father Mackey acquired his first jeep, a simple Indian-made Willys with a removable canvas top. He kept it in a shed just below Rongtong, where it fell victim to a freak accident.

The Dantak road construction crew was blasting nearby, and a chunk of rock flew off towards the makeshift garage. It arced perfectly to enter the open front of the shed and smash the windscreen of the jeep. Father Mackey asked Dantak for reimbursement, and was assured it would be forthcoming. Six months later, Dantak replaced the shatter-proof safety glass windscreen with ordinary plate glass. Fortunately, this stayed intact, and Father Mackey continued to use the jeep to travel to Samdrup Jongkhar — whenever he could.

The biggest problem he faced was the slide, especially during the monsoon season, when rain destabilized the mountainsides. A traveller could encounter rock, earth or mud, or a spot where the road itself had slid away. Being caught in a serious slide could mean injury or even death. Fortunately, the odds on this happening were low. As for blocked roads, the traveller adapted as best he could. He could clear a few rocks by hand. And a road crew, if one were nearby, could clear a moderate blockage in hours. A badly breached road could require days, weeks or, in the worst cases, months to restore.

When Father Mackey first got his jeep, the roads were new and unstable, and delays of several days were common. He often had to trans-ship, as on his first trip to Paro in 1963. Even so, during these early days in Tashigang, jeeps were a relative luxury. And buses did not exist. Slow-moving eight-ton trucks from India were the principal means of transport, both for people and goods. They would carry passengers but had little space in the cab, so most people rode on top, sitting on the freight.

Travelling down to Samdrup Jongkhar from Tashigang, this freight would probably be potatoes. That made for a fairly comfortable ride, as one could usually make a place among the burlap bags of potatoes and hold onto a rope that encircled the load. The trucks travelled slowly, never more than forty kilometres per hour, and averaging only twenty, but the road was unceasingly winding. The traveller had to seat himself well to be comfortable over the ten to fourteen hours of the trip.

If the load were mixed, as it tended to be on the return trip from Samdrup Jongkhar, a traveller might have difficulty finding comfortable seating amidst the crates, oil drums, pots, plastic containers and whatever else. The cab would be more comfortable, though often crowded, because it offered some protection against cold and rain. And whether inside or out, motion sickness was common on these winding roads, especially among Bhutanese not used to motor vehicles.

The teachers normally travelled at the end and the beginning of each school year. They would try to arrange their travel in groups of four, so they could play cards. The Keralan game of "28" would occupy about half the trip. The rest of the time they would talk, look at the scenery or, given a comfortable, secure spot, sleep. In December and February, when teachers usually travelled, they didn't have to worry about rain, but riding outside could get cold.

This was wintertime, and at certain points elevations could range around 2,800 metres. Also, a cold, damp mist could invade sections of the route at just about any time of year. Barring serious delays due to landslide or breakdown, a truck leaving Tashigang early in the morning would reach Samdrup Jongkhar by nightfall. Travelling by jeep, Father Mackey could make somewhat better time.

He'd spend the night in Samdrup Jongkhar with friends, in the government guest house, or in one of the Indian-style hotels which grew up as the town developed. Next day, if he were heading to Siliguri or beyond, say to Darjeeling, Father Mackey would go to Rangia, on the rail line in Assam, in hopes of catching the train that night. But reservations were almost impossible to get and riding without a reservation was a nightmare. It meant riding third class, sitting up (if a seat could be found) in a carriage that was probably already packed when the train left the rail head at Gauhati.

In this situation, Father Mackey found a bottle of Bhutan's Apsoo rum invaluable. He would go to the ticket counter and politely explain to the agent, "Look, we couldn't get reservations, but we'd like to get seats on the train tonight. Would you see what you can do?"

He'd place the bottle on the counter, then turn away as the agent got on with his business. When the rum disappeared, he knew he had his reservation. The following morning he'd arrive in Siliguri, where the station was in the middle of town — not at New Jalpaiguri where it is now. He might stay a day or two in Siliguri before proceeding to Darjeeling by bus.

The return trip was the same in reverse. The bus ride from Darjeeling to Siliguri did not take a whole day, but Father Mackey would usually leave early in the morning. Jesuits in Siliguri would usually arrange train reservations in advance. The train he caught to go east came from Patna, and would stop in Siliguri for a couple of hours. Gone were the days when you could set your watch by trains like the Darjeeling Mail, and usually Father Mackey's train was late.

Very early the next morning, it would pass through Rangia, where Tashigang-bound travellers would get off and make their way to Samdrup Jongkhar. Father Mackey might have a jeep waiting for him. Otherwise, he would look for a lift or share a taxi with others heading the same way. In Samdrup Jongkhar, a traveller had to wait until a truck was heading up the road. This could be days. For the trip up, one had to remember to have some warm clothes handy. Temperatures could be balmy in Samdrup Jongkhar, but once in the mountains, the air was usually cool and often freezing cold. The entire one-way trip, which could take a week in those days, now takes two days.

* * *

While most villagers in Eastern Bhutan had never seen cars or trucks, many had seen airplanes, or at least one airplane. In Tashigang they called it the Tawang *gora*, the Tawang horse. The plane was a Dakota which flew past Tashigang once a week. It carried supplies to Tawang, a large town in Arunachal Pradesh, near the eastern border of Bhutan. The flight took a short cut across Eastern Bhutan. It followed the main chain of valleys up from Samdrup Jongkhar, past Tashigang and then turned east for its last leg. Father Mackey was told that the pilot would count the main side valleys. When he came to the fifth one, he would turn east and follow it to Tawang.

One cloudy day, a pilot new to the route mis-counted and turned at the wrong valley. He just never arrived, and authorities had to assume he'd crashed. They began a search north of Tashigang, believing that he'd missed the first valley and overshot his turning point. Helicopters and planes of all sorts swept the maze of deep, heavily forested valleys and ravines among the mountains, but found nothing.

Meanwhile, Father Mackey was teaching at Tashigang school. As soon as the initial excitement caused by the aircraft settled down, classes went on as usual. Then, one afternoon, a fluttering sound announced the approach of a helicopter. Father Mackey looked out in time to see a French-made Alouette pass overhead. It landed on the football field. Leaving his students to work on their own, Father Mackey went up to see what was going on.

He climbed the hill behind the school. When he reached the playing field, he found the helicopter pilot surrounded by Bhutanese soldiers from the small cantonment just above the football field. Father Mackey went closer and listened. Both sides were frustrated because they had no language in common. The soldiers were demanding to know why the pilot had landed without permission. They were prepared to hold him under armed guard.

The pilot noticed Father Mackey and asked: "Do you speak English?"

He told the Jesuit that a sighting had been reported. He was supposed to pick up Colonel Lama, the Dantak officer in charge at the construction site at Kanglung. But the pilot did not know the terrain and couldn't find his destination. When he saw the football field at Tashigang, he thought he'd better land and find out where he was.

Father Mackey explained the situation in a mixture of Sharchopkha and Nepali. Then everything was all right. But the pilot still had to get to Kanglung. He asked Father Mackey if he knew where it was, and the Jesuit described how to get there: "See that point on the spur there? Go straight that way and you'll hit Rongtong and then Kanglung. It's two minutes."

The pilot looked around at the mountains, one of them much like another, and asked Father Mackey to show him the way, promising to bring him right back.

The Jesuit was quick to accept. He'd flown in old Indian helicopters, but never in one of these beautiful French Alouettes. They took off and Father Mackey savoured the fabulous view of the surrounding region. He directed the pilot to Kanglung and indicated where he might land. There were people at the site, apparently waiting for the helicopter.

When Colonel Lama saw Father Mackey, he said, "What are you doing here?"

"I'm the pathfinder on this deal. Now he's going to take me back."

"No, he's not," said the Colonel. "We just got an urgent message with some new information. We've got to move immediately."

"What about me?"

"My vehicle will take you back."

The road was not yet through to Tashigang, but would get him to Phomshing. Just below Rongtong, however, the road was blocked, as usual. The helicopter flight had taken three minutes, but the trip back took more than three hours. It would have been quicker to walk, but Father Mackey decided to sit in the vehicle until the road was cleared.

He never learned where exactly the Tawang *gora* had crashed, only that it was north of Rangthang Woong, somewhere around Tashi Yangtse. Having turned up the wrong valley in the mist, the pilot hit a mountain and died.

* * *

Even today, despite roads, people in Eastern Bhutan travel more miles on foot than by vehicle. Thousands of rural people make their way along narrow trails, up and down and across mountains, where no roads exist. It seems unlikely that all the rural areas of this country, made up entirely of mountains, will ever be served by roads. And while efforts are being made in remote areas to build and improve suspension bridges, a traveller still finds much more primitive means of crossing mountain streams.

Father Mackey encountered one such contrivance during a trip to Shinkharlauri, a village in south-east Bhutan. Visitors usually approached by travelling south from Merak-Sakteng, or east from Khaling. On this occasion, Father Mackey was walking to Shinkharlauri from Khaling with Doctor Anayat, Kipchu from Tashigang Dzong, and Cyril Namchu of the agriculture department. The four men came to a ravine cut by a river flowing far below. The distance across it was the width of a football field. The means of crossing? A bamboo ropeway.

It was made of a heavy rope of twisted bamboo and anchored to big trees on both sides of the ravine. From it hung a basket supported by two large bamboo rings, one at each end. This basket, too, was made of bamboo, and was just large enough to hold one person. Tied to the basket were two lighter ropes, one running to each side of the ravine. While in those days this type of crossing was not uncommon, it did not inspire a lot of confidence in this group.

When the four friends arrived, the basket was on the far side of the ravine, so they took the light rope attached at their end and pulled it across. Then they faced the big question. Who would be the first to cross? Nobody was keen. But the others agreed: "Okay, Kipchu, you're the Bhutanese, you get in."

Before Kipchu got into the basket, Mr. Namchu said, "Wait a minute. This may be the last time we're here together. Let's have a bit of holy water." From his rucksack, he produced a bottle of Apsoo rum and the four men drank. Then, with words of encouragement from his pals, Kipchu got into the basket and let it slide down the supporting rope to the middle of the ravine. Far below him, the small but violent river churned. By pulling on the rope attached to the far side, he hauled himself up and across.

The other three pulled the basket back to their side and Mr. Namchu asked, "Who's next?"

Father Mackey was quick to propose Doctor Anayat: "Doc, a medical man's required." So they put the doctor in. He slid down and pulled himself to the other side.

Then Mr. Namchu said, "They may need the priest on that side." So Father Mackey got in and made the trip.

Finally, Mr. Namchu pulled the basket back for himself. He looked at the river below, he looked at the basket and he looked at the bottle. He said, "Let's finish this to get a blessing from Sangye [Lord Buddha]."

Mr. Namchu polished off the bottle, got in the basket and crossed the river.

12/

One May morning in 1964, the King's helicopter landed on the football field behind Tashigang school. His Majesty, King Jigme Dorji Wangchuck, climbed down and, ducking to avoid the wash from the helicopter blades, walked to the group waiting to greet him.

The King was of medium build and height, a little shorter than Father Mackey. His somewhat softened Mongolian features were not striking, but he was a good-looking man. Though still in his thirties, he was balding and his hair was cut very short. He was neatly dressed in an unpretentious *go*, and the impression he established was one of comfortable confidence, intelligence, warmth and good humour.

Father Mackey, wearing traditional Bhutanese dress, was introduced to the King, who complimented him: "You look nice in a *go*."

Father Mackey was part of the group that accompanied the King along the path of pine needles and grass — a kind of "red carpet" — laid out to the Guest House. He was invited in while the others stayed outside. The King's helicopter was going to pick up his guests, and he asked Father Mackey what they could do while they waited. Father Mackey suggested a visit to the school.

As Father Mackey and the King walked up the trail from the Guest House, the Thrimpoen and the other officials who were some distance away assumed that the King would be going down to the Dzong and they started heading that way by a short cut. Father Mackey tried to get their attention by waving at them behind the King's back and, by pointing, to indicate that they were going to the school.

The King asked, "What are you doing, Father?"

"Nothing, Your Majesty."

"You're doing something."

"No, no, I'm just walking behind you."

They got to the school and walked towards the kitchen at the far end, where the students were eating lunch. The area was muddy. From a spring higher up the hillside, water was piped down to the school through tubes and troughs made of bamboo and rubber piping. The water couldn't be turned off and the excess ran across the area below the kitchen. There was a walkway of raised stones along the path to the kitchen so the King and Father Mackey could stay out of the mud.

But the Royal Body Guards, who had just been issued new uniforms from Switzerland, were required to fan out in protection of the King. There they were, unceremoniously and laboriously making a "gluck, gluck, gluck" sound as they slogged through the mud. The King took a plate of rice and dhal and squatted to eat with the boys. Doctor Tobgyel, the royal physician, was beside himself when he arrived on the scene because one of his duties was to taste everything the King ate, to guard against the unlikely possibility of the King being poisoned.

On the way back to the Guest House, the King looked in on Father Mackey's quarters. He showed immediate interest in the collection of books he found there. He took down one book after another and examined each. Outside, the rest of the party wondered what could be keeping the King in Father Mackey's one room. The King finally asked if he could borrow a couple of books. The two would exchange books until the King died.

* * *

On the morning of another, more formal, visit by the King, Babu Tashi was making a last-minute check of the area around the football field, hospital and school. He came rushing over to Father Mackey and asked, "Where's your gate?"

Father Mackey looked blank: "Gate?"

Traditionally, every community or institution would build a temporary ceremonial archway or gate for the arrival of a high-ranking guest on a special occasion. It was usually built with a light wood frame covered with flowers and fresh boughs from trees and often had a banner across the top, welcoming the guest. The army had one in front of its little cantonment and there was another on the way to the Dzong.

But the King would be walking from the football field towards the school, and Father Mackey had not realized he should have a ceremonial gate to greet him. He thought: "Wait a minute now, what to do?"

He asked Babu Tashi, "Have you got an extra banner, one of those banners with the greeting on?"

"Yes."

"Can you get it for me?"

When the banner arrived, Father Mackey located two bamboo poles and tied the banner along them. Then he gathered a dozen of his best gymnasts.

The King's helicopter landed and the army greeted him with a guard of honour. Father Mackey stood in his *go* and *kabney*, along with the other officials turned out for the arrival. While the King inspected the guard and chatted with the officers, Father Mackey slipped away, down to the school where his gymnasts waited.

As he went, he noticed that some of the people around wore odd expressions and acted strangely, as if holding their breath. What he learned only later was that when he left the official party, one of the Royal Body Guards followed him with a Tommy gun in case he was up to no good.

Father Mackey was waiting when the King led the procession of officials down the hill towards the school. The King came down the steep path, looked up and saw Father Mackey standing there. Apparently used to Father Mackey's unorthodox behaviour, he said: "Oh, Father, what are you up to now?"

Father Mackey blew his whistle and the boys sprang into action. In seconds they had built two pyramids, each of them with three boys on the ground, two on their shoulders and one at the very top. Each of the boys on top held one end of the banner greeting His Majesty. The King was amazed. "This is very interesting," he said. "I want to take a picture."

Father Mackey was a bit worried. The boys couldn't hold their difficult positions for very long. He thanked God when he saw Doctor Tobgyel pull a camera out of his *go* and hand it to the King. His Majesty clicked a picture and passed through the gate. The boys were getting shaky and as soon as the King passed through, Father Mackey blew his whistle and everything collapsed. Doctor Tobgyel, the Thrimpoen and the rest of the officials were surrounded by tumbling boys.

Father Mackey and the King got to know one another better during this visit. The next day, Father Mackey was called to the Dzong, where the King was staying. As they sat cross-legged on small rugs on the hand-polished wooden floor, with cups of tea, the King said, "Father, I want you to tell me, in brief, the essence of your Catholic faith."

"In brief?" Father Mackey said. "If you love God, you prove it by loving your neighbour."

That impressed the King.

Then the King asked, "Have you got anything on the life of Christ?"

"I've got the gospels, the New Testament."

"Okay, come down tomorrow with the New Testament."

Father Mackey brought the book next day. The King looked at it with some dismay. It was too long to read in the time he had.

"Take one gospel, a short one," Father Mackey said. "It won't take you more than an hour, an hour and a half. Read it through in one sitting and you'll get a better idea. Don't read it as little bits but read the whole thing through at once. Take Luke — it's the shortest — and read it though."

The King read the gospel and talked again with Father Mackey. "These cures," he said, "these miracles, whatever you want to call them — are they true?"

"Well, Your Majesty," Father Mackey said, "I've seen strange things happen in Buddhism which I would call miraculous." He described a case in which the Yonphula Rinpoche said prayers over an old man who seemed certain to die, and the man recovered. "There was something very, very special there."

The King, of course, did not wish to become a Christian. But he was interested in religion. As well, perhaps, being impressed by Father Mackey's devotion and work, the King wanted to know what made him tick.

Father Mackey and the King not only respected each other, but shared a down-to-earth sense of humour. They met whenever the King visited Eastern Bhutan, and from time to time Father Mackey was called to the Palace.

On a couple of occasions, while travelling in royal convoys, Father Mackey ran into permit problems. As a foreigner he was obliged to stop at the border check post at Jaigaon in India, opposite Phuntsholing, and present his papers — particularly his transit permit. But as Father Mackey said, "When you're in a royal convoy you can't say, 'Look, I want to go into the police.' They'd just whizz right by."

The Indian border officials did not accept this argument.

The far north-east of India has been a restricted area for more than a century. In Father Mackey's time, foreigners were restricted from travelling north into the Darjeeling hill area and Sikkim (until the 1970s a nominally sovereign state), across the border into Bhutan or east to Assam and other areas.

To travel through this restricted zone, a transit permit was required. It specified details of the trip — exact date, route, mode of travel, reason for travel, identification details of the traveller and so on — and remained a nuisance to foreigners over the years.

Foreigners like the Jesuits at Darjeeling had residence permits that allowed them to stay within specific restricted areas (it was this permission that Father Mackey was denied in 1963). But India also required knowledge of any foreigners in Bhutan.

So, Father Mackey had to have two types of Indian permits: a transit permit for crossing the border and travelling through the restricted Indian territory, and permission to remain in Bhutan. The residence permit, issued from Calcutta, was good for six months and could be renewed regularly. But the transit permit, from the Indian Embassy in Thimphu, was issued only for specific trips and had to be applied for well in advance.

What made the travel permit regulation particularly bad for Father Mackey was the lack of an east-west road within Bhutan. The only way to travel between Eastern and Western Bhutan, apart from walking, was to go through India, crossing Indian territory between the border towns of Samdrup Jongkhar and Phuntsholing. So, to go from one side of his country of residence to the other required a special permit, with all the particulars of the trip specified two months in advance. Bhutanese citizens could cross the border and travel in this area with no restriction.

Fortunately for Father Mackey during his days in Tashigang, and even for a while after he moved to Kanglung, there was no Indian check post at the Samdrup Jongkhar border crossing. While technically prohibited from travelling south of the Bhutan border without a transit permit, he could actually move quite freely, up to a point. He could travel to Gauhati, the nearest city in Assam, where he occasionally had business to transact. He could also travel to the area just south of Phuntsholing.

The hitch was that he could not cross back into Bhutan at that point without the permit. It all seems quite ludicrous, but if Father Mackey had to meet the education director, Dawa Tshering, at short notice, he would do so at a tea estate near the train station at Hasimara, just a few kilometres from Phuntsholing but inside India. The Jesuit wasn't supposed to be there, but nobody bothered about it. However, if he tried to cross into Bhutan at that point, there was usually hell to pay.

When he travelled beyond the border areas, to Darjeeling or to Calcutta via Gauhati or Siliguri, he would obtain a transit permit. For one thing, such trips were usually planned well in advance, with time enough to apply. But apart from that, he knew he would probably be noticed and checked at Gauhati airport, the Siliguri railway station or the airport at Bagdogra, or else in Darjeeling where he was well known.

Following his first encounter with Indian border officials, after running the border in a Royal Convoy, Father Mackey had a chance to discuss the matter with the Indian Ambassador, who said there was no problem. Unfortunately, there is a big difference between chatting with the senior diplomat in Thimphu and confronting a border guard indoctrinated into taking a narrow, inflexible position. They were not about to stop the King of Bhutan just because his convoy included Father Mackey. After the fact, however, they could give the priest a hard time.

On one occasion, an Indian border guard wanted to stop Father Mackey because on his previous crossing, in the second jeep behind His Majesty, he had failed to report.

Father Mackey challenged the guard, "Report! How can I stop the Royal convoy?"

"You should."

"Look, I've sorted this out with your ambassador in Thimphu. If you've got any problems, phone him."

"No."

"Please lend my your phone."

"What are you going to do?"

"I'm going to phone your ambassador."

Father Mackey was let through.

It hadn't been so easy at Jaigaon, when Father Mackey crossed on a uniquely intriguing mission. He was responding to a wireless message from Dawa Tshering that began, "His Majesty is pleased to command . . ." It required him to come to Thimphu and report to the King. But Father Mackey didn't have a transit permit. He would not normally have attempted such a trip without one — he tried to follow the rules as best he could — but this was special. He said to himself, "Let's try, take my chances." He got a ride down to Samdrup Jongkhar and from there took a bus to Phuntsholing. He almost made it.

Jaigaon in those days was little more than a dusty street, the Indian check post and a few shops. At the little Indian immigration building every bus going to Bhutan was stopped at a pole barrier lowered across the road. Father Mackey's bus stopped at the barrier and an Indian official got into the bus. He normally gave only a perfunctory glance around. Father Mackey was sitting near the rear by a window. The immigration man missed him. He gave the okay to the driver and stepped down from the bus. Just then, one of Father Mackey's old students from Darjeeling, standing outside, recognized the priest at the window. He called out, "Hey Father, what are you doing here?"

The official climbed back into the bus and demanded Father Mackey's permit. As he had none, the priest had to get off the bus and go into the little office. He explained that he had to go to Thimphu and that he had applied for a permit (actually for a later trip to Siliguri) but didn't have it yet. The border official wouldn't accept that. Even the wireless message which Father Mackey thought would be his trump card made no difference. "We don't take orders from the King of Bhutan."

"Well, I do!"

The man didn't want any complications. He said, "Just go back to Samdrup Jongkhar."

But Father Mackey had come this far and was under orders from the King. "I'm not going back," he said. "I've got this order, I'm staying. You can do what you like, I'm staying."

Father Mackey would have to be detained. But the border guard didn't know where to put him. Just across the border the sub-divisional officer in charge of Phuntsholing was waiting for Father Mackey with a Royal Body Guard jeep to take him to Thimphu. It was mid-afternoon, and when the Bhutanese authorities found out what was happening they brought Father Mackey tea and snacks.

The normally quiet Sunday afternoon was disrupted for the wireless and telephone operators. They were kept busy for the next few hours as border officials sought a solution to the problem. Dawa Tshering had been informed and Bhutanese officials were trying to contact the commissioner of Jalpaiguri who was in charge of Jaigaon District. He had the authority to allow Father Mackey to cross into Bhutan, but he was out playing tennis.

So, the guards kept Father Mackey — not in a formal lock-up, but in the check-post office that contained a desk and a few chairs. He read the newspaper and dozed off in his chair. At seven that evening, a full meal arrived for him from Phuntsholing. The border official was getting tired of this unwanted guest in his office, and he was even less happy about Father Mackey eating his meal at the desk. But Father Mackey saw no other place to eat. He picked up the fellow's newspaper and said,

"Okay, we'll keep your desk clean with this," and he laid it out as a place-mat.

Later, the border official said: "Now, where are you going to sleep?"

Father Mackey shrugged: "I can sleep anywhere. I've got a sleeping bag and I've slept in worse places than this. But," he continued, "there's a guest house over there." He pointed towards Phuntsholing. "I could sleep there — they're waiting for me."

The guard glowered at the smart-alecky priest.

A nearby government building served as quarters for the check post staff. A spare charpoy, the basic Indian bed, was found there for Father Mackey. Escorted to his room, he opened his sleeping bag, crawled in and was asleep in moments. About ten o'clock that night, the Bhutanese finally got things straightened out with the Indian commissioner. Word was conveyed to the border post and the Royal Body Guard came to collect Father Mackey. They woke him and brought him across the border to the guest house in Phuntsholing.

Father Mackey still didn't know why the King had summoned him. He arrived in Thimphu late the following evening and stayed the night with his old friend Tamji Jagar. Next morning, he went to the Palace at Dechencholing, a few kilometres north of Thimphu. He arrived about eight-thirty and the King called for him immediately. But at the door he was stopped by a Royal Body Guard and a servant: "Where is your *chanjey?*"

Father Mackey was not aware that a person summoned by the King was expected to bring a gift — more specifically, *chanjey*, a gift from a lower person to a higher person. He would have given it to the servant who would have carried it in to the King. The guard and servant found Father Mackey's lack of etiquette very irregular, but who could understand foreigners? They let Father Mackey proceed.

The room he entered served as a bedroom and was a mixture of simplicity — polished wooden floors, sparsely furnished — and exquisite woven fabric and painted adornments around the windows and on *choedroms*. There were no Western-style beds but traditional Bhutanese "beds" — essentially, cotton mattresses on the floor. The King and Queen and their five children were all there together. They received Father Mackey warmly and gave him tea and cakes and cookies. He was impressed by the abundance of love the parents exhibited towards their children. This looked to the priest like a close-knit family in an ideal home.

The royal parents told Father Mackey that they wanted him to spend a month with the three eldest children. But he, audacious foreigner that he was, said, "Well, I'd like to get back in two weeks' time because it's the end of the year and exams are coming up."

The King said, "Well, we'll see after two weeks."

Then he explained that his son, the Crown Prince, had been attending school in England but had run into problems. The boy, Jigme Singye Wangchuck, had been put out of the school after arriving late a number of times. The King did not know if the boy was below average in his intelligence, or just where he stood. The King wanted Father Mackey's assessment. The priest was to teach the three children and see how they did.

Father Mackey later pieced together an explanation for Jigme's problem with the English school. It had nothing to do with his intellect. When it was time for the boy to return to school after spending a holiday at home, he would obviously have to travel. The Buddhists of Bhutan believe that there are better and worse times to undertake certain actions. To ascertain when it is timely to act, many people consult religious astrologers.

To pick an auspicious time for the Crown Prince to travel back to England, the Queen would consult the appropriate astrologers. In a science that is very precise for the Bhutanese, but allows a lot of leeway (one day might be okay, another better, another better still), these senior monks may have leaned towards letting the boy stay longer with his mother. They knew she hated to see him leave. There might be a series of postponements, as they looked for an auspicious date for the boy to travel, and his return to school would be delayed.

The boy himself was probably not overly eager to return. Though he knew better than anyone when he had be back, he didn't try to ensure that a propitious date was found well in advance. And once on his way, when he had to stop at places like Calcutta and Delhi, he probably didn't hurry, accepting any opportunity to dally. As for hosts in these places, they were probably inclined to hang onto their prestigious young guest as long as possible.

So, by the time he reached England he could be quite late. Apparently the school authorities were not prepared to forgive this transgression often, and he was finally refused readmittance. After trying unsuccessfully to get around the problem, his father called the boy back to Bhutan.

The morning of Father Mackey's first class, he encountered a Royal Body Guard standing at the door just inside the room he was to use. The guard wore the traditional "uniform": a *go* with the trim *kabney* which was like a flat, four-inch-wide cloth belt slung over one shoulder and hanging to the waist under the opposite arm. This identified him as a Royal Body Guard.

As Father Mackey entered, stepping over the high threshold, the man, holding a rifle (it looked pretty useless to Father Mackey), snapped to attention so smartly that the priest just about tripped and fell. But besides being startled by the reception, he thought, "My God, I don't want this guy standing here the whole time."

He said to Jigme (Father Mackey still pronounces it "Jimmy"), "Get this guy out of here, will you, Jigme? I don't want to have him in here. Let him stand outside if he wants, but he's not standing inside the classroom."

The guard seemed happy enough to leave.

The tutoring went well and Father Mackey enjoyed it. He taught a bit of English, French, plus some maths and science. His three students, just entering their teens, had very different personalities. The eldest girl, Sonam, was serious and quiet, while her sister Dechen was quick and outgoing. Dressed in their ankle-length *kiras*, both were attractive and conscientious students. Jigme did not lack intelligence, but he was not very interested in school. A good-looking boy, at the same time cute and quite distinguished in his *go*, he acted like the schoolboy he was.

For one thing, he didn't like homework. Father Mackey assigned some the first day. Next morning he checked the boy's work and it seemed all right. That evening, he assigned more homework. The following morning, he found that the homework had again been done, and quite well — but the handwriting was different. It was not difficult for the Crown Prince to find someone to do his homework for him, but the same person wasn't always available, and here he'd slipped up. He hadn't bothered to copy the work himself.

Father Mackey told the boy: "You may do that in England, Jigme, but you don't do it here."

During this time, Jigme stayed with his father at Tashichoedzong, the huge dzong in Thimphu that houses the national government. The girls stayed at the Dechenchoeling Palace with their mother. Father Mackey was accommodated at the Palace during his stay. That afternoon, when the Royal Body Guard arrived to return the prince to the Dzong,

Father Mackey said: "Nothing doing, Jigme. He can wait while you sit here and do your homework."

Father Mackey kept him for an hour and a half. This did the trick: the boy hated being kept late. He promised to do the work himself if he could take it home.

A few nights later, Father Mackey was in Thimphu and Doctor Tobgyel managed to find him. The small bespectacled physician said, "For heaven's sake Father, don't give that kid French homework. Nobody here knows any French. We spend hours trying to do his homework for him."

While the homework exposé showed him he couldn't fool an old hand like Father Mackey, Jigme didn't abandon pranks. One morning the priest arrived for class and sat down to begin the lesson. He normally sat on a low Bhutanese bench that was covered with a small rug and some cushions. This morning when he sat down, there was movement under the rug. Father Mackey didn't bother to look and see what it was. He said: "Jigme, take this thing out of here will you?"

The boy removed a tiger cub from under the cover.

Father Mackey was expected to teach from nine in the morning until noon, and then from one in the afternoon until two-thirty. This much time with just three kids was a bit much. So for a break, he fell back on an old favourite — gymnastics. He knew any kid would enjoy that, and he did too. Outside was a well-kept lawn, perfect for a bit of tumbling. He had no horse, of course, but for a bit of fun with these youngsters he could make do with a couple of *choedroms*. He said to the three, "Look, I want these outside. Bring them along."

And he leant a hand himself.

As soon as they stepped out the door, servants came running to carry the things for the royal children. Father Mackey stopped them, saying, "No, no, they're carrying these things. Just leave them. They can carry the stuff."

That sank in after a couple of times. When Father Mackey led them out of the class, the guard at the door would come to attention. Then the guard and the servants hovering nearby would watch the little procession go on outside. Father Mackey was sure he saw grins on their faces as they watched the prince and princesses parade by with their load. The guards and servants were also very interested in the goings-on out on the lawn. They had never seen anything like that at the Palace. The priest had the kids tumbling, standing on their heads, diving through each other's legs, doing somersaults and all sorts of things.

The servants were not the only ones to take an interest. Word got to His Majesty about the informal gymnastics, and he asked Father Mackey to bring the children to his office in Tashichoedzong for a command performance. There, where Father Mackey found a couple more tiger cubs wandering around, the children gave a gymnastics exhibition for their father.

In his science lessons, Father Mackey used the "magic" tricks that had so enthralled students in Lhuntse and Mongar. The royal students were just as intrigued with the egg wiggling into the bottle, the air pressure keeping water in an upside-down glass and the other tricks. Jigme, in particular, wanted to do all of them himself. So Father Mackey showed him how and the boy took great pride in showing his parents. First, they did a science show for the queen, the younger children and their teacher. Then, when the King heard about it, he said, "I want to see that too." So the children repeated their performance in the throne room.

Father Mackey, in turn, was impressed by the mini-zoo at the Palace, apparently Jigme's project. There seemed to be thirty or more different animals, especially young animals — tiger cubs and other wild cats, jackals, monkeys and a great variety of birds. Father Mackey learned that the boy had taken part in catching many of these animals. His father had passed on a great interest and knowledge of wildlife and nature.

While in Thimphu, Father Mackey also came to appreciate His Majesty's knowledge of agriculture. Every once in a while, the King would drop by and pick up Father Mackey and the children and take them to see something. Once he took them to the agricultural research station at Simtokha, just south of Thimphu. There, while touring the facility, Father Mackey looked on as the King debated, with obvious knowledge, the merits of various types of corn with the Indian expert on hand.

Ashi Kesang, the charming and beautiful Queen, though very aristocratic, could also be counted on for diversion. During Father Mackey's stay, she and the children moved for a few days to the Palace at Paro, below and across the river from Rinpung Dzong — and the priest went with them. While there, Her Majesty came to him one morning and said, "Father, let's go for a picnic."

Father Mackey loved the idea. So the Queen, the children, the priest, a couple of servants and two drivers set off in two jeeps. They drove towards the Confluence and parked across the river from the old Tachogang Lhakhang. This is sometimes referred to as the Drubthob temple, after Drubthob Thangton Gyelpo, the fifteenth-century lama famous for building durable chain suspension bridges. In fact, it was one of his bridges that this party crossed to get to the temple for their picnic. Father Mackey was impressed by the huge, elongated links that made up these "iron bridges." They were strong enough to last centuries and did not rust.

The grass on the surrounding mountainsides was turning brown as autumn progressed. The picnic was not laid out on the grass, however, as Father Mackey had expected, but on the upper floor of the temple, or *lhakhang*. It was a delicious lunch, but again, more typical of a Bhutanese meal than a Western-style picnic — no potato salad or sandwiches, but fresh-cooked rice and meat. This was followed by dessert cakes.

After lunch, Jigme proposed a fishing trip. Father Mackey was no fisherman. The only fishing he'd ever done was back at the Jesuit villa in the lakes of Muskoka, when he'd trail a line behind his canoe. But he went to fish with the boy.

Jigme had a very modern casting rod and reel. For a while, the boy cast the line and reeled it in. Then he gave the rod to Father Mackey and told him to try. The priest had never even held a casting rod. He made a fair cast into the river and reeled the line in. Jigme said, "You're not throwing it far enough. Throw it harder."

Father Mackey wound up and gave a great heave. But instead of going further out over the water, the hook caught the back of his neck. The boy said, "Here, I'll take it out, Father."

The priest wondered if Jigme had a glint in his eye as he yanked the hook out, taking "half the neck" with it.

The two weeks of tutoring passed and Father Mackey was growing anxious about exam time back in Tashigang. He wanted to return. He also found living in the Palace unnerving. Having servants hovering and catering to his every need was driving him up the wall. He mentioned his concern about the exams to the Queen a couple of times. She said, "We have to get His Majesty's permission."

Father Mackey told Jigme to ask his father if he could return to Tashigang. His Majesty agreed to let the priest go. But before he left, they had a concentrated discussion about the priest's experience with the children, Jigme in particular.

Father Mackey assured the King that all the children were intellectually sound. The King also sought the priest's ideas on the further education of the children. When he was leaving, the King and Queen both thanked him personally. For the trip back, the King provided

Father Mackey with a Royal Body Guard jeep, food, drink, everything he might need — and also took care of the border crossing. As a special token of appreciation, His Majesty gave Father Mackey an old Tibetan coin, a traditional gift.

Father Mackey and the Royal Family maintained a cordial relationship. The King, during the last eight years of his life, visited Tashigang, Kanglung and Yonphula once or twice a year. During these visits, he would invite Father Mackey to functions or just to chat privately. His Majesty would usually visit the school as well.

Several times during this period, the King celebrated the Bhutanese National Day, December 17, at Deothang, with Dantak playing host for the event. Just eighteen kilometres up the road from Samdrup Jongkhar, Deothang was Dantak headquarters. On these occasions Father Mackey would be invited. This gave him a chance to see the children again, as the King usually brought them to these celebrations. In the years to come, Father Mackey would be dealing with them, especially Ashi Dechen, as young adults with heavy responsibilities.

He also remained a trusted friend of the Queen Mother, as she became, following the death of her husband and the accession to the throne of her son, Jigme Singye Wangchuck — the king who, as a boy, had hid a tiger cub under Father Mackey's bench cover.

13/

E arly one morning, as Father Mackey was getting ready to leave for Gauhati on a shopping expedition, a boy named Rongtong Sangye ran up and asked him to get some hair dye for his mother, a woman known as Abi Gombo (Granny Gombo) because of her premature grey hair.

By this time, 1966 or '67, the road came up to the hospital, though not to the school. Father Mackey no longer had to keep his jeep at Rongtong, or on the other side of the Dzong where the road used to end. It was not unusual for people going to Gauhati or Samdrup Jongkhar to have a long list of things to buy for other people. But this was out of the ordinary.

"Hair dye? What kind of hair dye? Have you got a bottle or something?" The boy ran back to the small house above the school where he and his mother stayed, and got an empty bottle with the label showing what the woman wanted. Father Mackey put it in his pocket and set off.

When he arrived back in Tashigang, he parked his jeep where he usually did, next to the hospital gate. As he pulled up, everyone gathered around — Phongmey Dungpa, Ten Dorje, Doctor Anayat and several of the teachers. Father Mackey noticed Abi Gombo. He said, "Ah, Abi Gombo, here's your hair dye."

Well, with Phongmey Dungpa and Doctor Anayat in the group, this meant only one thing: Abi Gombo was Father Mackey's wife!

They teased the priest unmercifully. The joke reached even the King. Next time he saw Father Mackey, he asked: "Who's this Abi Gombo?"

167

Many years later, around 1988, when Father Mackey visited the Palace school at Dechenchoeling in an advisory capacity, he asked the teachers, "Any problems?"

The headmaster said, "There's only one problem. We've got this old *abi* here and her darned cows and horse keep coming in. The kids plant a garden and her animals eat everything."

"Well," Father Mackey said, "give me her name. I'll go up and make a complaint. What's her name?"

"Abi Gombo."

The joke about Abi Gombo lives on, much to Father Mackey's delight. Old friends like Lhendup Dorji ("Lumpy" from his Darjeeling days) and Paljor Dorji ("Benji") will still occasionally ask, "Hey, Father, where's Abi Gombo?"

Father Mackey blames Doctor Anayat for these kinds of stories, but Bhutanese from Phongmey Dungpa to Lhendup Dorji, even the late King, usually nudged them along as well.

If all the teasing about wives were based on fact, Father Mackey would have been a polygamist. Of course, it is not uncommon for a person to have more than one spouse in Bhutan, although the additional spouses are usually sisters or brothers. Still, a number of women have been called Father Mackey's wife over the years.

Another was Miss Brozy, a German health care worker who ran a mobile health unit based in Khaling in the late sixties. At Losar one year, she came to Father Mackey as everyone was getting ready for the new year's archery competition. "Everybody's getting dressed up," she said. "Where can I get a Bhutanese outfit?"

Father Mackey said, "Well, I can lend you the one I'm sending to my sister."

Miss Brozy took the *kira* and headed for the guest house. As she was leaving Father Mackey's quarters with the *kira*, however, she ran into Phongmey Dungpa. That was all it took. Father Mackey had just given a new *kira* to his new wife! (This was Bhutanese custom.)

Now it happened that Miss Brozy's vehicle horn made a distinctive sound, like a sharp, nasal "pin-pin" as pronounced in French. And at the archery match, Phongmey Dungpa and company imitated that sound to razz Father Mackey every time he went to shoot an arrow (a male symbol) at the target (considered female). For months afterwards, Miss Brozy was known as Father Mackey's girlfriend, and referred to as "pin-pin."

At his schools, anytime a good-looking Indian teacher joined the staff, she would automatically be identified as Father Mackey's wife or girlfriend. Often, according to Phongmey Dungpa, Father Mackey would have at least two wives. And even today, no less a figure than Lhendup Dorji teases Father Mackey about his "girlfriend" or "wife," Mrs. Wilkie, his own mother-in-law. Mrs. Wilkie, it might be noted, has done a lot herself to improve education in Thimphu at the Lungten-zampa school, particularly through her work with the library.

Father Mackey usually gets an invitation from Dasho Lhendup for Mrs. Wilkie's birthday parties. As soon as he arrives, the teasing begins: "Go right in and see Ama, she's been missing you terribly, you haven't been here for such a long time, why have you kept her waiting?"

The priest does nothing to suppress the joke, and usually plays it up. At the end of the evening, when everyone is kissing people goodbye, he doesn't hesitate to give Nana (as she is known) a peck on the cheek, much to the delight of the rest of the gang.

* * *

Generally, Father Mackey's health was good. He seldom missed work because of illness, which is remarkable considering the rough and ready life he lived in circumstances rife with dangers to health. One of the few specific complaints came to a head in Tashigang. He had experienced trouble with his teeth off and on for years. He blamed his diet as a First World War baby. While in Kurseong and Darjeeling, he could easily get dental help, but Eastern Bhutan had not a single dentist.

The closest thing to dental assistance was Doctor Anayat, who had some injectable "freezing" that didn't really work. So in 1966, when his teeth bothered him, Father Mackey went to Calcutta at the end of the school year. He travelled by train from Rangia, arrived in Calcutta on the first of December and went to stay at St. Xavier's. The very next day he went to French Brothers, the dentists the Jesuits used in that city. He told one of the dentists that he wanted all his teeth out.

The dentist said, "No, no, we can save them."

"Maybe you can, but where I live there's no dentist and I have trouble with my teeth, so I want them all out. They're my teeth, I want them out."

The dentist remained reluctant to remove all the teeth, especially all at once. But Father Mackey was adamant. Finally the man agreed: "Okay, all the bottom today, and all the top tomorrow."

A few teeth were already gone, maybe seven or eight, mostly at the back. Still, it was painful, even the first day, getting the bottom teeth out. Nevertheless, Father Mackey went back again the next day: "Okay, all the top out."

These were worse, especially the eye teeth, whose roots didn't seem to be sufficiently frozen. "Boy, I jumped!" he said later. But he thought, "I've been through so much already, get it finished."

The first day had been bad enough, but the second knocked him out. When he got back to St. Xavier's, he stopped in to see Father Henrichs, Minister of the House — sort of a house manager. It was the third of December, the Feast of St. Xavier, a big day at the College, and Father Mackey was invited to the special dinner. He told Father Henrichs, an old friend from Kurseong days, "Look, I'm not coming down. Maybe send a bit of something up, but I don't think I need anything. I'm going to bed."

At dinner time, Father Henrichs brought a bowl of soup. Father Mackey was not enthusiastic. His visitor asked, "How about some ice cream?"

Obviously, he knew Father Mackey well.

"Well, okay," Father Mackey said, "I'll try the ice cream."

Father Mackey rested for two days. He didn't get his false teeth immediately — he had to let his gums settle — but later, during a visit to Darjeeling.

When he got back to Tashigang with his false teeth, he was a sensation. Nobody had ever seen such a thing. Slick cleansing powders hadn't yet reached Bhutan, so Father Mackey had to brush his teeth every morning and evening, and leave them in a glass of water overnight. He'd go to the stand pipe, turn on the water, take out his teeth and brush them.

This astonished the boys. Word spread through the school and boys came running to see. Soon the news went beyond the school. Everybody wanted to see Father Mackey's teeth. The first reaction was usually surprise. Little kids sometimes started to cry, but others got interested. They couldn't figure it out. Some asked if he could take his tongue out, too. This was the most amazing thing they had ever seen. Even today, Father Mackey is not above capturing the attention of children by taking out his teeth.

* * *

Father Mackey had not been back to Canada since 1951-52, so in 1967 he decided to visit. During the previous fifteen years a lot had changed. First, the trip itself was dramatically different. Instead of the slow pace of ships and propeller-driven airplanes, large jet planes took him home with a speed that was hard to comprehend. And the planes took him from the quiet, natural life of the Eastern Himalayas to the technological world and radical attitudes of the late Sixties. He found things "topsy-turvy."

Staying with his brother, Father Mackey tried in vain to understand the dinner conversation of his teenaged nieces. "What are they talking about?"

His brother shook his head and said, "I don't know."

"Thank God you don't know," Father Mackey said. He would have questioned his sanity otherwise.

Another shock was the price of haircuts. He knew the economies of Canada and the Sub-Continent were different, but his first twelve-dollar haircut stunned him. In Bhutan or India, he paid two rupees — maybe thirty cents.

Then there were the students. During his stay, Father Mackey agreed to give retreats in various parts of the country, including three to high school students. The first was at St. Paul's, a big Jesuit school in Winnipeg. He started off full of enthusiasm and with a wealth of stories to use in the retreat. But he seemed to exhaust his stock without raising a shrug of interest from the teenagers. He couldn't understand it. To the head of the school, he said: "My God, how can you keep these kids interested?"

The man said: "Look, you're doing well. We could never do what you're doing."

"Well, thank God for something."

Father Mackey swore never to give another retreat to Canadian high school students. But he ended up giving them in Halifax and St. John's, where he was assured the students would be more receptive.

These retreats were three days long, with four meditations a day. Father Mackey would talk for thirty-five or forty minutes, after which the students would go out and pray for fifteen minutes. The talks were on subjects like sin, salvation and prayer. But the students seemed totally uninterested, blasé, with no desire to sit peacefully and think anything through.

When Father Mackey had been in high school, boys wore ties and even jackets. During a talk or a sermon, they'd sit up straight in their chairs and pay attention. The students now slouched in their seats, stretched their legs and slung their arms over the backs of their chairs. They showed no sign of interest.

Father Mackey later realized that they were, in fact, listening. They just didn't adopt the attitude he expected. And while he assumed from their lack of response that they were totally against religion, he learned that this wasn't true either. The students just didn't follow the old conventions.

In the classrooms, Father Mackey felt frustrated with the teachers. Instead of telling a student to do something, they'd say, "Don't you think it's a good idea to do this?" The priest wanted to say: "Now sit down and shut up." From his disciplined upbringing and having worked where discipline was accepted, this new era was a radical change. He didn't condemn it, however: "Good or bad, I wouldn't know. But it's certainly different."

Father Mackey established better rapport with a Tibetan group he addressed in Milwaukee. Besides being interesting on its own, his presentation on Bhutan included enough cultural material and identifiable images that the Tibetans felt homesick. Father Mackey used Dzongkha names and terms like *dzong* and *thrimpoen* that were similar to Tibetan, and showed pictures and descriptions of Tibetan Buddhist practice and celebrations that the Tibetans could relate to directly. The show went over so well that the group insisted Father Mackey give a repeat performance the following night — and gave him a generous honorarium before he left.

Besides a change in the young people, Father Mackey noticed a change in speed. Not just the speed of transport, but in people's lives generally. Nobody ever took a walk or relaxed. Everybody seemed under constant pressure and in a continual rush. He didn't mind working while he was in Canada, talking about the missions and giving retreats, but every so often he'd take a day off, saying, "Today, nothing. I'm going for a walk. You can do what you like."

He would walk for a couple of hours, drop into a restaurant for lunch, then walk back again. After a shower and a change of clothes he felt refreshed and ready to carry on with his schedule.

Father Mackey was also struck by the reduced role of the family home, which he discovered when, about ten weeks into his visit, his father died. When his mother died, she had been mourned and waked at home. But as soon as his father died, the body was taken away and the family only saw it the following morning in the funeral home.

He could see some benefits in the new way, but felt also that it took away from the family. Once centred in the home, birth, marriage and death were now distanced from it. Births took place in hospitals, marriage receptions in hotels or clubs, mourning in funeral parlours. Children lived much of their lives not at home but at school and outside clubs. As a family institution, the home had dwindled.

As for the funeral parlour, Father Mackey could meet more people in less time, but the whole process seemed less friendly, less intimate. People would stop in, say hello, and in five minutes be on their way. Before, in the home, people would be fed. They'd drink and enjoy conversation. Even with the body present, it seemed more like a reunion — and much more human. That old style was also what Father Mackey was used to in Bhutan, with the Bhutanese cremations.

Then there was television. When Father Mackey first left Canada in 1946, he had never seen television. During his last trip home, he'd seen very little. But now television was everywhere. Father Mackey liked the sports, especially the hockey games, and the news. And he was impressed with programmes that had educational or scientific aspects, even the weather reports. He picked up a lot of ideas that he took back to Bhutan to use and share with other teachers, especially for geography and science.

But Father Mackey also felt television had invaded people's social lives. When he visited friends, the television would be on when he arrived, and no one would bother to turn it off. These people might be used to it, but he found it distracting and off-putting. The social attention was lost, whereas in Bhutan, social interaction and attention to people were foremost.

Certain other technological advances caught Father Mackey off guard. One day at Windsor Station, he piled out of a taxi with his bag in hand and went to push open the station door. He quite literally almost fell over when it opened automatically. He walked through and turned to watch as it closed behind him. In Bhutan, he had read magazine articles about the technology of space travel and satellite communication — but that hadn't prepared him for the little, everyday things. He found himself looking for the *doens* or devils who must be working things like automatic doors.

14/

The building of the new school at Kanglung was a slow, painful process that bogged down in endless meetings, plans and, apparently, a political standoff. In January of 1964, the prime minister asked the chief Dantak engineer, Brigadier Jaganathan, if Dantak would build the school. Jaganathan seemed keen but needed authority from Delhi. Meanwhile the Bhutanese began preparations, acquiring the land and hiring Indian town planners. They hoped the school could open the following year.

Nari Rustomji, the energetic and enthusiastic Indian advisor to the King, and a close friend of Jigmie Dorji, got involved and was confident of an early opening. In April of 1964, the prime minister's assassination brought everything to a halt.

In May, the town planners returned and Father Mackey and the *thrimpoen* met them at the site. Some work on the ground had been started. But the plans were "hopeless," Father Mackey said. "The playground was on a forty-five-degree slope above the road and the kitchen was in the middle of the football field."

In July, the deputy education director, a Mr. Bose, visited. He agreed that the job should be handed over to Dantak who, as Father Mackey said, "knew the road, the mountains, the conditions." They met with the Dantak people and Mr. Bose gave them a free hand. In September, the head of Border Roads Projects, the parent organization, visited to discuss plans for the school. But by November, Dantak had not yet received clearance from Delhi, and had done nothing on the buildings. Father Mackey postponed the school opening by one year.

In January of 1965, the King visited Deothang, Dantak headquarters, and applied pressure. The Brigadier insisted that he needed Delhi's sanction. In May, the chief architect for Dantak's Eastern Command visited Kanglung with Father Mackey and discussed plans. The Jesuit suggested less planning and more actual work. This was the fifth set of plans, but they proved the best, and were eventually used.

Another round of talks ensued in July, as officials came from Delhi to visit the site and talk with Father Mackey and the *thrimpoen*. The chief engineer then went to Thimphu and Paro to finalize plans, expecting to start work soon after. But by October, when the King visited Tashigang, no progress had been made. Father Mackey talked with the King for two hours and showed him around the site. His Majesty said he would take up the matter personally in Delhi, and also asked the Brigadier to try to get sanction.

But the second winter slipped away, apparently because the Dantak bosses had their own agenda. They liked the idea of producing a showplace institution, and of producing something particularly fine for the King. However, they also wanted to build a road north from Tashigang towards the Tibetan border. Many think that, behind Dantak, the Indian government wanted to build roads that would be of strategic use in the event of war with China.

The Bhutanese government, presumably jealous of its sovereignty and concerned about these military implications, apparently didn't want such roads. Father Mackey was not especially interested in the political jockeying. But he found the delays frustrating. Sometime during the process, as well, Brigadier Jaganathan, who had been a good friend to Father Mackey, was succeeded by Brigadier O.P. Datta.

Finally, in 1966, the parties reached agreement. On June 27th, Ashi Chhoeki Wangmo, half-sister of the King, visited and laid the foundation stone for the new school. The King had already given it a name — Sherubtse. Sherubtse (the more common transcription would have it spelled Sherabtse), can be reasonably translated as "peak of knowledge" or "peak of learning." The full name was Sherubtse Public School.

Father Mackey hoped to open Sherubtse at the start of the next school year — March, 1967. He visited Brigadier Datta, the man in charge, who told him yes, no problem. Father Mackey worked towards that deadline, choosing materials and supplies for the new school, and also selecting a staff. But in early 1967, when he arrived back from his winter break, the brigadier told him a March opening was "impossible."

Father Mackey was furious. He sent off a wireless message to Dawa Tshering that read, "Delay not understood. Insincerity unpardonable."

Given the etiquette of Bhutanese protocol, and Indian sensitivity, in his words, "All hell broke loose."

Now Brigadier Datta was upset and Dawa Tshering came to Tashigang. He told Father Mackey, "You just can't do that sort of thing. Not in this situation. We need these people."

Unintimidated, fed up with years of delay, Father Mackey said: "Look. He told me to go ahead. I selected teachers, I selected students, and it was all hit on the head."

"I understand," Dawa Tshering said, "But we're dealing with a political issue." The problem wasn't Datta's insincerity, but orders from higher up. Dantak had slowed work at Sherubtse because they had not received permission to continue the road north.

Father Mackey decided that this was a good time to take an overdue break, and in August of 1967 he left for Canada on leave.

* * *

Father Mackey returned to Bhutan in January of 1968. A few days later, the King visited and officials set an opening date: May 2nd, 1968, the King's birthday. Meetings followed, over the number of boys to attend the new school (eventually, 100). In February, boys heading for Sherubtse began arriving in Tashigang. They were accommodated and taught in new agriculture department buildings.

Yet another postponement came when the prime minister of India decided to visit Thimphu and Paro around the King's birthday. The inauguration ceremony was rescheduled for the 25th and 26th of May, and preparations went ahead. Early monsoon rains poured down on May 22nd, when the boys had to move to Kanglung, most of them walking.

Three days later, the main guests arrived, among them Dawa Tshering, now secretary-general of development as well as director of education, and Tamji Jagar, now home minister, and finally, at three in the afternoon, His Majesty. The King went directly to the Dantak officers' mess, where he would stay, and where Father Mackey met him. In the evening there was a variety show. The tiny village of Kanglung overflowed as five thousand people from neighbouring villages gathered for the event.

The big day was May 26th. Boys from seven schools lined the road to greet His Majesty when he arrived in his jeep. Lamas preceded him slowly to the administration building, and boys walked in procession behind him. The full Bhutanese tea ceremony was enacted with pomp and dignity, everyone wearing his best *go* and *kabney*. The tea servers' *kabneys* swayed as they entered, bowed, poured the tea and receded.

Brigadier Datta made a speech, and then His Majesty officially opened Sherubtse Public School by cutting the ceremonial ribbon. The inauguration plaque was unveiled. Then the guests visited the administration building, the classrooms, the dormitories and the staff quarters. The King rounded out his morning by having tea with the boys.

At noon, His Majesty ate lunch with the tradesmen. The afternoon events included a Fun Fare — a Dantak-organized, Indian-style *mela* or fair, with snack stalls, games of chance, and so on — as well as a programme of drill and gymnastics by the boys of Tashigang and Sherubtse, and a performance by the Royal dance troupe from Thimphu. Both the King and Father Mackey were most in their element that evening, as they enjoyed a campfire and the enthusiastic comradeship of 400 boys.

A few days later, the Indian newspaper *The Statesman* carried an item headlined: "Bhutan's Biggest Public School Inaugurated."

* * *

The facilities at Sherubtse were impressive enough that for years people came from all over the country to see this marvelous institution. Dantak, too, used the school as a showplace, and brought every important Indian visitor to see it.

With its two generators, the school was the only place in the whole region (apart from the main Dantak camp at Gomchu, further down the road) to have electricity. Nobody had ever seen electric lights, which were perhaps the greatest marvel in a world of marvels: desks and benches, windows with glass in them, bathrooms and showers and indoor plumbing, the dining room, the big kitchen with its huge iron stoves.

Anyone who came and saw these things returned to their village with fantastic stories. Word spread across the country about this wonderful place. Adults wanted to visit and see these amazing things, and students wanted to attend this school, just for the facilities.

For the boys from Tashigang, moving to Sherubtse meant stepping into another world. As Father Mackey put it, "They jumped from the Middle Ages to a modern school in one day."

Their old classrooms and facilities for sleeping, dining and toilet were, at best, basic. Classroom windows let in little light and could be closed only with heavy sliding shutters made of wood. There was no glass. Students sat on their haunches on the floor and used benches to write on. The boys lived in the attic of the school building and the few girls boarded with families. Tashigang boasted no dining room and the students would have their *bangchungs* (woven baskets) or wooden bowls filled at the kitchen, and then eat wherever they could find a spot.

When it rained they would sit under the eaves of the buildings or in the doorways. And as at home, where they would sit on the floor, in traditional Bhutanese fashion, they ate with their hands. Also traditional was the toilet. Outhouses, or pit latrines, were extremely rare in Bhutan and people followed the age-old practice of relieving themselves in the fields.

Pit latrines were coming in — very simple affairs without toilet seats. The wooden floor of an outdoor toilet would simply have a gap where excrement could fall into the pit. The Bhutanese didn't follow the Indian practice of cleaning themselves by applying water with the left hand, but usually used some natural material, like leaves, or even sticks or stones.

All of this changed drastically at Sherubtse. The classroom walls, instead of being dark, were plastered and painted. The light colour, along with the large glass windows, made for brighter rooms. And instead of sitting on the floor, students sat on benches in front of desks designed for three or four together. The dining room offered tables and benches and metal plates. The boys had never eaten like this in their lives.

But Father Mackey's main concern was the plumbing. Flush toilets with porcelain fixtures from India provided the kind of sanitation required of a modern institution that would grow to hold hundreds of students. There was also a faucet beside the Asian-style (floor-level squatting type) toilet bowl to provide water for cleaning in the Indian manner.

Here was a problem. Children from a closed, rural background were required to change a basic habit. This was one of Father Mackey's priorities when the boys arrived at Sherubtse to occupy the new hostel. Before they even got into the dormitories, he gave them a clear, explicit talk about the facilities and how to use them. He said: "Now look, you are not going into bathrooms or toilets where you can use sticks and stones and throw everything down the hole. And you're not going outside to do what you want to do around the building."

Then he squatted and gave a bit of a demonstration. "You squat, and you use your left hand with water. Because there's water there and if you start putting in paper, the next thing, you'll be using a cover from a book, and then you'll block everything. So only water, nothing else. No sticks, no stones."

And every morning when the kids awoke and went to the bathroom, he had a school captain at the toilet door reminding them to use water and only water.

For the Jesuits, too, Sherubtse was a marvel. Situated on a small plateau high up on the side of a major river valley, it had a magnificent view. And Father Mackey found the climate perfect. Tashigang had been a little too hot for his liking. But Kanglung was higher (at 2,100 metres) and cooler, though snow was very rare. It got lots of sunlight and avoided excessive cloud or rain.

Even more marvelous were the facilities themselves. When they moved to Sherubtse, Father Mackey said later, "We thought we were moving into modern apartment buildings or sort of Canadian houses, because Dantak really set up lovely quarters." This included the teachers' residences.

Father Mackey and Father Coffey lived in two small detached bungalows, each built to house one person. Nearby, in a separate building, was their mess. Each of the "Fathers' quarters" had three main rooms, with the front two opening onto a small verandah. The largest of these Father Mackey called his "office-cum-bedroom." It had a desk, a bed, a large clothes cupboard and a fireplace.

Both front rooms had fireplaces, but they didn't work well and were never used. The other front room served as a parlour or sitting room. It had comfortable chairs and padded benches around the walls as well as bookshelves. Behind this room was a small bedroom, which worked well as a guest room. In the back part of the house was a washroom, a self-contained toilet, and a shower. The washroom had nice mirrors and cold running water. There was also a small kitchen and pantry, which the Jesuits never used as such.

The third building, the mess, was large, considering that it was catering at first to only three Jesuits. The kitchen was almost the size of a school classroom. The rest of the building, which was rectangular and bigger than two classrooms, was originally open, but Father Mackey had a partition built to create a good-sized chapel at one end, which left a large dining-room/sitting-room. The Chapel would hold twenty people. Besides the Jesuits and Sisters who would come later, many of the Indian teachers were Christians. The dining room had windows at the end and an attached bathroom. It had attractive shelves and cupboards, comfortable chairs and padded benches.

Brother Quinn's accommodation was next to the infirmary. He had a large bedroom, a small reception room, a kitchen and a bathroom. Given Brother Quinn's medical "portfolio," the place was perfect. The infirmary had a dispensary and two small wards.

In the boys' dormitories (at first there were no girl students), there was a warden's room and bathroom off the end of each of the two floors. Later on, when Sherubtse offered class ten, Father Mackey would sleep in the warden's room, on the floor accommodating the class ten students. This meant he was on hand to help them and to keep an eye on their studies. He kept his clothes and other things in his bungalow. If he needed a quick shower after sports, he could take it here in the dorm, but otherwise used the facilities in his bungalow.

For the most part, Father Mackey was able to leave behind the candles and troublesome kerosene lamps. A generator produced electricity for evening light. As Dantak also drew its electricity from this source, they provided a man to operate the generators, only one of which worked well. Apart from special occasions, electricity was provided only from about six to nine in the evening.

In the winter, the electricity allowed Father Mackey and others to enjoy the heat of basic electric space heaters that could be purchased in India. While not effective in large rooms, in a small one this was a good alternative to the troublesome and inefficient fireplaces. Once the electricity was turned off for the night, people went straight into bed, the only other way to keep warm.

Electricity also provided a way to heat water for a bath on a winter's day. Immersion heaters were available in India, and could heat a bucketful from which one dipped hot water for the economical "bucket bath."

* * *

When Father Mackey moved to Kanglung in May of 1968, he remained principal of Tashigang school. It was now a high school, with students in class ten who would write their Bhutan Matriculation exams in December. He left behind a teacher-in-charge who ran the school on a day-to-day basis, but he visited at least once a week.

Besides having administrative responsibilities, he taught class ten mathematics. The jeep was not always available, nor completely reliable. Neither was the road, especially during the monsoon. So often he made the visit on foot. He would leave Kanglung after the second period on

Friday, and hike quickly to the Bamrichhu, the river that ran down the major valley between Kanglung and Tashigang.

Depending on how deep the river was (it could be a metre and a half), he would remove whatever was necessary and ford the river while holding his clothes above the water. He'd dress and proceed up the trail to Tashigang. He'd teach and do his other work that afternoon and on Saturday morning, then hike back to Kanglung. The first hike, downhill from Kanglung, would take just over an hour, and the return trip, three and a half.

Father Mackey left the library intact and began to build one up at Sherubtse. His father and other relatives and friends continued to send books from Canada. His brother Jim worked for Reader's Digest, and arranged for Father Mackey to receive a series of books published by that company. Written in simple English, these were graded for different levels of reading ability. They became some of the most-read books in the Sherubtse library.

The move to Kanglung coincided with a relaxation of the Jesuit dress code. The cassock had always been a nuisance to keep clean, especially in the rainy season when the long garment would pick up mud. Elsewhere, during the previous couple of decades, Jesuits had moved from cassocks, through "clerics" (suit and "dog collar") to casual lay clothes.

The change came later in Bhutan because of the tradition-oriented environment. Now, the Jesuits switched directly from cassocks to lay clothing, and were relieved to do so. Father Mackey still required the Jesuits and other teachers to wear a tie, at least in the classroom, and if not a suit or sports jacket, at least a jacket of some kind or a cardigan sweater. The Jesuits continued to wear cassocks, white or black, on special occasions.

Keeping clothes well-pressed was not easy, and Father Mackey preferred permanent-press garments that did not require ironing. Only in the winter, when Kanglung could get quite cold, did he switch to the old style woolen trousers. A few warm sweaters, a decent windbreaker and "a good solid pair of boots" rounded out the winter wardrobe.

* * *

Much was new at Sherubtse, but many challenges remained the same. For example, the boys still had to be fed. Father Mackey received a stipend for each boy and continued his arrangement with Moth & Co.

for supplies. The basic diet remained unchanged: rice, dhal and vegetables. The rice and dhal came by truck from Samdrup Jongkhar, and this presented an occasional problem.

The trucks carried a varied load, plus passengers, most of whom brought large containers of kerosene. If these leaked, as they often did, the oil would make the rice inedible. At times, full sacks of rice had to be discarded or fed to the pigs, because the boys simply would not eat rice tainted with kerosene.

Fresh vegetables came from the school's own garden, so during certain times of the year there were none available. And only at peak season — August-September, late monsoon — was there much variety. The common vegetables were potatoes and a local spinach, called *saag* (the boys called it "grass"). The boys were lucky to eat meat once a month, as it was both difficult to find and expensive.

Father Mackey would buy quality meat from local farmers if the price was right. So if a cow died, a farmer would visit Father Mackey and offer it to him. The Jesuit would have it checked out and determine why it had died. A beast killed in an accident, perhaps falling down the mountainside, would probably be fit to eat.

It might be noted here that the Bhutanese Buddhists would not kill cattle, nor any other animal (except sometimes pigs). Outsiders have sometimes speculated that cattle were "encouraged" to step off cliffs, as the Bhutanese love to eat meat. Pigs are very low on the Buddhist scale of beings and some Bhutanese will kill them for meat, though they prefer to find someone else to do it. Pork is the meat most commonly available, and the Bhutanese like it very, very fat and boiled with hot chillies.

Father Mackey tried to keep pigs on hand at the school. There was usually plenty of scrap food left over from the boys' mess, and fattening up pigs was a good way to use it. The school might have as many as thirty pigs at one time. The winter vacation posed problems, but even then Father Mackey tried to have a couple of pregnant sows left at the end of the school year, and would set aside food for them. This ensured a batch of pigs that could be fattened up once school resumed.

Pork was seldom used to augment regular meals. Pigs were wanted for celebration feasts, sports days, picnics and other special events. Most of these took place later in the year, so it was usually possible to ensure that a fat pig was available for the feast.

Kitchen stoves were (and still are) fueled by wood. Early on, Father Mackey used the same collecting process as in Tashigang. The boys gathered wood from the mountainside. Within a year, however, the local supply was exhausted. Carrying on would have meant cutting into forest that the local farmers used, and sometimes even owned.

After some complaints, Father Mackey had to find wood elsewhere. He received an increase in the student stipend and arranged to buy firewood from the forest department. He was allotted a concession, a section of forest where wood could be cut for the school. This was too far from the school for the boys, so the priest turned the work over to an agent who had men collect the wood. He paid for it by the truckload — 200 rupees a load (about twenty-five dollars then). Today the price is 4,000 (over 150 dollars at today's exchange rate).

Paying for all these supplies remained complicated. Sherubtse had an account at the State Bank of India in Gauhati, and the department of education would send demand drafts there. It would inform Father Mackey by wireless message. Still, Gauhati was a four-day trip: one day to Samdrup Jongkhar, next morning drive to Gauhati, stay overnight at the Salesian college, back to Samdrup Jongkhar the next afternoon, and return to Kanglung the following day. Fortunately, there was as yet no check post at the border crossing, so Father Mackey or another Jesuit could cross without transit permits.

On one occasion Father Mackey delegated the banking to the school hostel matron, a Mrs. Joseph, better known as Juni. She and her husband, Peter, had taught primary school at St. Alphonsus in Kurseong. They had been devoted, honest and reliable, and when Father Mackey needed someone trustworthy to look after rations and school stores, he'd invited them to Sherubtse. So it was Juni that Father Mackey sent to Gauhati with a cheque for 40,000 rupees. This was a staggering amount and she was frightened stiff.

Father Mackey told her: "Look, go to the bank. Go in and see the bank manager in his office. Give him the cheque and get the money. Put the darned money in a bag in the office and out you go as if nothing happened."

Juni didn't have a bag, but she had a wicker basket. She filled it up with vegetables — carrots, eggplant, okra, a variety of things — and followed Father Mackey's instructions. In the bank manager's office, she wrapped the money in a piece of cloth and stuffed it in among the carrots. Then she walked out, certain that every eye in the bank was on her.

She had entered the bank as soon as it opened, at ten or eleven in the morning, and then waited nervously for the afternoon bus that would take her to Samdrup Jongkhar. She stayed there overnight and travelled back to Kanglung the next day. She told Father Mackey she hadn't closed her eyes from the time she got the money until thirty-six hours later, when she arrived back at Sherubtse. And she added: "I'm not going again. No. Send anybody else, I'm not going again."

In 1972, the Bank of Bhutan established a branch in Samdrup Jongkhar and later, another in Tashigang. This made things much easier, at least when the bank had money (often it didn't). And Father Mackey didn't really have to worry whether he had money in the school account. Pasang, the manager, an old student of North Point, would advance him ten, twenty thousand rupees without hesitation. And most subsequent bank managers were cooperative. Sherubtse was the bank's biggest customer.

15/

In November of 1968, as the first school year at Sherubtse drew to a close, Tashigang students prepared to write the first Bhutan Matriculation examinations. Only Tashigang had class ten students ready to write, and the exams were held at Sherubtse. The results came out in December. Of the twenty students who wrote the exam, one got a first-class mark, eighteen a second-class and one a third. Nobody failed.

Those who wrote the exams included many who later became highly placed officers in the government service. One of them was Lhatu Wangchuk. He had been a kindergarten student at Tashigang when Father Mackey arrived in 1963. But he was already eleven years old, an oversized school boy destined to drop out. Following normal advancement, he would have been at least twenty-one by the time he wrote the new class ten examination.

Father Mackey recognized, however, that Lhatu was bright and hard-working. He wanted to see the boy move ahead quickly, but Mr. Kharpa was of the old Indian school and wanted Lhatu to do his full two years in kindergarten. Father Mackey said: "Mr. Kharpa, nothing doing. I'm putting him up right away to class one."

Mr. Kharpa protested: "No, he needs the foundation."

"He can read a bit, write a bit," Father Mackey said. "I'm putting him up."

Ultimately, Father Mackey was the boss. He jumped Lhatu to class one, then to class three, then to five, then to seven and finally to ten. The boy was obviously able to handle the school work. And he did other work as well. He was willing, in fact eager, to stay at the school during vacation periods and do chores and to profit from any extra tutoring the Jesuits could give. A few boys liked doing this and the Jesuits gave generously of their time.

When Father Mackey needed a typist, he chose Lhatu. This benefitted the boy, as he spent extra time working in English. The salary he drew didn't hurt, either. On at least one occasion Lhatu even travelled with Father Mackey to Hasimara to meet with Dawa Tshering. This would prove important to the boy.

Father Mackey had a portable typewriter and knew it would be a great help to have his top-notch clerk with him. As his first session with Dawa Tshering drew to a close, he called Lhatu in and gave him instructions — told him to organize the notes in a certain way and type them up. When the boy went out, Dawa Tshering asked, "Can he do that?"

"You wait a while and you'll see."

Dawa Tshering was impressed with what he saw. If the boy had not still been in school, he probably would have stolen him from Father Mackey then.

Lhatu moved to Kanglung with Father Mackey, studying for the Bhutan Matric exam while working at Sherubtse. After passing his exams, he stayed on for two more years, then went to Thimphu with a letter from Father Mackey, in search of higher education. When Dawa Tshering heard Lhatu was available, he recruited him for the development ministry and sent him to Mysore, in south India, to get his BA degree. Lhatu moved on to the foreign ministry where he handled posts outside of Bhutan as well as in Thimphu. He also studied for a year in the U.K. and took university night courses while posted in New York. In the early 1990s, Lhatu held the position of Deputy Permanent Representative for Bhutan at the United Nations in New York.

* * *

One of the main criteria for admitting boys to Sherubtse was age. It was common to find boys in their teens, like Lhatu Wangchuk, in primary schools. Father Mackey and his colleagues did not want this in the new school if they could help it. They wanted boys whose age suited their level of education, and with whom they could build a strong foundation for the school.

New students plus some chosen from Tashigang made up the hand-picked complement at Sherubtse, classes one through four. Boys who were not suitable, mostly because of their age, continued their schooling at Tashigang.

There was one particular seven-year-old brought to Sherubtse, seeking admission. He was unusually intelligent and Father Mackey accepted him. But being very bright did not keep him from being a little boy. On one occasion he had to be called to the office, where Father Mackey admonished him, "You *badmash!*" The Jesuit had a light bamboo stick that he called "Lopen Shing" (Lopen "Stick"). He lifted the back of the boy's *go* and administered three quick whacks to the bare behind. Then the boy went on his way.

As was his practice after administering punishment, Father Mackey called the boy back a short while later. He had a small errand that needed doing — something to be taken somewhere, or fetched from the bazaar. "Now, this is very important," he would say, sending the boy off. When the boy returned, Father Mackey would give him a treat and a pat on the back.

One day, a year or so after he had joined the school, three Royal Body Guard jeeps arrived at Sherubtse. Each was carrying three or four lamas or senior monks. An officer who was with them told Father Mackey that the boy was thought to be Dzongsar Khyentse Rinpoche, a reincarnation of a very high Tibetan lama who had died in 1959, and this delegation was here to examine him. He would be asked questions and shown certain objects, and his responses would reveal whether he was indeed the reincarnation.

Father Mackey was not involved, though he chatted with the monks from time to time. They stayed in the infirmary and the school *lopens* provided their food.

After a few days, the officer told Father Mackey that they would be taking the boy. The Jesuit knew they had permission to do so if they wanted, and so accepted this. Having recognized the boy as a high lama of Tibetan Buddhism, the monks took him to Enchey Gompa, a monastery at Gangtok, Sikkim, for his enthronement. His education would continue in the monastic tradition.

About a year after the boy had left Sherubtse, Father Mackey learned that his former student, now the Dzongsar Khyentse Rinpoche, would be visiting Tashigang. As he passed through Kanglung, the staff and students of Sherubtse lined the road to greet him. Father Mackey wore a *go* and bowed low with all the others, holding his *kabney* in the honorific position of greeting. The procession slowed to a halt and

Father Mackey didn't know what was happening. A thought ran through his mind, "I wonder if he's remembering my stick."

But when the procession stopped in front of him, the young Rinpoche and a senior lama from Gangtok both placed white scarves around Father Mackey's neck. As a teacher of Dzongsar Khyentse Rinpoche (albeit not for very long), he was to be revered.

Father Mackey's former student went on to Tashigang to give public blessings called *Wang*. As he was still just a boy, he was carried in a simple open litter by monks. He had a stick with which he touched the heads of those who came for his blessing. Usually he administered just a gentle touch, but now and then, for whatever reason, he'd give a real bang on the head with the stick.

Over the years, the young Rinpoche and Father Mackey became friends. When he travelled to Eastern Bhutan to visit his mother's family, the young man would visit Father Mackey, and they would meet from time to time when the Jesuit went to Thimphu. As a young adult, Dzongsar Khyentse Rinpoche visited Father Mackey and asked where he could study Christian theology. Father Mackey was taken aback: "Wait a minute!"

The young man quickly reassured him, "No, no, I don't want to become a Christian." But he was interested in getting a broader view of Buddhism, and wanted to learn something of Christian theology to better understand how different religions relate meanings and words, often having different ways to express the same reality. "He brought that out very clearly to me," Father Mackey said. "That the distinction between religions — say, Catholic, Protestant, Buddhism, the Jewish religion — that often it's in the words. The reality is there, but when we try to express it in words, we interpret it differently."

Dzongsar Khyentse Rinpoche's quest for broader and deeper knowledge led him to travel extensively, touring many countries in Asia, America and Europe, as well as Australia. Later, Father Mackey would reflect, remembering the arrival of the monks: "They certainly chose a fantastic person," he said. "Reincarnation or not, don't ask me. All I know is they chose a very, very talented, brilliant, good, solid person."

* * *

Prayer has been and remains an important aspect of school life in Bhutan. Besides a short prayer at assembly, just before classes begin, there is usually a prayer period late in the day. When Father Mackey arrived in Bhutan, there was an early morning prayer, whose length depended upon the *lopens* in charge. Most of them had been monks, but had left the monk body. They became Bhutanese language teachers quite naturally because they belonged to the minority who could read and write Choekey.

Because prayers were written in Choekey, and most of the *lopens* had a religious background, they naturally oversaw and led the prayers. They also gravitated into roles having to do with Bhutanese culture.

Usually they conducted morning prayer as soon as the boys got up — after washing, but before morning study or breakfast. The more zealous *lopens* insisted on long sessions. Lopen Phuntsho in Mongar was known for his hour-long morning prayers, for which his students had to rise at 4:30 a.m. It was almost the same in Tashigang when Father Mackey arrived. He found that the boys were saying the monks' morning prayer. Over time, the Jesuit moved to having a standard morning prayer period of fifteen to twenty minutes. More recently the education department has eliminated the early morning prayer.

Father Mackey, who was keenly interested in Buddhism, would try to sit in on the evening prayer himself. He insisted that each of the students have a prayer book. It cost them seven rupees (about one dollar), and looked like the standard books of prayer found in a monastery — unbound loose sheets, roughly ten centimetres by forty centimetres.

As students read from these books, written in Choekey, they would flip sheets over into a second pile. When not in use, the sheets that constituted the book were tied together between wood or cardboard "covers," then wrapped in a piece of cloth. While the students were reciting from their prayer books, Father Mackey would be reading from his breviary. He found this a positive experience, "a very prayerful thing." There was a rhythm that had a psychological effect.

For the students, his presence reinforced the idea of prayer. He would say, "I'm reading my prayers, you're reading your prayers."

Father Mackey's insistence that each student have a prayer book was not purely religious, although he placed high value on their prayers. He knew that reading prayers in Choekey twice a day over many years could be very beneficial to their Bhutanese language studies.

While keenly interested in Buddhism, Father Mackey left the teaching and practice of religion to the *lopens*. He also felt he needed someone who really knew Bhutan and its culture to guide him in these matters. Mr. Kharpa was not a Bhutanese language teacher, but he was Father Mackey's first such right-hand man.

When Father Mackey moved to Kanglung, Mr. Kharpa moved with him as senior teacher. But he was getting old, and in 1970, while walking down the corridor one day, Father Mackey heard a great commotion in one classroom. He opened the door and looked in. There was old Mr. Kharpa sitting at his desk at the front of the class, his head in his hands. The class went silent when Father Mackey appeared. He asked, "Mr. Kharpa, you're sick?"

"No," came the weary reply, "I just can't control them anymore."

Not long afterwards, the King visited Eastern Bhutan to open the road between Tashigang and Mongar. Father Mackey suggested to him that Mr. Kharpa should be retired and given a pension. The King agreed. "He was one man who deserved it," Father Mackey said, "because he did a lot for education in the country, as did many old *lopens* like him."

With the departure of Mr. Kharpa, Father Mackey would lose his Bhutanese guide and guru. Seeking another one, he spoke to Tamji Jagar, who responded: "I know one man, but he has terrible handwriting."

"Well, if it depends on handwriting, you'd better get rid of me," Father Mackey said, without exaggeration. "My handwriting's the worst."

So Lopen Jamphel Dorje came to Father Mackey. He had been a monk in a monastery in Bumthang. When the monastery sent several monks to Lhasa, Tibet, for further studies in religion, he was not one of them. But he wanted so badly to go that he went anyway, without permission. He stayed in Lhasa for a dozen years or more and became quite a scholar in Choekey. But back home he was an outlaw. He had run away from the monastery.

In 1959, when the Chinese invaded Tibet, Lopen Jamphel had been forced to flee, and so returned to Bhutan as a fugitive. He was held in the monastery in Tashigang for about a year, as a kind of honoured prisoner, and then discharged from the monk body. But he remained a religious man.

Father Mackey found Lopen Jamphel to be learned, sensible and down-to-earth. His knowledge of Buddhism and of Bhutanese culture, both north and south, was even greater than Mr. Kharpa's. Father Mackey particularly liked his ability to explain Buddhist holy days and festivals to the students. Often such events as Tshechu, days commemorating the ascent or descent of Lord Buddha, or Blessed Rainy Day are observed without real understanding. And many *lopens*, even if they understood the meaning, were unable to make the students understand.

Lopen Jamphel, however, would talk to the kids before each festival, and so give much more meaning to the celebration. Even on prayer and scripture he was able to give meaningful explanations to the students.

In matters of discipline, Lopen Jamphel was doubly valuable. First, because he had stature as an upright and holy man, he could mete out tough discipline without inspiring rebellion. Second, and even more important, Lopen Jamphel understood the religious and cultural psyche of the Bhutanese, which is such a mystery to outsiders, but which explains so much behaviour.

Lopen Jamphel could understand why boys acted in certain ways — actions that might appear to be simple naughtiness to an outsider, or even to a less insightful Bhutanese. With his depth of understanding, he could help Father Mackey judge a situation and choose the most appropriate discipline, and also, to some extent, help Father Mackey understand the intricacies of culture and religion.

The term "*jagar*" provides a simple example. To Father Mackey, this word meant "Indian" — perhaps not a name that a Southern Bhutanese wanted to be called, but hardly cause for the intense rage that ensued when a Northern Bhutanese called a Southern Bhutanese by that name. Lopen Jamphel explained that the word had taken on extremely offensive connotations, something like "foreign bastard" but worse.

Lopen Jamphel told Father Mackey that "if the Northerner used that term, '*jagar*,' then the Southern kid had full right to do anything, use a stick, beat the guy up — he had full right."

In such a situation, Lopen Jamphel could step in and, using the respect he commanded, show the offending party the error of his ways, so eliciting an apology. His broad knowledge of Northern and Southern culture could solve ethnic problems going either way. Father Mackey saw that without the advice of a Lopen Jamphel, outsiders like himself could have serious problems.

Lopen Jamphel also made a major contribution in the development of Dzongkha at Sherubtse. Rather than being one of the old school who resisted the use of Choekey script for the writing of Dzongkha, he helped promote it. He worked at trying to make the language more relevant and less complicated. Later, using his abilities to select material and produce Dzongkha text, Lopen Jamphel was instrumental in having Dzongkha taught beyond the class-ten level.

16/

A t the end of 1968, during his annual break, Father Mackey acquired a motorbike, a Jawa, the Czechoslovakian bike that later became the Indian Yezde. For the mountains of Bhutan he wanted something more powerful than the ill-fated scooter he'd had in Darjeeling, and the motorbike, while modest by today's standards, was better than a scooter.

He bought it in Darjeeling and began the trek home. The first day he rode down to Siliguri, where he spent the night. The next day he rode to Samtse, where he gave a three-week course in mathematics to the first second-year "batch" (as they are called on the Sub-Continent) of student teachers at the Teacher Training Institute. While in Samtse, the head of the local distillery came to see him.

Father Mackey had helped the man get his grandchildren into good schools in Kurseong, and now he insisted on giving the Jesuit a sample of everything in the distillery. He gave him twelve bottles — a full case. Father Mackey managed to fit the box onto the back of the motorbike along with his other things and left for Kanglung.

Between most if not all states in India, one finds check posts, mainly for the taxing of inter-state commerce, but also to stop illegal imports. One such check post existed between West Bengal and Assam. The latter was a "dry" state that prohibited liquor. Only trucks are required to stop at these border check posts, and Father Mackey on his motorbike could have driven right through. But he found it convenient to stop for lunch at a good Punjabi restaurant located at the crossing. He ate at an outside table, enjoying the winter sun.

As he finished his tea, Father Mackey saw an Assam policeman come out of his check post. The policeman walked over to the bike and studied it, then walked back towards his office — hesitantly, it seemed. As Father Mackey looked on, he thought of the box full of liquor and realized that it was clearly marked: "Bhutan Distillery." What to do?

While keeping one eye on the policeman, Father Mackey paid for his meal. He waited until the policeman was far enough away from his motorbike, then hurried to the machine, key in hand. He hopped on, started up the bike and roared away before the cop could get back. Father Mackey waved as he drove off.

He stopped at the first stream he saw. He dismounted, scrambled to the edge of the stream and gathered up as much mud as he could. With this he smeared the box, covering the tell-tale "Bhutan Distillery." Then went on his way.

On the still-new road to Tashigang, the motorbike was totally foreign to the dogs. Normally they would chase vehicles, but this one was different. "Every bunch of dogs that saw me started running," Father Mackey said later. "I chased dogs all the way up."

The priest also caught a goat by surprise. It ran down onto the road in front of him, leaving him no time to stop or turn. He ran over the goat, but it jumped up and ran away and Father Mackey kept going.

* * *

Not long after he bought the motorbike, Father Mackey had to prepare for a Royal Visit. His Majesty was bringing his mother, Ashi Phuntsho Chhoedron, the "Royal Mother," to open the Sherubtse Auditorium. The Royal Party was to stay at Dantak quarters above the school. However, there was a shortage of appropriate furniture, so Dantak asked to borrow some from the Jesuit residences on the far side of the campus.

Father Mackey rode his motorbike to his residence to meet the Dantak crew and give them what they needed. He was preparing to leave when some lamas arrived at his door. They were going to say prayers at the opening and wanted to discuss that. This took five or ten minutes, and again Father Mackey started to leave. In the meantime, the Dantak people who had left his residence shortly before, in their jeep, realized that the Jesuit wasn't with them. They turned back to see what had happened.

As Father Mackey roared around the first corner, trying to catch up, he met the Dantak jeep coming towards him at a good speed. He shoved the bike at the jeep and took off into the air. Fortunately, the ground here was flat, with neither a rock face nor a dramatic drop-off at the edge of the road. He landed in the grass at the side of the road, turned a somersault and landed on his feet. He remarked later, "Thank God for gymnastics."

Father Mackey was only slightly hurt, having banged his knee and broken the ring finger of his right hand. The Dantak doctor, who happened to be in the jeep, fixed the finger as best he could and ordered Father Mackey to bed for the afternoon. Next day, he was back in action again.

His small injuries gave him some trouble as the celebrations unfolded. During the school's gymnastics show, he found himself flipping boys over the horse, an awkward job with a broken finger. His knee, which had dented the petrol tank of his bike, was also stiff. He had difficulty bending his leg to sit on the floor when the assembled group took their meals in the traditional Bhutanese manner. He realized he was providing a good display of his underwear when His Majesty and others started joking about it. Father Mackey very deliberately pushed his *go* down between his legs.

* * *

The King visited Eastern Bhutan about once a year. Dantak liked having him attend their functions, and invited him at every opportunity to open a piece of road or another section of Sherubtse. Always he would spend some time with Father Mackey. Sometimes they would discuss serious matters like education, but mostly they enjoyed lighthearted chats, with lots of joking.

In 1970, His Majesty came East for the official opening of the Tashigang-Mongar road and used Sherubtse as his base while in the area. Dawa Tshering called Father Mackey on the Dantak line from Samdrup Jongkhar. He asked the priest if there were anything he wanted on the programme.

Father Mackey requested two things. First, he wanted an hour or so with the King to discuss improving the education system. Second, he wanted the King to visit the classrooms and talk to the students.

On the morning of the formal opening of the road, His Majesty put the Sherubtse school captains in his jeep with him and the driver —

no bodyguard. At the opening, the King would speak to the public in Dzongkha, but many of the Indian road builders would not understand. The King wanted a translator.

He called the school captain, a very clever boy named Tashi Bidung, and asked him to translate into English. The boy was scared stiff. He was just finishing class six. But he did a superb job. The boy did so well, in fact, that when the Indian Brigadier spoke a little later, he asked the youth to translate his speech from English into Dzongkha. (Tashi Bidung continued his education, and later became head of Bhutan's department of mines.)

That afternoon, back in Sherubtse, His Majesty said he would now talk to the boys. Father Mackey gathered the students in the auditorium. The Brigadier and the other Indian officials had expected to attend this gathering, but the King said: "No, this is for the Bhutanese students and myself."

Father Mackey was the only non-Bhutanese in the room.

The Jesuit and the King sat on the stage of the auditorium and the King gave a short talk on development. Then he said, "Have you got any questions?" Father Mackey had primed some of the boys to ask certain questions — to make certain points for the benefit of the students, to get some answers that he was looking for and to make sure there was no awkward silence. The students were forthcoming and a good dialogue was soon underway.

Neither the boys nor the King were concerned about *driglam namzha*. According to this code of traditional Bhutanese etiquette, the boys should have kept their heads bowed and placed a hand in front their mouths when they spoke. But they spoke and acted naturally. One boy, whom Father Mackey called Apa ["Father"] Kinley, was very animated, pointing and banging on the edge of the stage. His Majesty listened and nodded, "Yes, yes, mhmm, yes." He was obviously comfortable with all this and impressed by the boys. He enjoyed the meeting so much, it lasted for more than two hours.

Meanwhile, the Indian officers stood outside freezing. They had come up from the plains and wore only light clothing. They hadn't expected a meeting between the King and a bunch of students to last this long. They paced up and down, trying to get warm.

During this stay, the King also visited each of the classes. Then at a concert one evening, when he was sitting with Father Mackey, he pointed to one of the boys and asked, "Father, who's that kid?"

"That's Thin [Thinley] Tobgye. Why?"

"When I was talking the other day, he didn't agree with something I said. I saw him shaking his head. I'm going to Yonphula tomorrow morning and he's coming with me."

After the concert Father Mackey found the boy and asked him about this: "I didn't see what you were doing, but what did you disagree with?"

The boy reminded Father Mackey that His Majesty had been comparing Bhutan to a jeep. Then the boy said, "I disagreed with what he was saying. He said that Bhutan is a jeep and His Majesty is the wheels. The development minister takes the jeep and drives it up the development path. Then the agriculture guy takes the jeep and drives it up the agricultural path. That's not right! His Majesty's not the wheels. They're the wheels and he's the driver!"

Father Mackey heaved a sigh of relief: "Okay, fine, tell him that, no problem."

* * *

In 1970, a Salesian Father came to visit Sherubtse.

The Salesians had started the Don Bosco industrial school at Kharbandi, near Phuntsholing, in 1965, and were interested to hear that the Jesuits had started a vocational section at Kanglung. It was a modest programme initiated by Brother Quinn. He envisaged an alternative for students not involved with games, and set up practical courses like typing and tailoring. It was nothing on the scale of Don Bosco.

The Salesian school carried on at Kharbandi for a few more years. They had an excellent reputation for industrial or vocational schools in India, and were expected to turn out much-needed tradesmen from the Don Bosco school in Bhutan. However, a combination of difficulties involving quality of students available, disagreement on academic training and the Salesians' penchant for proselytizing led to conflict with the Bhutanese government. After ten years of operation, the school became Kharbandi Technical School, and eventually severed all connection with the Salesians.

A visitor from another religious order facilitated a major change at Sherubtse. The government wanted girls to study at Kanglung, and this was okay with Father Mackey. He wanted nuns present to take care of them, however, and invited the Mother Provincial of the St. Joseph of Cluny Sisters to see about sending some nuns. At the time, Sherubtse had 134 boys spread among classes one to five, for an average of twenty-seven per class. But no girls. Girls did attend school in Bhutan, but in much smaller numbers and never as boarders.

Early in 1970, four Sisters of the St. Joseph of Cluny order arrived to look after Sherubtse's first girl students, who would start school that year. Until then, there had been only a few women on the campus — mostly wives like Juni Joseph and Mr. Kharpa's wife. Now females would achieve a critical mass and have a real presence on campus.

When Sherubtse opened in 1968, it had four classes — one to four. In 1969, the students moved up one class and a new class one came in. By 1970, the school included classes one through six. The girls were installed mainly in the lower classes, so they would ultimately fit in better. But a few went into higher classes, including three into the top class.

This brought about a change in some of the older boys. Until now, they had been unconcerned about their dress and grooming. They weren't filthy, but neither were they particularly clean. They were just naturally sloppy. But when the girls joined the class, the boys cleaned themselves up and made sure their *gos* were straight. "The arrival of those girls," Father Mackey said, "had a very definite influence on the boys."

Mother Peter Claver, Superior of the Sisters, was well known to the Royal Family, having taught the Queen, Ashi Kesang in Kalimpong. A couple of years younger than Father Mackey, she combined a look of propriety with a down-to-earth attitude. Her bright eyes could be sharp and observant, but also warm and friendly. She came from a wealthy European family and was herself brilliant, a linguist, and very intellectual. She was also talented in music and art. "She'd come into a place," Father Mackey said, "and within a week, it would be a beautiful place whatever she had. She was interested in beauty."

Mother Peter's upright background set her up for some amusing situations in rural Bhutan. On one occasion, Father Mackey invited the army from Yonphula to attend a concert rehearsal. Mother Peter, with her great talent in music, did a lot of work on the concerts, including playing the piano. She adapted nursery rhymes to the local context, including one that went "Dasho Dungpa Had a Farm, ee-ai-ee-ai-oh." It included all the usual animals.

When this song came along, Mother Peter was delighted to hear the audience of soldiers warm up. When the students sang the line about Dasho Dungpa's chickens, "with a chick-chick here and a chick-chick there, here a chick, there a chick, everywhere a chick-chick," the soldiers clapped and cheered and stomped on the floor. Mother Peter beamed and bounced on her piano stool and played all the harder.

Father Mackey stood at the back of the auditorium wondering how to handle this. Watching the soldiers' reaction, he realized that "chick-chick" had a local meaning unknown to Mother Peter. It referred to sexual intercourse. The students knew what it meant, and when they heard the audience reaction, they played it up, augmenting the words with classic finger gestures. At the piano, Mother Peter couldn't see any of this, but the audience was going wild and she thought she had a real hit on her hands.

After the dress rehearsal Father Mackey approached the woman about the song: "Mother Peter, please don't use chickens."

"Why not?"

"Because it's very obscene."

"What do you mean?"

"Well, you ask one of the girls what 'chick-chick' means and you'll get an answer."

Mother Peter thought a moment, then looked at Father Mackey, "Is it bad?"

"Yes, very bad."

"Okay, I'll leave out the chickens."

Another little surprise for Mother Peter arrived courtesy of another barnyard animal. Pigs were kept at Sherubtse to make use of the abundant scraps and to provide the traditional food for celebratory feasts. When the school seemed gripped by an epidemic of diarrhoea, Doctor Anayat was asked up from Tashigang to investigate. His first approach was to have all the servants tested for parasites that might be transferred to the students through the kitchen and dining room.

He did stool tests and found that virtually all the servants had parasites. He prescribed a treatment programme, and gave the food handlers instructions on cleanliness. There was some improvement in the incidence of diarrhoea, but a problem remained. Doctor Anayat said, "Maybe it's the pork. Give me some of the *tati* [stool] from the sows and we'll have it tested."

The school had half a dozen big sows, and a stool sample was taken from each. To identify the sample, each sow was given a name. As they were females, each got the name of some local woman, one of the wives. This was an internal matter, so indelicacy was of no concern. Even Lingshay, Doctor Anayat's wife, was not spared.

The samples had been collected, wrapped and identified, and were sitting on Father Mackey's desk awaiting dispatch to Tashigang Hospital when Mother Peter happened by. She saw the six neat packages on the desk. "Father, what are in all these little parcels?" She picked up a couple and began squeezing them, "What is it?"

"Well, Mother," Father Mackey said, "it's the *tati* from the pigs. I'm going to get it tested at the hospital."

Mother Peter dropped the packages and exclaimed, "Oh, and I squeezed it!"

At the hospital the samples were tested and the results returned to Doctor Anayat. As he read the test results, he didn't pay much attention to the names of the pigs until he came to Lingshay: "Who is this Lingshay?!"

Bhakte, the compounder, responded, "Oh, that's not your wife. Father Mackey put down the names of his sows and one of them is Lingshay."

Smiling enthusiastically, the compounder added: "Lingshay's the one with the most worms."

Doctor Anayat went looking for Father Mackey.

* * *

Phallic symbols are commonplace in Bhutan, often appearing in the form of a carved wooden penis or a penis painted on a wall. But they can sometimes take the uninitiated by surprise. Father Mackey was quite used to seeing wooden penises hanging on the outsides of homes. But on his first visit to Rangchikhar, a village above Tashigang, he was taken aback as he stepped into the temple and found himself confronted with a huge penis on a table. He exploded with his standard Nepali exclamation: *"Bap-re!"*

Mother Peter got her awakening at a festival called Tshechu. Along with the *gelongs* (monks) and impressively costumed dancers, there were men who act as *atsaras* — jokers or clowns. Their paraphernalia nearly always includes a penis, perhaps thirty centimetres long, either hung from the head, or held and waved as in giving a blessing. At this Tshechu, one *atsara* was running around with a wooden penis, teasing the women. Mother Peter saw it and exclaimed, "Oh!" and lowered her eyes.

She quickly recovered and looked up again.

On another early occasion, Mother Peter was with Father Mackey when he stopped to see Phongmey Dungpa, who was building a new house. From each corner of the roof, he had hung a large wooden penis. She asked Father Mackey, "Is it what I think it is?"

"It is, Mother."

"Very good."

The Sisters were sensible people, Father Mackey says, "who understood life and had absolutely no prudery. They never let their hair down in my company, but as the Fathers together would have a lot of jokes, the Sisters probably had their own, too. When we were together it never came out. But they were down to earth, solid people."

Sister Leonard, Mother Peter's lieutenant, came by this more naturally. She was from a poor Nepali family and little educated. And while there was no nonsense about her when it came to the care of the girls in her charge, she had a soft, friendly face and was the epitome of down-to-earth warmth and common sense. She and Mother Peter formed a perfect team.

The Bhutanese were familiar with celibate Buddhists, both monks and nuns (*animos*), but some never did grasp the relationship between Fathers and Sisters. Father Mackey realized this one January morning when he and Mother Peter set off on a short excursion to Rangthang Woong, a village north of Tashigang.

They were to be joined by Mr. and Mrs. Namchu, who would meet them at the Khiri petrol pump, not far from Tashigang. Father Mackey and Mother Peter arrived first. It was a cold morning and they decided they'd rather wait down at the bridge below Tashigang, where it would be warmer. Father Mackey told the petrol pump operator, "Tell Mr. Namchu we've gone down to the bridge. It's too cold to wait up here."

Forty minutes later, when the couple arrived at the bridge, Mr. Namchu — he of the ropeway story — was doubled up with laughter.

Father Mackey asked, "Now what's up?"

Mr. Namchu said, "When we went to the petrol pump we were told that Father Mackey and his wife had just gone down to the river!"

When Father Mackey made an exaggerated protest, demanding to know how anybody could think such a thing, Mr. Namchu cited Mother Peter's strong personality: "All they see, Father, is that she's running you!"

17/

While at Tashigang, Father Mackey had received few visitors. The school there was ordinary, housing was limited and road conditions made the journey unattractive. Sherubtse, however, was a showplace for both the Bhutanese government and Dantak, and hosted many visitors over the years for that reason.

For the Jesuits, the school represented Father Mackey's "real" work. This was the institution he had been recruited to establish and run. Almost as soon as the school opened, Jesuit colleagues visited from Darjeeling. They were impressed with the facility and the students, especially their level of English.

In November of 1970, not long before His Majesty's visit, Father Mackey received a very special Jesuit visitor. Not only was Father Sheridan coming from Rome, where he was very highly placed, but he was an old school mate of Father Mackey.

They had both grown up in the Montreal neighbourhood of St. Henry, when Father Ed Sheridan was known as "Butch." He was three years older than Father Mackey and went to college before joining the Jesuits. This had made him junior to the younger man at Guelph, where he was one of Father Mackey's "students."

Now, Father Sheridan was an Assistant to the Father General, the head Jesuit in Rome. He helped keep the Father General advised of activities in the Jesuit provinces within his "assistancy." Father Sheridan's Assistancy included the Canadian Jesuits of the Darjeeling Mission, and hence Father Mackey.

201

Father Sheridan was visiting the Mission, and decided to make the jeep-trip to Bhutan. During his visit, Father Mackey took him to Tashigang Dzong. Father Mackey acted as if he lived there, and as they entered the imposing edifice, Father Sheridan asked, "Where are we going?"

"You're going to meet the head man, the Dzongdag." The chief administrator was no longer the *thrimpoen* (this position reverted to administration of the law only), but the "*dzongdag.*"

Kunzang Tangbi held this position now, and he greeted the Jesuit priests warmly. But he explained, "I'm very busy just now, but you're having lunch with me in about an hour."

Father Mackey said, "Don't worry, Dasho, I'll show Father Sheridan around the Dzong," and they set off down the dark passageways of the medieval structure.

"Where are we going now?"

"We're going up to see the Lam Neten."

"What's that?"

"You'd call him an abbot."

"But you can't just go and see the abbot of a monastery."

"Why not?"

"You need permission."

"Forget that. We're not back in Rome. Come on."

Father Mackey led the way up a steep ladder-like stairway. Father Sheridan had some difficulty. There was no electricity and the few small windows provided very little light. Emerging at the top, Father Mackey warned the taller man, "Duck now, or you'll bang your head on these beams." And at the Lam Neten's room, he told his friend, "Take your shoes off, Butch."

It's doubtful that in Rome Father Sheridan was often called "Butch."

"What? Do I have to?"

"Take your shoes off and don't argue! You can't go in there with your shoes on." They both removed their shoes and Father Mackey beckoned, "Come on in."

"But you knock."

"We don't knock here." The door was open and Father Mackey stuck his head in. "Lam Neten," he said.

The abbot hurried to the doorway and greeted Father Mackey even more warmly than the Dzongdag had, taking his hand and embracing him. Father Mackey gave the Lam Neten the gift he had brought, and then introduced Father Sheridan. When they were seated, a monk brought a large teapot of *suja*, or butter tea, and poured each man a cup.

Suja is an acquired taste for foreigners, and many do not care to make the acquisition. The prime ingredient comes in a form that looks like a cake of black tobacco or the droppings of a small rhino. The other main ingredients are home-made butter, salt and bicarbonate of soda. The expectation of taste at the offer of "tea" is misleading. The uninitiated would stand a better chance if it were called soup.

This was Father Sheridan's first time and Father Mackey anticipated his reaction. He said, "Butch, take a sip and leave it. Put it over towards me." The Assistant took one sip and the look on his face was precisely what Father Mackey expected. When the Lam Neten stepped out for a moment, Father Mackey grabbed Father Sheridan's cup and finished it in one long gulp. He said, "Don't let them give you any more. If anybody comes in to give you more, you put your hand over it."

As soon as the Lam Neten saw the empty cup, he called for more. Father Mackey said, "No Lam, you see, he's not used to it, so, please." The gracious host had a cup of ordinary tea brought for Father Sheridan.

The three religious men chatted until Father Mackey said, "Look, Lam Neten, we're having lunch soon with the Dzongdag and I want to take Father Sheridan to the temple."

"Certainly Father, go right ahead."

Outside, Father Sheridan shook his head, "You go into the Abbot's room, and you walk in and out as you like?"

"Come on," Father Mackey said, "I want to show you something about Buddhism." Inside the main temple of the Dzong, he showed Father Sheridan the murals that cover the walls. "What's this, Butch?" He pointed to a particular scene, then answered his own question: "It's the virgin birth. The Buddhist virgin birth."

"No. What do you mean?"

"Look, the darn kid is coming out of the side of the mother. That's the virgin birth."

"Hmm!"

They explored scenes of the Buddha's youth, then other scenes of the Buddha's life, involving an old man, a sick man and a dead man. Then came the cutting of the Buddha's hair, his life as an ascetic and his leaving that life, accepting the first bowl of food. Round a corner they encountered graphic depictions of temptations, like the woman with her skirt held up. A bit of extra illustration had been added, presumably by some young monk. A little farther came the descent of Lord Buddha.

"See Butch, he went up into heaven to teach Buddhism to his mother, and then came back down again."

"Butch" was becoming dazed. Father Mackey admonished him: "You don't know anything about Lord Buddha's life. But he's more Christian than we are."

Father Sheridan looked at Father Mackey in amazement.

Finally, they came to the reclining Buddha, the last scene. "Now Butch, look. There you have a synopsis of Christian theology."

This to the theologian from Rome.

"What do you mean?"

"You've got no eye. Open your eyes, Butch. What's he doing?"

"He seems to be sleeping."

"No, he's dying. But what's he lying on? Look, what's over there?" Father Mackey pointed to the shelves of religious texts — volumes of unbound ten-by-forty-centimetre pages, carefully wrapped in cloth, tied and stacked in pigeon-hole shelves. "They're the scripture. He's sleeping on the scripture. What are the sources of our faith? Tradition and scripture. That's what they taught me. We spent years studying the tradition of the church and scripture. Okay, here's scripture."

By now nothing could surprise Father Sheridan.

"Now what else do you see? What's the other source of religion?" his guide and tormentor asked. "Tradition. Scripture and tradition. Well, there you've got tradition."

"Where's tradition?"

"What are all those people doing around there?"

"They're crying. It looks like they're in tears or upset."

"Yeah, they're his disciples who are going to preach what he taught. Tradition." Father Mackey adopted a tone of friendly admonition. "You people, you know, you get into a book and you've got no sense of reality of what's happening in the world."

Another visitor, of a somewhat different kind, was Koley Lam. He was a senior expert on Bhutanese tradition and etiquette. In practice, this combination is called *driglam namzha*. It's a code that defines how people are supposed to behave, particularly in terms of ceremonial tradition. It includes marks of deference to persons of authority — the way the scarf or *kabney* is held, the depth of the bow required, the presentation of the honorific *kata* or white silk scarf. It also includes the elaborate ceremony, the pouring of tea and giving of morsels of food, that marks the opening of important gatherings. The study of *driglam namzha* can occupy a day, a week or a lifetime.

Koley Lam came to teach some lessons to the students of Sherubtse. He was well-tutored himself — part lama (hence the name "Lam") and part civil servant — and had served under all three kings. He supposedly still had marks on his head from disciplinary blows he received in training in the time of the first king. He worked under the second king and tutored the third. His personality and status made him an intimidating figure to the Bhutanese at Sherubtse, and the news circulated quickly when it became known: "Koley Lam is coming!"

Father Mackey set up a lecture in the school auditorium. As usual, the small boys were seated at the front, the older boys at the back. But for Koley Lam's lecture, absolute stillness was expected, no noise, no movement. The little boys did their best as they sat in the big auditorium seats. But their feet didn't reach the floor and after an hour of serious presentation they started to wiggle. This did not fit with *driglam namzha* or Koley Lam's strict discipline, and he gave them a good bawling out.

The material he covered was pretty deadly stuff for young school boys, especially in subsequent years, when some students heard Koley Lam repeat it year after year as he made regular visits. But if he could be led astray, into his own stories, he had fascinating tales to tell.

Father Mackey prepped the captains to ask questions that would lead him into stories of his youth and life with the three kings. "What was the first king like?" "What did he do?" "What did you learn?" "Where did you go?" When Koley Lam got off on one of these tangents, he was good for an hour. This was living history, and probably a lot more valuable to the kids than the programmed material.

For the second day's lecture, Father Mackey put the small boys on the balcony at the back in hopes that their inevitable wigglings would escape the harsh eye of Koley Lam. He stationed a captain on the balcony to make sure there was no discernable movement among the young audience. "Nobody's going to move," Father Mackey told the captain, "I don't care what happens."

The last boy to sit down was Bomba, the son of Tashigang's chief of police. Bomba had arrived late and rushed into the auditorium without having had time to go for a pee. As the lecture proceeded, his need grew stronger and stronger. He turned to the captain and gestured that he had to go out. The captain shook his head. The situation got worse and Bomba gave the older boy an imploring look.

But the captain had his orders and his attitude was, "Nothing doing! Nobody's going to move." He made this clear to Bomba. The expression on the little boy's face turned to pain and he held the end of his penis. Then slowly, trickle, trickle — and a wet spot grew on the balcony floor.

Bomba became Bhutan's first airline pilot.

* * *

A local man called Mim Dorje had a farm just over the hill from the Fathers' mess at the edge of the campus. Mim was short for Meme, which means "grandfather," and "Mim Dorje" would translate roughly to "Old Man Dorje." He was a few years older than Father Mackey. From time to time, Mim Dorje's animals would ravage the school's vegetable garden. The pigs would root up the potatoes and the cows would eat anything above ground. But the mules were particularly troublesome because of their greater intelligence.

They were pack animals used to carry supplies to the Wing 4 army camp up near the Tibetan border. After a long trek, they would return with a voracious appetite and raid the school garden, led by the lead mule. The garden gate consisted of wooden bars that were slid into slots in the gate posts on either side. But the lead mule learned how to take hold of a bar with its teeth and slide the bars, one at a time, out of the slot, so gaining entry to corn or other delights.

After years of friendly bickering over this, Mim Dorje came to Father Mackey one day. He said, "Father Mackey, I'm going to die."

Father Mackey replied typically: "You can't die, Mim Dorje. You've got a long time to go yet. You're younger than I am."

"No, no. I'm going to die."

He was serious, and Father Mackey was struck by the man's lack of fear. It was just a matter-of-fact conclusion. Two weeks later, he came back and again said he was going to die.

Father Mackey countered: "You told me that a couple of weeks ago but you're still alive."

"Yes, but now I'm going to die."

Two days later Mim Dorje's son came and told Father Mackey that his father was dead.

Father Mackey went to the family's home to pay his respects. The *phajo* came. A *phajo* is normally a soothsayer, but apparently this one was also something of an astrologer, for he would determine the auspicious time for the cremation and the direction to take when leaving the house with the body. If the device used indicated a direction other than where a door or window existed, a hole would have to be made in the wall to allow the body's removal. For this reason the body was often kept outside the house.

The *phajo* set the cremation for the following Sunday, and said to take the body from the home at six-thirty in the morning. Crops were still in the fields, so the cremation could not take place around the farm house. This would be inauspicious for the harvest. At such times, cremations were done at the river. This one would be at the Drangmechhu, which was one kilometre below Kanglung, and almost straight down.

Father Mackey was at the house when the body was taken, but he had to return to the school to say Mass for the Sisters at eight. He explained and said: "You carry on and take the body down. I'll move fast and catch up with you around nine o'clock."

He delivered a short sermon that morning, got away shortly after eight-thirty and set off across the campus towards the river. Just over the lip of the Kanglung plateau, where the hillside slopes steeply down to the river, he found the villagers waiting for him. Father Mackey joined them in a cup of *ara* before setting off down the mountainside.

The first cup was offered to Mim Dorje, who was tied up in the fetal position in a large basket. Until the cremation was finally completed, he would be treated as a living participant — part host and part honoured guest. After the *ara*, the funeral party proceeded down the hill, gathering wood for the pyre as they went.

Once at the river, the mourners built a wooden platform on a base of rocks that jutted out into the stream. They piled the wood on this platform, then placed the body, still tied in the fetal position, on the pyre. Mim Dorje had been the village *champoen*, the master of the dances, leading the masked dancers at religious festivals held at the old temple near Kangma, not far away.

Each year at the local Tshechu, Mim Dorje and other dancers would dress in elaborate costumes and formidable carved wooden masks to act out historic and morality plays from the Tibetan Buddhist tradition. So when he was placed on his pyre, before the fire was lit, the basket holding his body and the pyre were adorned with some of his costumes and head-dresses. This was acknowledgement of his role as *champoen*, and would help bring the merit earned by his religious work.

In due course the wood was ignited. Being out in the river, the pyre got lots of oxygen to help it burn, but the wind also carried away some of the heat needed to consume the body. To help things along, oil or diesel fuel would usually be poured onto the pyre. It takes a lot of heat to burn a body. To be traditionally correct, butter should be used for this purpose, but these village folk could not afford such an extravagance. One of the many reasons for Father Mackey's popularity was that he could always be counted upon to supply some old oil from his generators or maybe diesel fuel for a cremation. In two hours the body of Mim Dorje was just about reduced to ashes.

Before the fire consumed the body completely, a meal was served, with Mim Dorje still the host. The people ate in good spirit and the *ara* flowed. Except for the occasional bout of weeping by a close relative, a cremation like this one is not a scene of sadness and pain. Mourners tell stories and jokes. The deceased is not really dead but will be reincarnated — with any luck, to a stage closer to nirvana. Despite the sins of his mules, Mim Dorje could probably expect a higher state of existence in his next reincarnation.

With the friends and relatives gathered for the meal, Mim Dorje's eldest son gave a silver Tibetan coin to each of those who had helped, thanking them for their participation in the ceremony. Then the ashes and anything remaining on the platform were pushed into the river. A final cup of tea was served, then Father Mackey and the others walked back up the hill.

* * *

Mim Dorje's cremation was not the first Father Mackey attended, and it would not be the last. When people died in the community, the Jesuit would do what he could to help with the cremation, often taking some of the senior students to lend a hand. To the Bhutanese Buddhists, death is the most important event in a person's existence in the world, but it remains a natural event. And children from an early age take the reality of death in their stride, accepting cremations as a normal part of community life.

Deaths occurred even among Father Mackey's students. A clever class-five boy named Kinzang Dorji came from Tashi Yangtse, but had been more or less adopted by his uncle, who had a shop near Yonphula. At the beginning of June, 1977, Kinzang had gone to spend a two-day holiday with his uncle's family. When he returned to the school he had stomach trouble, but this was attributed to the water at Yonphula. He improved somewhat over the next few days, but a week later he was complaining of headache, fever and his stomach again. He was put to bed and given some medicine used for common stomach problems or the flu. He did not improve and other medicines were tried.

By mid-month he was still not responding, so Father Mackey sent him to the hospital. The doctor there considered tuberculosis and obstruction of the intestine. Ordinary medicines and then stronger and stronger antibiotics failed to bring improvement. The doctor considered surgery, but still did not know what the problem was. And there was no anaesthetist. The doctor said, "There's not much hope." The boy died on a Monday night, just before midnight, the twentieth of June. Cause: unknown.

Through most of this period, Kinzang's uncle stayed with him, and he was there at the end. Father Mackey had spent the final Sunday and Monday with the youngster as well. His parents had been informed by letter and two messengers, but they had not come down from Tashi Yangtse. Father Mackey met with the boy's adopted father and another uncle.

It was very hot in Tashigang and the body could not be kept long. The uncles decided to cremate the body the next day, Tuesday. As it was June, crops were in the fields, and again the cremation would take place on a bank of the Drangmechhu, but this time below Tashigang. Father Mackey went to see his friend the Lam Neten, abbot of the monastery in Tashigang Dzong, who said he would bring some monks down.

The uncle from Yonphula organized the cremation and had the boy's body taken from the hospital about noon. Father Mackey got the hospital's ambulance to carry the relatives and the body. Boys from the school collected firewood and a public works department truck helped carry the wood, food and senior boys to the site. Deda Tashi, head of the police in Tashigang, had his men there helping as well. He was always supportive of the school. At the river bank the body was stripped and washed in the river, then forced back into the fetal position and tied up. As you come into the world, so you go out.

The pyre for a cremation is built up with most of the wood well below the body. The body starts out on top but sinks down as the wood burns. As the body sinks it catches the intense heat from the lower wood. It's difficult to get everything burnt — especially the skull and the abdomen, the centre of the mass as the body is tied up. Any parts that are not completely burnt to ash can be pushed into the river, which is regarded as an appropriate receptacle for such remains. As the cremation started late, it was evening when the ashes were finally pushed into the water. Darkness falls quickly in Bhutan, even in June, and by seven it was dark. It started to rain.

Now the boys had to get back to the school. Healthy school boys can run down the short cut in less than an hour, but walking back up as evening came on was another matter. Some did hike the short cut and some took the longer route, following the road. They had all had a good meal at the cremation, provided by the dead boy's uncles.

The bigger boys, from class ten, who were helping out, had to stay later, and Father Mackey wondered if they would have to walk all the way back to Sherubtse in the dark. He couldn't fit them all into the school Land Rover. But by chance a Dantak truck came along the road from Mongar. Deda Tashi stopped it and said: "This is an emergency. Put these kids in the back and take them to Kanglung."

The truck was travelling only as far as Rongtong, but given the police chief's instructions, the driver took them right to the school. By nine-thirty all were back at Sherubtse.

When Father Mackey went to see the Lam Neten and offer something for the services of the monks, he was told, "Father, I won't take a thing. For the school and a school boy, I would not accept a donation for saying prayers. I don't want to displease you, but I would feel it unjust for myself to take something from you for this boy. That's my job. You're teaching and doing a lot for the school. My job is to take care of this."

Kinzang Dorji was a popular student and his fellows collected money for butter lamps for offerings at the temple. Special prayers were said at the school on the seventh, fourteenth, twenty-first and twenty-eighth days following his death.

* * *

On the morning of July twenty-first, 1972, Father Mackey received a wireless message saying that His Majesty, Jigme Dorji Wangchuck was dead. The King had died of a heart attack in Nairobi while on a hunting safari. His mother, Dawa Tshering, now the foreign minister, and the Crown Prince were with him. The body of the late King arrived at Dum Dum Airport, Calcutta, at three in the morning. It was then flown by the Indian Air Force to Hasimara, and then taken to Thimphu by road, accompanied by lamas and an entourage.

The King, though still only forty-four, had suffered from a bad heart for many years. This had occasionally slowed him down, but he had tried to live a robust life in the service of his people. Some have suspected that he knew the end was near when he planned the trip to Kenya. Unease had lingered in Bhutan since the death of the prime minister,

Jigmie Dorji. People wondered about distrust between the Wangchucks and the Dorjis. And there was concern about the "Tibetan factor."

Some saw a Tibetan hand in the assassination, and distrusted a Tibetan "princess" who was very close to the King. Also, one or two attempts had been made on his life. So, some suggested that the King chose to die outside Bhutan, where it would be difficult to lay blame, point fingers or manufacture an assassination scenario. And indeed, no such insinuation established itself. The King's untimely death and the coronation of his young son may in fact have laid some ghosts to rest and allowed old wounds to heal.

This time there was no reservation on the part of those around Father Mackey. The Jesuit called an assembly, and he and Lopen Jamphel talked about the late King. Father Mackey spoke for over half an hour, citing the major accomplishments: establishment of the National Assembly and the High Court, redistribution of land, abolition of serfdom, Bhutan's joining the United Nations, the modernization of the education system, including the adoption of English medium.

Father Mackey also spoke in personal terms about the King as a human being. They had been friends, and Father Mackey respected and liked the King very much. He had found the King down-to-earth, intelligent and good humoured. He pointed out to the students that one might not pick the King out of a group because he wore no fancy clothes: he was one with his people. Father Mackey told them: "He loved the people. Driving along the road, if he saw somebody walking along, he'd stop the jeep and say, 'Where are you going?' Then he'd put them in the back of the jeep and drop them closer to wherever they were going. He was very, very close to his people."

He told them about the King's high standards and his confidence in his officers, the public and the country. And he told them of the King's interest in books and of their friendship — how they had met and how they would chat and exchange books.

The next afternoon, the *lopens* organized a ritual in the temple, and the boys recited prayers for the dead. Later, Father Mackey said Mass in the auditorium. This was one of only two times he said Mass in public in Bhutan. Usually he said it in the small chapel he maintained in his home or in the Fathers' mess.

Father Mackey closed the school for a week and prayers continued in the temple, sometimes officiated by the local lama, the Kanglung Rinpoche. On the twenty-sixth of July, the boys went on a pilgrimage to various *gompas* and *lhakhangs* in the area. The religious actions of these students reflected the sadness of the ordinary people, who mourned the loss of the King for whom they had strong love and devotion. Father Mackey later commented on the students' tears of reaction to the King's death: "They felt a personal loss."

Father Mackey had sent a message of condolence to the Royal Family, and later received letters back from the new King, Jigme Singye Wangchuck, and his sister, Ashi Dechen. Both expressed thanks for the prayers and message of sympathy. The young King wrote, "My father was highly appreciative of the good work you and your colleagues are doing towards the cause of education in Bhutan." And Ashi Dechen said, "My father admired the way you ran the Public School."

The full period of mourning for Bhutanese Buddhists is forty-nine days. Common people cannot always afford the daily prayers and attendant expenses of a long mourning, and in hot weather cannot keep the body that long. They then shorten the mourning period to twenty-one or even seven days — some multiple of seven. For the King, of course, the full mourning period was observed, and the auspicious time for the cremation was found to be later still.

In October, Father Mackey travelled to Thimphu, visited the Royal Family and spent a morning with the Royal Body. When he stepped into the Royal Cottage, where the body was resting, his presence was announced to the late King: "Your Majesty, Father Mackey has arrived."

The late King was resting, in the fetal position, unseen, within a *chorten*-shaped construction, beautifully adorned with *katas*, coloured scarves and flags, statues, butter lamps and *bumpa*, the holy water vases. Father Mackey stepped forward and laid his *kata* on the bottom of the *chorten*.

Ashi Kesang, the late King's widow, was waiting for Father Mackey. He paid his respects and offered his condolences. Then he asked, "Would you mind if I say some prayers?"

"No, Father, go ahead." She was familiar with Catholic prayers from her school days at St. Joseph's Convent in Kalimpong.

Father Mackey knelt and prayed. In the quiet, he was impressed at the traditional embalming which had kept the King's body fresh for almost three months. After he'd finished praying, a Royal Body Guard brought Father Mackey tea — presenting it first to the late King, and setting it down at the front of the *chorten*. The priest didn't touch his tea until the guard indicated that His Late Majesty — as he was thereafter referred to — was asking him to drink it.

The late King had been a chain smoker. So all the time Father Mackey was with His Late Majesty, a Royal Body Guard lit a cigarette every fifteen minutes and placed it on the front of the *chorten* for the late King to enjoy.

Father Mackey was considered an old friend of the family, and he talked with Ashi Kesang for some time. As noon approached, Ashi Dechen, the late King's second eldest daughter, came to Father Mackey and asked if he would mind feeding her father. He said he'd be honoured.

On the four sides of the *chorten*, on a ledge, were bowls. Father Mackey was given larger bowls of traditional Bhutanese food — meat, vegetable and cheese dishes, and rice. He took one at a time and went around the *chorten*, in the proper clockwise direction, and placed a portion of each dish into the bowls on each side of the *chorten*. Then he sat down and food was brought to him. His Late Majesty and Father Mackey ate a last lunch together.

18/

S herubtse school had few support staff but many jobs that needed doing. Every student not only participated in sports, but also helped out in some way — in the library, for example. The first half hour of evening study period was compulsory library reading. It was common for a student to get interested in his or her book, forget the homework and carry on reading for an hour and a half. Father Mackey usually let this go, as he felt that students got as much out of reading as doing homework.

The library was open after lunch every day and on Saturday and Sunday afternoons. Father Mackey found responsible, interested kids from classes eight and nine and put them in charge. Class ten students, who would write their final exams in the fall, were excused or barred from most of these kinds of jobs because of their heavy work load.

The librarians were conscientious. They not only issued books, but made sure they came back on time, especially at the end of the year. The job was not really a burden. Those who took it were interested in books and reading, and when it came time for class ten exams, those who had been librarians usually came out on top.

When the science teachers complained that they had no lab assistants, Father Mackey had them pick three students each for physics, chemistry and biology. They were trusted with keys to the laboratories, and would help set up lab demonstrations and also take them down and put away apparatus. Father Mackey stressed the idea of responsibility and they lived up to his expectations.

Some boys served as dormitory doctors. Kids were continually turning up with cuts and bruises, wanting to run up to the small Dantak hospital above the school. Brother Quinn could not man the infirmary continually. But before a student could leave the campus for medical reasons, he had to be cleared by the dormitory doctor. This student could take temperatures and clean and dress superficial wounds. On hand he had plenty of iodine, cotton wool and sticking tape. At least two of these dormitory doctors went on to become real doctors.

Father Mackey also started a gymnastics group, of course, and a drill team, a dance group and other entertainment groups. He delegated responsibilities through the school captains. Some jobs were attractive, like those involving staging shows for the community. Others were dirty little jobs like making sure the footballs were returned each day after sports period.

A captaincy was in itself a responsibility. The school had a captain and an assistant captain, and so did each residential "house." This included the girls' houses, under the tutelage of Sister Leonard. The captains had a lot of authority and a lot of responsibility. It could be tough, especially, to have their fellow students yelling at them. Sometimes, one would come to Father Mackey: "Father, please, it's too much."

He'd say: "No, you're learning a valuable lesson in how to handle people. You'll appreciate it later on. It's going to help you a lot when you leave school. You must face responsibility, and this is fantastic training for you."

Father Mackey believes this has been borne out: "We turned out some fantastic people who were thinking of others, could take responsibility, and see a job done."

In 1974, class seven students at Sherubtse wanted to do "social work" — something to help the local people. They wanted to take a certain amount of time each week and go out into the community. Father Mackey said: "Fine, why don't you do something to teach the kids?"

This took them by surprise, but a lot of children around Sherubtse had no school to attend. The enrolment at Sherubtse was limited and drawn from a wide area. Besides, the school was dropping lower classes as it added senior classes and sections. Students from class seven started teaching the children of school servants, kitchen help, sweepers and so on. Every afternoon, during the sports periods, and every holiday, these children would learn reading, writing, mathematics, even some Dzongkha. Gradually, some of the local kids from off campus were brought in. This informal "school" grew to have scores of students.

One year a boy named Karma, who particularly enjoyed this work, asked if he could stay over the winter vacation and carry on. He and two others gave regular classes through December, January and February until Sherubtse opened again. The informal school carried on like this until a Royal Visit, when Father Mackey said to the King, "Your Majesty, come and see what the boys are doing."

The King was amazed: "Why, this is a regular school!"

Father Mackey said, "I know, but I can't get a teacher. The education department should take it over."

This suggestion reaped results, for soon afterwards, in 1979, the full-fledged Kanglung Primary School officially opened. Karma became a real teacher. He trained in England and went on to be become a teacher trainer.

Students also pursued unstructured individual interests, like chess. Back in Tashigang, one of the teachers had started teaching boys to play. When Mr. Bose, the deputy director of education, visited the school, he asked Father Mackey if any of the boys played chess.

When Father Mackey said yes, Mr. Bose said: "Send one or two down to me. I'll teach them a few things."

Father Mackey picked two good players and Mr. Bose sat down to teach them. The first boy beat him. The deputy director insisted on a rematch. The boy beat him again.

That was the last time Mr. Bose sought out Father Mackey's chess players.

* * *

Father Mackey's Land Rover had been donated by a man named John Goelet. He was a multi-millionaire married to a friend of the Queen, Ashi Kesang, who had gone to school in England. The Goelets visited Bhutan from time to time, and the man became interested in Father Mackey's work and in Bhutan's agricultural development. He approached the Canadian Jesuits about getting someone with an agricultural background to come to Bhutan.

Brother Nick Johannesma, a naturalized Dutch-Canadian already working in India, came to Sherubtse in 1971 to teach in the lower classes and run an agriculture programme for the older students. He later branched out into other aspects of agricultural development.

To Father Mackey, he was yet another distinctive colleague. The stocky "Wild Dutchman" was a practical, no-nonsense man with a fiery tempcr. His manner did not always endear him to his bosses, but apart from the occasional flare-up, he and Father Mackey got along well.

A year or so after Brother Nick arrived, John Goelet gave both him and Father Mackey 450-cc BSA motorcycles. Father Mackey's new bike was a lot more powerful than his old Jawa. It took the hills with ease and was great on the winding roads — at least until the priest had an eye operation.

By 1972, Father Mackey realized he was developing cataracts. During a visit to Calcutta he saw a doctor to have them removed. The doctor examined him and said: "Your cataracts are not ripe yet. You'll have to wait another year." So Father Mackey went back to Sherubtse and carried on, but with increasing difficulty. He found himself kicking objects on the floor and banging his shins on low furniture. Finally he decided to travel to Canada for the double cataract operation.

Not long before he was due to leave, Doctor Anayat visited Sherubtse with a colleague. In the evening, they organized a rubber of bridge in Father Mackey's quarters, with Father Coffey rounding out the table. After the first hand Father Mackey rose and went to the bathroom. In the tiny toilet cubicle, he thought he saw something move. He called out, "Hey, there's a snake in my bathroom!"

Doctor Anayat yelled back, "You're blind! There's no snake in your bathroom."

Father Mackey said, "Well, there's something."

Doctor Anayat came to have a look. Sure enough, there was a snake curled up in the corner. He ran and grabbed a poker from the fireplace and poked at the snake. When it raised its head, Doctor Anayat, who knew snakes, cried, "My God! It's a king cobra!"

He went after it with a vengeance, hammering and bashing, but the snake slithered behind the toilet bowl. Father Coffey had yelled for Prem, Father Mackey's driver. He looked at the snake, dashed outside and grabbed a big rock from around the flower garden. He rushed back into the bathroom and hurled the rock at the snake. Unfortunately, the rock was too big to fit between the wall and the toilet bowl and a piece of porcelain went flying.

Brother Nick arrived on the scene. He took a look and ran to get the metre-long piece of pipe he kept in his vehicle. Finally, having reduced the bathroom to a shambles — floor tiles chipped, walls dented, a big chunk gone from the toilet bowl — the men managed to kill the snake. Out of the wreckage, they pulled a metre-and-a-half black cobra.

They decided it must have entered through the window, from the peach tree just outside. The very next morning, Father Mackey had the tree cut down. And for the next five nights, whenever he got up to answer nature's call, he chose to go outside.

Father Mackey left for Canada in April 1973. In Toronto, the Mission office had made him an appointment with Doctor Callaghan, an eye specialist. He took one look at Father Mackey's eyes and exclaimed, "My God, man, you're blind!"

"I know I am! Just look at my shins!"

"Okay, Tuesday we'll do one. Then the other a week later."

Father Mackey found the procedure less rigorous than the pulling of his teeth.

By the time he returned to Bhutan, his eyes were almost healed. Brother Quinn and Brother Nick came to Gauhati to meet him. Brother Quinn had just been bitten by a dog suspected to be rabid. He had received the anti-rabies treatment of multiple injections in the abdomen and was not comfortable. The Jesuits decided to go all the way to Kanglung that day, even though they got a late start out of Samdrup Jongkhar.

At eleven o'clock that night, near Khyengtongmani, about fifteen kilometres south of Kanglung, they ran out of petrol. In the rush to leave, Brother Nick had forgotten to fill the tank. So, to use a classic South Asia expression, "What to do?" Someone had to go for fuel. Brother Nick himself drove well, and had chosen not to bring a driver. He knew how to siphon gas from one vehicle to another, and had to stay with the Land Rover in case a truck came by. Brother Quinn was in no shape to walk. That left Father Mackey — or, as he puts it, "the blind man."

The dark, foggy night precluded short cuts. Father Mackey followed the road north, winding down from Khyengtongmani. In the fog, he could see nothing along the side of the road. After walking a long time, he reached a turning point he recognized — and knew he had gone past Sherubtse. He turned around and walked back, watching carefully. Now he found himself above the school.

Finally he located the upper gate and followed the road into the Fathers' quarters. By now it was two o'clock in the morning. He banged on the door of Father Bill Robins, who had joined the Sherubtse staff the year before, and told his sleepy colleague: "Get some darned petrol and take it up to Nick on your motor bike."

He explained the situation and went to bed. Father Robins put petrol in a tin and set off. The fog was so bad he had to proceed without his light, driving slowly and watching carefully to make sure he stayed on the road. Brother Nick and Brother Quinn could hear him coming and waited out on the road. It was four in the morning before they all got back to Sherubtse.

Father Mackey's eye trouble was not really over. His cataracts were gone, but the operation had left him with tunnel vision. He adjusted to this, and stopped bashing his shins on furniture, but driving his motorcycle became dangerous. He insisted on riding it because he enjoyed it and it was very handy.

But now he had no peripheral vision: if he looked forward, up and along the road, he couldn't see the roadway directly in front of him; and if he looked down at the road immediately ahead, he couldn't see what was coming. The obvious answer was to alternate between the two, and this would work well on a straight road. Unfortunately, the roads in Bhutan are anything but straight.

Still, Father Mackey managed reasonably well — though once in a while he would round a bend and see another vehicle approaching. His first impression was that the other vehicle was immediately in front of him. If he had a moment to adjust, he would usually see that he had time and space to edge over and pass safely. Often, though, his reaction was to slam on the brakes and head for the edge of the road.

The bike would slide in the loose gravel and go down, and Father Mackey would end up scraped and bruised. It was most fortunate, even miraculous, that none of these encounters sent him over the edge of a precipice to his death. He continued to ride his bike for two more years. But after taking some fifteen spills, finally he admitted: "This is getting too dangerous, boy, you'd better stick to a jeep and a driver."

Brother Nick became the proud owner of a second BSA.

* * *

During the day, Father Mackey taught classes and ran the school. He handled ordinary administrative work, dealing with teachers and their problems, disciplining students, and making sure the support side of the school was in order — the kitchens, the dormitories, the school vehicle and so on. He delegated as much responsibility as he could to his fellow Jesuits and other teachers, but the buck stopped with him.

Evenings afforded Father Mackey some time to get to know the students in an easier, more relaxed atmosphere. Like all the other teachers, he took a turn at supervising night study, and he might just wander around at any time. He knew all the syllabi and could tell from glancing at students' homework how the classes were progressing. If a teacher was falling behind schedule, Father Mackey could look into it. He did his best evaluating, he said, walking up and down, observing night study.

Although he always had living quarters of his own, Father Mackey lived much of each year in the boys' dormitory. He slept in a small room on the floor that housed the class ten boys. These senior students didn't have to go to night study with the others, but studied in their dormitory. So Father Mackey was always handy and available to help if a student had a problem, especially in maths, but in other subjects as well. Almost nightly he would circulate among the students, glancing at their work, chatting casually. He was aware of their weaknesses and could usually detect the presence of a problem, personal or academic.

Because of his involvement, Father Mackey had few discipline problems. When he did mete out discipline, he tempered it by re-establishing rapport afterwards. Problems rarely required more action. But there were exceptions.

Virendra Singh Allahwat was a Punjabi, but he did not wear the turban of the Sikhs. He was a good teacher of geography, a good organizer of sports, and he ran the staff team — a good all-round man for the school. For all his good points, however, Mr. Singh, as he was called, did have a temper. And on one occasion, in his first year, he lost his composure and sense of proportion.

In class one day, he punished the wrong boy for some infraction, now forgotten. Bhutanese students usually took rightful punishment without much fuss. They knew that if they did wrong, they would be punished, and they accepted that. However, they were not willing to accept the guilt of someone else. This was the case with a class-eight boy named Tenzin.

He, too, had a strong temper, and that day he stormed out of the classroom in a rage. He returned a few minutes later with a large stone in each hand, prepared to throw them at Mr. Singh. The teacher was checking maps drawn by three other class-eight students. The boys noticed Tenzin first and made themselves scarce. Then Mr. Singh saw his would-be assailant. His reaction was dramatic. He opened his coat, in a breast-baring gesture, and said bombastically: "My father won the Victoria Cross! He was an army man, a fighting man! Kill me if you wish!"

Tenzin was so taken aback at this outburst that he turned and walked out.

Mr. Singh went to Father Mackey in the heat of his anger. Father Mackey said, "Look, let's just keep it quiet for a while. This afternoon, after school, come and see me."

Mr. Singh had not cooled down when he returned. He said, "That boy must go, or I go!"

"Look, he's just a kid, a student, and he's in class eight. We can punish him."

"No, he must go!"

Father Mackey consulted with some of the other teachers. One spoke for the group, saying, "Father, it's tough, but he's really angry. He's a good teacher, a good man to have here. I think we'd better go along with him."

Tenzin was a good student approaching his important class-eight exams. Father Mackey couldn't bring himself to expel the boy, though he had to appease and stand behind his teacher. He called the boy into his office, "I've tried to get this straightened out but you have to go. We'll do it this way: You get all your books ready for tomorrow morning, and I'll take you to Tashigang. I'll arrange for you to join the class-eight there. And when the exams come, you'll appear as a student from here, but you may have to write with the students from Tashigang."

At Tashigang school he explained the situation to the headmaster: "He's not a bad kid, but he's got one awful temper. He lost his shirt and this is what happened."

The headmaster had no problem with the arrangement.

Back at Sherubtse, Mr. Singh had a change of heart. He came to Father Mackey, "Father, I made a mistake."

"Well, Mr. Singh, we all make mistakes."

"Can we bring him back?"

"No," said Father Mackey. "We've taken a decision and I wouldn't want to touch it now. But if he passes, then we can bring him back here for class nine."

"Oh, yes, Father, please bring him back!"

In Tashigang, Tenzin not only did well in academics, but also taught the drill team the routines he had learned in Sherubtse. He led them in an impressive drill display at that year's National Day celebration held in Mongar. After passing his exams, Tenzin returned to Kanglung the following year, and he and Mr. Singh became good friends. Mr. Singh later joined the National Sports Academy in India, and Tenzin became an officer in the Royal Bhutan Army.

The closest Father Mackey came to expelling students outright was for sexual activity. This had been one of Father Mackey's concerns when he refused to admit girls until he had Sisters to help. His confidence in the Sisters proved justified. Generally, the girls could take care of themselves and with the Sisters' help, they stayed out of trouble.

The exception that came to light was a rather brazen affair. Three nights in a row, during a series of evening educational films, a boy and a girl slipped away and made love. Then they were discovered. Mother Peter was not amused. The girl, apparently, was notorious among the boys even before this happened. Father Mackey would probably not have sent the pair away, but turning a blind eye to such an audacious breach of behaviour would invite imitators. He never considered just getting rid of the girl, as other principals have done. He said, "They're both involved. They both have to go."

Even so, he avoided total expulsion from school. Both individuals had been good students, and Father Mackey sent them from Sherubtse with letters indicating their academic ability, so that they could gain entry at other schools. The boy was put on a bus, and with his letter he was accepted at Punakha High School, the newly established Jesuit-run school in Western Bhutan. Father Robins took the girl on his motorcycle and delivered her to her home at Pemagatshel, 110 kilometres away. She went on to take teacher training and became a teacher.

* * *

The school was the centre of the community, and the source of most of its entertainment, and the local people came out in numbers for shows and concerts. But visitors to the community, especially Indian visitors to Dantak, could be brought to the school at any time. Sherubtse was a showpiece, and no visit to Eastern Bhutan was complete without seeing it.

Everyone at Sherubtse grew tired of this visiting, which, in the fall — peak Indian holiday time — threatened teaching schedules and exam preparation. Every visitor wanted to see classrooms with cute little Bhutanese children in them. Over time, Father Mackey and his staff developed a routine. They'd trot out certain show items to entertain guests.

One of Father Mackey's favourites was a long-division problem that looked impressive: divide a twelve-digit number by an eleven-digit number. Any primary student who knew his times tables could rattle off the answer in no time. The trick was that the eleven-digit divisor always began with the digits 9-8-1 or something similar. What the students learned, but the visitor would not realize, was that this number could be rounded off to the number 1 (actually 100,000,000,000). All the student had to do was multiply and subtract to complete the lower part of the long division process. The kids knew their multiplication tables so well they just flew through it — much to the amazement of the visitors.

The students were also ready with songs and recitations, and these would charm the visitors as well. And to ensure that the burden was spread around, and no one class got interrupted too often, a roster was maintained. If class 3-A got one group of visitors, then 3-B would take the next.

In science, Father Robins capitalized on community interest. At that time, the most important examinations came in classes six and eight. He divided these students into teams that included one of the better students, and one or two of the weaker students, then gave each team an experiment that would be its speciality. Every student did all the required lab work, but specialized as well. Then Father Robins mounted a science exhibition.

Usually, Father Mackey invited the soldiers first. They were the guinea pigs. As he included Indian soldiers, often based alongside the Bhutanese, these groups might ask questions in Dzongkha, Sharchop-kha, Nepali, Hindi or English. The students would do their best to explain the experiment in whichever language the guest spoke. This was great practice, both in language and in understanding the experiment.

The local people came the second night. They would speak Shar-chopkha, but would bring a different perspective, usually that of a farmer. The students usually had the most fun showing experiments to the locals, because they expressed more surprise. The third night was for students. The highlight of this evening was seeing the girls go after the boys and vice-versa, as students challenged each other's knowledge, with each team trying to show its expertise.

The final show was for the people from Tashigang, the Dzong and the town, who despite the hike still came to all the functions at Sherubtse. This show would be held on Saturday, when people would have time to walk to Kanglung and back. When there was bus service, they might be able to take the bus one or both ways.

After the four-day show, the students knew their own experiments inside out and backwards, and in five languages. They had also picked up a good understanding of everyone else's experiment as well — good enough to bring excellent exam results at the end of the year.

* * *

The students weren't the only ones who needed social activity, of course, and Father Mackey knew this. Apart from activities directly linked to school and students, the teachers had little to do of a social nature. They could socialize among themselves, of course, family with family, but natural barriers prevented a lot of mixing.

Socializing styles varied among the three groups that made up the staff — Bhutanese, Indian and Canadian. Each group felt most at ease speaking its own mother tongue, and even among the Indians there were different language groups. Responding to this situation, Father Mackey set aside one Saturday night each month for a teachers' get-together.

This gathering included wives and children. The first month the Fathers would host the party, and the next month the Sisters hosted. The *lopens*, the teachers from Kerala (the Keralites), and then the non-Keralite Indian teachers — everybody took a turn, and then they'd start over again.

The food for the dinner was the usual fare. Father Mackey provided rice and dhal from the school stores, and those who had gardens would bring vegetables. Whoever was hosting the party would provide drinks. The *lopens'* wives often made *ara*, and twenty rupees would buy five bottles of rum — more than enough.

Father Mackey found that these gatherings did more towards building spirit and staff unity than anything else could, and he established this programme in each of his schools in Eastern Bhutan.

Each year, as well, the teachers and students gathered in mid-August to celebrate Father Mackey's birthday. This was just past the midpoint of the school year, at the height of the monsoon — an excellent time to raise spirits. Brother Quinn had instigated the celebration, and it had become an institution. Ultimately, Father Mackey's birthday became only one aspect of the day, the impetus for a grand celebration in recognition of all the teachers, which in turn became the first half of a two-day celebration of teachers and students.

The birthday party was organized by the senior students, the class tens, who would be graduating at the end of the year. They would collect money and buy a pig. Boiled pork heavily spiced with hot chillies is the basis of any big Bhutanese party. The school provided everything else, including the liquor. The party was always held on a Saturday or Sunday night, and class-ten students did the cooking.

They would also organize a programme of dancing, singing and skits. Class-nine students were apprentices and did the serving. During the evening, class ten would express appreciation for what the teachers had done for them. The climax was a presentation to Father Mackey of an impressive and beautiful painting done by their best artist, and incorporating small photos of every class-ten student, as well as one of Father Mackey. The priest still treasures these paintings, and shows them proudly to every visitor.

The second half of this pair of parties honoured the class-ten graduates, and was hosted by the staff just after exams. Father Mackey provided all the food, including the pig. Class nine cooked and served dinner. The teachers brought the liquor, and if the senior students wanted to drink a bit of *ara*, they were welcome. They were grown up and ready to leave school.

After the meal, before the party broke up, Father Mackey brought out his stack of school registration cards. He never cared for registration books, but preferred to keep each student's important information on a card. This included vital statistics, parents' names, home village, exam results and any interesting or important facts or personal characteristics.

Father Mackey would read aloud from each student's card, spending three to five minutes on each student. He would focus on what the student was good at, and what contribution the student had made to the school. This might take a couple of hours, but everybody listened and applauded each graduate — a farewell from Sherubtse that would become a cherished memory.

*   *   *

On Bhutan's National Day, the seventeenth of December, 1973, Father Mackey, as he loves to point out, officially became an "S.O.B." He received the prestigious Druk Zhung Thuksey Medal for his contribution to education in Bhutan. Along with the medal came a title in Dzongkha, which has a very honourable and profound meaning, but is difficult to translate precisely. But one translation was, "Spiritual Son of Bhutan." A colleague in Darjeeling focused on the last three words and exclaimed that Mackey had finally been acknowledged as an S.O.B.

Seven months later, on June 2nd, 1974, Father Mackey led a group of staff and students from Sherubtse to the coronation of the new king.

After his short period with Father Mackey, Jigme Singye Wangchuck had received more schooling and spent considerable time with his father. In May 1972, he had been installed as Tongsa Poenlop, which denoted officially that he was to be the next king.

Just two months later, three days after the death of his father, Jigme Singye Wangchuck had become King of Bhutan. Now, almost two years after his accession to the throne, a grand coronation would take place.

This was truly a festive royal celebration. The shadows of the past had been dispelled. There had been an attempt on the new king's life, and a coup plot had been uncovered, but this had been dealt with and people were ready to move forward. Father Mackey was one of many honoured guests, and so had no opportunity to speak privately with the young King.

After Mother Peter's teams of girls and younger students put on their drill and some singing and dancing, and Father Mackey's gymnastic team put on their show of horse work, jumping through rings of fire and so on, His Majesty phoned down from his pavilion to the staging area to personally congratulate Father Mackey.

During the week-long celebration the dignitaries would deliver their felicitations to the King in his throne room in the Dzong. Father Mackey was one of those who was called in turn, and who brought the traditional white silk scarf and a gift — in his case, a historical book that he knew would interest the young King.

Father Mackey found the coronation especially remarkable because it mended rifts that had arisen after the assassination of the Prime Minister, Jigmie Dorji. Part of the Dorji family had left the country and not returned. However, they were all in Thimphu for the coronation, and Father Mackey credits Ashi Kesang, now the Queen Mother, for this. Her brother, Dasho Lhendup, and sister, Ashi Tashi, both returned from self-imposed exile in Nepal. And, as far as Father Mackey is concerned, it was Ashi Kesang and possibly her mother, Rani Chuni, who brought the Royal Family back together.

19/

The idea of a Bhutan Matriculation fit well with the Bhutanese sense of independence. His Late Majesty didn't like the Cambridge system, feeling that it produced graduates who were too big for their britches and didn't fit in when they returned to Bhutan. But neither did he want to use (directly, at least) the more ordinary Indian systems south of the border, which used Hindi, Bengali or Nepali. The Bhutanese had opted for English. They mandated Father Mackey to come up with a made-in-Bhutan system, and Bhutan's first class ten graduated after writing final examinations in December of 1968. Then came the snag.

Back in 1964, when Father Mackey modeled Bhutan's system after the one in West Bengal, everybody assumed that graduates would encounter no difficulties entering Indian universities. And, indeed, Nari Rustomji, the Indian advisor to the King, had said that any Bhutanese graduate would be given entry to an Indian university.

What nobody had reckoned on was an Indian requirement that students moving from one state to another have a Migration Certificate to continue their education. The Indian government and its agencies apparently viewed Bhutan as they would an Indian state, in terms of education. However, there was no provision for Bhutan to issue Migration Certificates.

So graduates from the Bhutan Matriculation were not able to enter Indian universities. This was overcome in the short term by finding places for them in other countries. Quite a few went to Australia or New Zealand on Colombo Plan scholarships. But this was not a real solution for the longer term. Something had to be done.

In India, the Council for the Indian School Certificate Examinations administered the Cambridge Syndicate Examinations. These examinations, originally conducted out of Cambridge, England, were being adapted to meet the needs of the countries, like India, where they were taken. In India education was a state-level responsibility, but the Council was a national body which administered a country-wide system and could issue Migration Certificates.

In the late 1960s the Council granted the Indian School Certificate (ISC) based on its own secondary-school curriculum, with final examinations coming after eleven years of schooling. In 1969, the Bhutanese authorities realized they could not continue with the Bhutan Matriculation, so, at the end of that year, Father Mackey went to New Delhi and started the process of affiliating Bhutan's high schools with the ISC system. This meant acceptance of the "Cambridge system" previously rejected, but the system was sound, was adapting to local needs and, indeed, would soon adapt to accommodate Dzongkha as an examination subject.

Over the next half dozen years, the systems overlapped as Bhutan switched from a class 10 Bhutan Matriculation to the ISC 11, and then a little later, to the next (10+2) generation of that system. This produced the class 10 Indian Certificate of Secondary Education (or ICSE 10) and the class 12 Indian School Certificate (ISC 12). Lead time was needed to get students onto the appropriate curriculum, and there were gaps as when the first ICSE 10 class graduated with no class eleven to attend within Bhutan. Those who continued had to go to India.

In May 1976, Sherubtse was upgraded and became Sherubtse Junior College. The College offered class eleven that year (1976-77) and moved up to class twelve the next (1977-78). The higher secondary classes, eleven and twelve, followed an academic year that started later than the lower classes. Twenty-three students from Sherubtse's first class twelve wrote the ISC 12 exams in 1978, and every one of them passed. By the time the results came out, Father Mackey had left Sherubtse.

* * *

While Father Mackey was at Sherubtse, Bhutan's schools introduced written Dzongkha. Dzongkha, the language of Western Bhutan, derived from Tibetan, the early Bhutanese having come from Tibet. Over the centuries, in the valleys of Western Bhutan, the language changed significantly in becoming twentieth-century Dzongkha. Before the 1960s, Dzongkha was a spoken language only, and its common use was limited to the West. Official documents were written in Choekey, the Classical Tibetan used in religious texts. In schools a limited amount of Choekey was taught, although the only use made of the language at school was to read Buddhist prayers.

The decision to make Dzongkha the written, national language seems to have come around 1960, like so many other modern initiatives. This meant adopting a script, and the authorities chose Tibetan script. To an outsider, this would seem to be an obvious decision. First, Classical Tibetan and Dzongkha were related in terms of sounds and actual words. Second, Tibetan script was familiar to a fair number of people, including those dealing with government documents and all the *lopens* who were already teaching in the schools. Trouble was, the people most familiar with Tibetan script were the monks. To them it was the script of Choekey, the language of Buddhism — a sacred language, a holy thing.

Government actions or decisions were not usually announced or publicized in those days, and maybe this enterprise was deliberately down-played. Learned scholars, monks in fact, of a liberal or progressive disposition were recruited to undertake the necessary work. But, as Father Mackey puts it, when non-religious books started to appear, "All hell broke loose!" A great many monks were shocked and outraged to find their sacred script being used to describe things that were not holy.

Opposition to the use of Tibetan script for the Dzongkha language remained strong for many years. But less conservative, more forward-looking *lopens* and monks worked at developing written Dzongkha and taught it in the schools. Father Mackey credits Lopen Nado, a monk scholar who worked extensively with the department of education, with the most substantial contribution. Lopen Nado had been asked by the King to lead this critical and sensitive undertaking. Father Mackey worked with the monk from time to time, at Sherubtse and later in Thimphu. He respected him as a scholar, an intelligent and religious man, and enjoyed his friendship.

Father Mackey also appreciated having *lopens* at Sherubtse, like Lopen Jamphel, who were not locked into old attitudes and who adopted the new language and did their best to foster the teaching of Dzongkha. Those *lopens* who opposed this change, he said, sometimes regarded it as an unwanted challenge. Up until the creation of written Dzongkha, the only material the *lopens* had to learn and teach consisted of religious texts, which they had practically (if not completely) memorized in the monasteries where they were educated. Now they were forced to deal with new, non-religious material, and this meant more work.

* * *

The first "batch" of class-eleven students at Sherubtse included some who had just passed the ICSE 10 in Bhutan, and others who had passed class ten in good schools in India. These latter students didn't especially want to go to Sherubtse. They had been conditioned to believe that they were already attending the best schools, and didn't look favourably on a school in Bhutan.

But a more tangible consideration was the matter of perks at the posh Indian schools. There, being outside of Bhutan, students had received travel allowance and pocket money. They were also used to good food and a good life generally. They were the elite of Bhutan, and they rubbed shoulders with the elite high school students of India.

By mid-year there were problems.

The new students complained about pocket money, food and their routine. Father Mackey was vehemently opposed to the idea of pocket money and, anyway, had none to give. He received the same food stipend for each student, fifty-six rupees per month (approximately seven dollars), and this allowed no broadening of the diet. As to the routine, the class elevens called themselves "collegians" and wanted special privileges. Father Mackey said: "As far as I'm concerned, there are no special privileges. We follow one routine and where we have the number we follow the number." Class eleven numbered about forty students out of more than 300 on campus. "I'm not making any exceptions for forty kids."

Some of the students, however, came from important families, and their complaints went high up. In July, Nado Rinchen, the education department head, brought a group of officials to Sherubtse to look into the problem. They arrived unannounced and said they'd come to discuss whether or not to continue the College.

Father Mackey told them it was their choice, but if they stopped the College, they'd never start again. He suggested a meeting with the collegians. They could tell their side of the story and he'd give his.

The Jesuit, the officials, and all class-eleven students gathered in the large library room. Only about half a dozen students were complaining — mainly those from St. Paul's in Darjeeling, and from big families in Thimphu. First, they said they wanted much better food.

Father Mackey admitted that the food was not the greatest, but said: "If you give me the ordinary stipend, I can't buy extra food. Every cent I get for food is spent on food. They get solid food: they get good rice, they get dhal, they get vegetables, and maybe once a month or so they get some meat."

A student said, "We want meat every day."

"You give me the money," Father Mackey said, "and you'll get meat every day. But I can't give it to you on the present stipend." The argument went back and forth a bit, and Father Mackey said to Nado Rinchen, "If you want meat, you give me the money and they'll get meat." And then to the students, "How about vegetables?"

"We don't get vegetables."

"Oh?" Father Mackey responded, "Every meal, at noon and in the evening you either get *saag* or you get potatoes."

"*Saag* is grass, that's not a vegetable."

"Okay. What about potatoes?"

"We don't want potatoes."

Father Mackey turned to the officials again, "What am I going to get? Give me the money." He paused, and then said, "Okay, you get that settled."

He felt he got his point across.

Then came the issue of a special routine and he said, "Look, I've got over 300 kids in the high school and to make a special concession for forty kids . . . no, I can't do that. They follow the mob."

Finally came the matter of pocket money. Father Mackey said, "I refuse to give pocket money. If these kids have to be paid to come to school, then I don't think much of them."

They said, "We got it in Darjeeling."

"So you got it in Darjeeling. The other three hundred kids are quite happy here not being paid." Turning to the officials, he said, with a shrug, "If you want to pay the kids . . . I'm not paying the kids."

And he left the meeting.

After the two-hour discussion, six of the students refused to remain at the College. Nado Rinchen and the others came to Father Mackey. He said, "Well, get rid of them. If there are six guys, get rid of them."

After further discussion, these students were sent home. But pocket money remained an issue. Father Mackey said, "Dasho, I will not give pocket money."

Jigme Thinley, one of the officials, said, "Let's leave that pending. We'll go back and talk with the people higher up. And if they insist . . .?"

"If I get a direct order from higher authority, I'll give it," Father Mackey said. "But otherwise it will be over my dead body. I'm not in favour of giving money. We're lowering our standard of education if we have to pay kids to come to school."

Eventually, the senior students were granted pocket money.

* * *

While at Sherubtse, and through no fault of his own, Father Mackey once again got embroiled with Indian authorities. This happened in 1976, when Father Robins, the science teacher, came back from Hazaribagh in India after completing the last few months of his spiritual training.

In anticipation of Father Robins' return, Father Mackey had written to the Indian Embassy in Thimphu for a permit allowing the Jesuit back into Bhutan. He was expected in June, and the request specified the crossing date at Samdrup Jongkhar as the 20th of June. In early May, Father Mackey sent some mail with someone going to Darjeeling, which was quicker. He included a letter to Father Robins, care of Father Van Walleghem. As the letter came hand-delivered, Father Van thought, "This must be very important, sent by personal runner" — and he opened it.

He read the letter, which was dated early May, and which said to Father Robins, "Please be at Rangia station on the 20th [no month specified]. A jeep and permit will be waiting for you." Father Van looked at the calendar. The 20th (of May) was just a few days away! He got on the phone to Hazaribagh and told Father Robins to leave for Rangia immediately.

Father Robins arrived at Rangia on the 20th of May and found no jeep and no permit. He shrugged and got on a bus, knowing he probably wouldn't be checked. Sure enough, he passed through the Indian check-post and, once in Bhutan, had no problem. He proceeded to Kanglung.

Meanwhile, Father Mackey had been in Thimphu. He almost fell over when he arrived back to find Father Robins. "My God, what are you doing here?"

Father Mackey sent a wireless message to the education department and to Dawa Tshering, who was now foreign minister: "Robins in Bhutan without permit. Letter follows. Kindly clarify with India House."

The attitude in Thimphu was, "Ah, it's already gone two weeks, forget about it. India House doesn't know what's happening in Eastern Bhutan."

That may have been true, but it happened that Father Robins, keen to get back into the swing of things, had immediately requested educational films available through India House. He wrote to the First Secretary, who happened to be the official who also signed the permits, and who had just signed Father Robins' permit the morning he received the letter requesting the films. He said, "Wait a minute, now."

As Father Mackey says, "All hell broke loose!"

Father Robins was ordered out of the country. Father Mackey pleaded: "For heaven's sake, he's the only physics man we've got. Class ten are writing their physics and they've missed a couple of months already. Let him stay until the end of the year. As soon as exams are over, I'll be going down to Gauhati and we'll go together." With a lot of persuasion from the education department and Lyonpo (Minister) Dawa Tshering, India House granted the request.

On the thirteenth of December, a farewell lunch was held for Father Robins, and that afternoon he, Brother Quinn and Father Mackey left for Samdrup Jongkhar. They spent the night in the border town and rose early the next morning. After a quick breakfast of tea and cookies at five in the morning, they set off in Father Mackey's jeep with Prem, his driver.

A three-hour ride would get them to Gauhati. Father Mackey and Brother Quinn had tickets and reservations for the flight from Gauhati to Calcutta later that morning. Father Robins had a train reservation. As this was likely to be his last chance, he wanted to see as much of India as possible, and had chosen to travel to New Delhi by train. It was pleasantly cool in the growing light as they crossed the Bhutan border.

A couple of kilometres into Assam they forded a river, beyond which was the Indian frontier post. Here, at the Foreigner's Check Post, three jeeps sat waiting. The Indian police knew their travel plans from the information provided on the transit permit application, and knew the Jesuits would enter India early that day. They stopped the vehicle and asked for papers. The Jesuits showed their passports and permits. The police looked from one priest to another. And although the four men fit comfortably into the jeep, the police said, "Your jeep is crowded. We'll take him with us," indicating Father Robins.

Father Mackey said, "No, no, we're fine. There's no problem at all."

The policeman in charge, said firmly, "No. We'll take him," and escorted Father Robins to his jeep. He was, after all, the major criminal of the bunch. The attitude of the Jesuits was a mixture of humour and irritation. They all had experience with Indian officials and knew what to expect. They presented an air of innocence to the police, and while they couldn't help being irritated, they were men of good humour and made jokes back and forth.

One police jeep led the way, with Father Robins sitting in the back. Father Mackey's jeep came next, and the other two police jeeps brought up the rear in the little convoy. Halfway to Rangia, they stopped briefly at the police station at Kumarikata. No doubt they were communicating the fact that they had the criminals in hand and were heading for Gauhati.

Once in Gauhati, the police went neither to the train station nor to the airport, but to what looked like police headquarters — a big building. The Jesuits appeared to be under arrest. Armed guards escorted them to two different offices — Father Robins was put in one, the other two in another — where the accusations began. The officers demanded that each of the Jesuits sign a confession that he had broken Indian law. The police were also under the strong misapprehension that all three were going back to Canada.

Father Mackey asked, "Hm? What Indian law have I broken?" He looked at the sour-faced officer and pointed at his permit. "This is a permit issued by the Indian Ambassador to Bhutan, signed and stamped by him in Thimphu. It allows me to proceed on this day from Samdrup Jongkhar to Calcutta via Gauhati. To fly down and then come back on a certain date. It's all approved and stamped."

The policeman couldn't refute this, but maintained, "You must write a confession."

"I'm not going to write anything. What am I going to write? I haven't broken any law."

Brother Quinn took the same position. Father Robins was not quite so genuinely innocent, but he said, "Well, as far as I know I haven't actually broken any Indian law. I got an order from Bhutan, there was a misunderstanding, but I got an order and I was obeying orders. There was a mistake made but that's been cleared up in Thimphu. I didn't really break any law, so you people sort it out."

The Jesuits were brought together, and the officer in charge was visibly angry. He was stumped. It was true that the three had proper documents. But he had obviously been told that they were all going to

Canada, and that he should detain them and get confessions. He left the room and his prisoners.

Policemen with rifles stood guard outside.

While the officer was out, his phone rang and somebody stepped in to answer it. The officer was called to the phone. After answering in English, he paused, glanced at his prisoners, then spoke in Bengali. Father Mackey knew enough Bengali to follow the conversation. It appeared that the officer had tried to reach someone higher up in Calcutta or Delhi, and this person was now calling him back. The subject was obviously the Jesuits.

Father Mackey piped in: "Hey, if that's about us, I've got a ticket here. I want to get on that plane to Calcutta. Here's the ticket" — and he riffled the ticket in front of the officer. The Jesuits had been having difficulty convincing the police that only Father Robins was returning to Canada, and that Father Mackey and Brother Quinn were travelling only to Calcutta and returning to Bhutan in less than four weeks.

The officer growled something inaudible. And he got no satisfaction from his superior on the phone. He sat looking at the Jesuits: he in his clean, neat khaki uniform, them in clean, neat but casual civilian clothes.

All of a sudden, Father Mackey and Brother Quinn found themselves saying hurried goodbyes to Father Robins as they were hustled off into a flying-squad jeep and rushed to the airport, red lights flashing and siren howling. They were assured that Father Robins would be on his train. At Gauhati airport they were late, but the police escorted them through check-in, security and right out to the plane. They were on their way to Calcutta.

But it wasn't over yet. Leaving the plane in Calcutta, Father Mackey and Brother Quinn were met by more police and taken to the anti-hijacking department of Calcutta airport. The office is a glass room inside a large outer area, and the two Jesuits were brought inside this glass cage. Police took their passports and permits and went outside to examine them. Father Mackey and Brother Quinn watched as the officers passed the documents back and forth.

A new man would come along, look at the documents, look through the glass at the prisoners, give the documents back to the first officer and leave. This was repeated a number of times. Nobody could find anything wrong. Why had they been told to detain these men? Mid-day came and went. Brother Quinn needed to answer a call of nature. The ex-Mountie said to the guard, in his soft but authoritative voice, "I want to go to the bathroom," and raised his six-foot, two-inch frame to its full height.

The guard got permission and, as he obviously intended to escort Brother Quinn to the washroom, the Jesuit boomed, "I'm old enough to go to the bathroom myself!" But the guard insisted and went with Brother Quinn, rifle and all.

The airport police realized that something was wrong with the order they had received. The Jesuits' papers were completely in order. So, in the early afternoon, the police let them go, more or less. Father Mackey was about to get a taxi, but a policeman said, "No, no, we have a taxi here," and pointed to an aged Ambassador sedan some distance away from the taxi rank.

"Okay, if you've got a taxi, bring the taxi." Father Mackey and Brother Quinn remained chipper. It was obviously an unmarked police car with a driver that looked very much like a policeman. But they still had to pay him forty rupees when they arrived at St. Xavier's in downtown Calcutta. And they still had a plain-clothes policeman as their escort.

It was after two o'clock when they arrived, siesta time, and St. Xavier's was quiet. But Father Mackey and Brother Quinn knew the routines. They put their bags into the small elevator and stepped in themselves. Their police escort tried to squeeze in too. This was too much for Brother Quinn. He got out, slammed the elevator door and said, "I'm walking!"

The policeman decided to stick with Father Mackey.

The person in charge of rooms, "Father Minister," the Minister of the house, was having his after-lunch snooze in his room, which was very near the library. Father Mackey took a magazine from the library and sat down where he could keep an eye on Father Minister's door. And every time he glanced up, he could also see that his guard was still on duty. Finally Father Minister came out, "Ah, Father Mackey, good to see you," and he got keys for the rooms.

Father Mackey settled in and cleaned up, then went down for tea. All the while, the policeman on duty hung around in the hall. About four o'clock, while Father Mackey and Brother Quinn were drinking tea and chatting with their colleagues, one of the Jesuits came in and said, "Hey, the police are looking for you."

Father Mackey went out. Another policeman had arrived and he said, "We have to go to Lower Circular Road." The police station in Lower Circular Road housed a security section that looked after foreigners' activities, permits and the like.

"Why?"

"We have to go to Lower Circular Road. And bring Brother Quinn."

Father Mackey went back and said to Brother Quinn, "Get your papers, Mike. We're off to the police station."

Brother Quinn groaned and went back to his room. Father Mackey got his own papers and joined the police at the front door. They waited for Brother Quinn, but he didn't come.

Brother Quinn was staying in the College section, which had its own exit onto the street. Directly across the street was Park Street police station, with a big sign over the door. Brother Quinn had crossed the street, walked in and said, "What do you want now?"

It took a while to sort things out, but the two Jesuits found themselves in a Black Maria — a black caged police vehicle big enough to hold a gang of hardened criminals — heading for Lower Circular Road. Once there, they again went through the whole rigmarole. Documents taken, examined, handed on to someone else. Their papers were taken upstairs.

The policeman who stayed with them was an Anglo-Indian Catholic and he tried to play down the whole thing. "Father, it's just red tape. I saw your papers and there's nothing wrong. But these guys have to get permission here, permission there, you know."

They chatted amiably for nearly two hours, and then he was called upstairs. He came back shortly and said: "Everything's okay, there's no problem, stay in Calcutta. But when you're going back, we'd like to be informed."

The two Jesuits said no problem and went back to St. Xavier's, finally free from police surveillance.

But their adventure was not over.

The day before flying back to Gauhati, they notified the police at Lower Circular Road, as promised. They also told the police they would be going out to the airport that same afternoon and staying in the airport retiring rooms that night. This was much simpler than getting up before dawn and trying to get a taxi in time for their early morning departure. At the airport they went to get a room. They looked for the fellow they'd dealt with before, but they were directed to another spot a few metres away. "See over there? You go over there."

"Over there" were two men who, despite their civilian clothes, looked a lot like policemen — short hair and the military bearing. These men seemed unsure of procedures, but insisted that the only room available was room number five, an air-conditioned room. Air-conditioned rooms were more expensive and at this time of year, January, the natural temperature is perfect in Calcutta. Father Mackey said they didn't want an air-conditioned room. But they had no choice. They were escorted to "left luggage," where they checked their larger bags, and then up to their room. Father Mackey asked for the key.

"Oh — no key."

"Hm? What's the matter with the key?"

"There's no key. You won't need one. No, no key."

"Okay, no key," and they went into their room and got settled.

Then Father Mackey decided to visit the book shop.

Outside the room the escort asked, "Where are you going?"

"I'm going to get some books."

"Oh, I'll escort you."

"I know the way. You don't have to come."

"No, no, I'll escort you."

"Very good, come along," and Father Mackey led the way to the bookshop. Once there, he said to himself, "This guy's going to wait." He browsed and browsed and browsed, and finally he bought a couple of books.

At six-thirty, as both Jesuits lounged on their beds reading, the door opened. It was the changing of the guard. A new face appeared in the doorway and looked at them. Brother Quinn said, "Father, we're receiving very maternal care this evening."

The door slammed shut.

As they washed up for dinner, Father Mackey said, "Okay Mike, let's make this guy suffer." It was a little past seven as they walked to the airport dining room on the mezzanine floor. It was a good place to eat. Once inside, Father Mackey said, "Let's sit near the door and make that guy stand out there where we can see him."

They would watch the watcher. They strung out the meal, ordering a drink and a snack, and then an appetizer. At eight o'clock they ordered dinner, and then they savoured it. About nine they finished up with a coffee. Their guard stood outside the glass panelling the whole time, watching them.

Early next morning, when they started to go for their bags, the guard said, "Don't bother, we'll get your bags," and took their baggage checks. A porter was sent for the bags. At least they didn't have to pay for this, although it's doubtful the porter got paid.

The police escorted the Jesuits through check-in and into the departures lounge. Besides the six-thirty flight to Gauhati, they could see two other planes on the tarmac, preparing to take off. Six-thirty went by and the other two planes took off. An announcement said the Gauhati flight would be delayed. When asked, one of the escorts said it was engine trouble. But the Jesuits could see no mechanics working on the plane. An hour went by, then another. People read their newspapers a second and a third time. Finally, about nine o'clock, passengers were cleared for boarding.

At Gauhati, the Jesuits were met by a Bhutanese policeman, Ugyen Tenzin. He said, "I've been here for hours. What happened?" Father Mackey described the morning's events in Calcutta. "Oh," he said, "that explains all this running around and people coming and going."

Ugyen Tenzin, who had been a student of Father Mackey, had witnessed a flurry of police activity around the airport.

From Calcutta, Father Mackey had written to his old friend Tamji Jagar, the home minister, outlining what had happened during their trip. Now the home minister was in Samdrup Jongkhar and wanted to see Father Mackey while he was in the neighbourhood. He had sent Ugyen Tenzin to pick him up and bring him to lunch. It was getting late and Ugyen Tenzin wanted to get moving.

Father Mackey's driver Prem was also at the airport, so they gave him the baggage checks, and left him to take care of things. Father Mackey and Brother Quinn jumped into Ugyen Tenzin's jeep and they tore off. Confusion ensued as the Indian police tried to figure out what was happening. They had been watching Father Mackey's jeep and driver. Now they realized that Father Mackey was leaving in the Bhutanese police jeep.

Two Indian police jeeps roared after them. Ugyen Tenzin looked back: "Ah, they're with us, okay. Well, they're going to have to drive fast, because I'm going to drive like mad."

Roaring at full throttle down the highway, and then bumping along the secondary road that turned off at Rangia, Ugyen Tenzin left the Indian police far behind. At the Indian frontier post, the barrier blocked the road. They had to stop, and the border official seemed to drag out the formalities of entering the Jesuits' names in the big book kept to register foreigners, and then to stamp their permits and passports. He knew Ugyen Tenzin, who said, "Look, we're in a hurry!"

The official just said, "Yes, yes, yes," and found more things to do. Finally the Indian police jeeps appeared. A signal was given, and the chase was on again. In the four kilometres between the Indian check-post and the Bhutanese border, Ugyen Tenzin lost the Indians again. Immediately inside the border, just before the Bhutanese barrier, a small road led off to the left. Ugyen Tenzin went this way, directly to his house, and explained, "Father, I have to get dressed for lunch."

Father Mackey said, "That's okay, we'll walk over to the guest house."

A few minutes later, the Indian police pulled up at the Bhutan border barrier. The officer asked, "Where's Father Mackey?"

"I don't know," the Bhutanese border guard replied.

"But he's crossed in here."

"No."

"He must have!" the Indian policeman insisted.

"No, Father Mackey did not pass through this gate," the Bhutanese guard answered with careful honestly. The Indian police turned around and drove back slowly.

At lunch, the home minister insisted on hearing all the details of the story.

Several months later, Father Mackey was driving up towards Yonphula one day when he met an Indian police jeep heading to Kanglung. On the narrow road, Father Mackey was easily recognized and waved down. A senior police officer got out to speak to him. He asked a lot of questions about what had happened on the trip to Calcutta and back.

Obviously, the home minister had taken up the matter with the Indian authorities and wanted an explanation for what was seen as very bad treatment of highly-regarded residents of Bhutan. This man had been sent to investigate the matter and would report back in person to the home minister. Father Mackey answered the officer's questions and said: "Somebody made a mistake. Don't ask me who it was, but somebody made a mistake. We were held up, delayed. They weren't disrespectful but the guy got the wrong information. There's no problem as far as I'm concerned."

As for Father Robins, he made it back to the U.S. in time for Christmas. He avoided the Indian authorities for a number of years, but ended up working in Nepal. Nowadays he passes through India without problem.

* * *

Throughout his tenure at Sherubtse, Father Mackey enjoyed the full support of His Late Majesty and then the present King, as well as Dawa Tshering and Ashi Dechen, the young King's sister. Ashi Dechen, when she was just seventeen years old, had been appointed as the King's representative in the ministry of development. This position, which continued when her younger brother assumed the throne, was a major responsibility. In 1972, when Dawa Tshering moved from being minister of development to foreign minister, it was tantamount to being minister of development.

At one point Ashi Dechen wrote Father Mackey a letter saying, "You have full permission to do whatever you think is good for the country." He made much use of this letter. Whenever an official in the education department or elsewhere appeared to be baulking at a request, Father Mackey would pull out this letter. Usually, it produced results.

The letter came in handy as the old ways passed away and bureaucratic red tape started to slow the efforts of freewheelers like Father Mackey. In Tashigang and the early days of Sherubtse, the Jesuit could do pretty well everything he wanted, on his own, or just by checking with his friends at the Dzong. For tougher problems, he had his ally Dawa Tshering in Thimphu. Father Mackey's talents, the needs of education in Eastern Bhutan and the uncomplicated system fit together perfectly to get the job done and provide the Jesuit with great satisfaction and joy.

Things changed in the mid-seventies. The upgrading of Sherubtse to junior college status, for example, brought problems like the demands of the disgruntled half-dozen class-eleven students in 1976. And as the changing times brought less freedom of action, Father Mackey also realized that he was happier with school than with college. But he carried on.

By the mid-seventies, department of education officials had begun to think that Sherubtse was no longer a place for lower classes. The school now had the image of a junior college that might offer degree programmes in the near future. Father Mackey was unaware of this thinking. And while he was perhaps not overjoyed with the higher classes, he was happy enough to be running Sherubtse.

He did hear rumours that the school at Tashigang (now downgraded to a junior high school) might be moved to Khaling, thirty-two kilometres further south along the road from Kanglung. Tashigang school had been all right as a small school, stuck on the side of a steep hillside as it was, but the pressure of student numbers and the lack of space for expansion as the town grew became a chronic problem.

Father Mackey knew Khaling, once a sheep farm, as a cold, wet, miserable place. But the moving of Tashigang school did not involve him and he took little interest. He'd also heard talk of the establishment of another school, but Father Mackey assumed he'd be carrying on at Sherubtse for some time.

But by 1977, he had learned that Khaling would be the site of an entirely new school, not just Tashigang Junior High transplanted. Furthermore, this would be a high school started with the lower classes from Sherubtse. Sherubtse would concentrate on being a college, but keep classes nine and ten for now. This worried Father Mackey. Just what did the future hold for him? College was not his cup of tea, but he didn't care for the idea of moving to Khaling.

He wrote to Ashi Dechen, making the rather audacious suggestion that, as the college really only comprised two classes (eleven and twelve), why not move the college to Khaling and keep Sherubtse as a high school? This time Ashi Dechen was neither positive and compliant nor particularly gentle in her response. Father Mackey recalls the letter he got back as being "a bit of a stinker." In plain language, it said: No.

Ashi Dechen wanted Father Mackey to stay on as principal of Sherubtse and have Father Coffey head up the new school in Khaling. After considering the situation, even with the unattractiveness of the Khaling site, Father Mackey decided to move with the school. And heaved a sigh of relief: "Thank God I'm getting out of this."

He quickly got involved in the building going on at Khaling, especially to get the sports facilities he wanted. At this school, in addition to a good football field, he wanted a covered basketball court.

20/

The terrain of Bhutan makes for significant climate variation within small areas. Some is due simply to altitude, but mountain ridges and valleys also alter the climate. Tashigang is hot because of its elevation, and the surrounding hills are relatively dry because of the lay of the land. Kanglung is cool because of its altitude, but it gets lots of sun and has a moderate rainy season.

Khaling is cool partly because of its altitude, but the surrounding mountains also dictate plenty of cloud and rain. Outside the monsoon season, when most of its neighbouring communities are sunny, Khaling tends to be, as Father Mackey puts it, "cold, wet and miserable." Leeches thrive in the dampness and can be picked up even in the campus grass. Khaling had been a sheep farm and seemed well suited to that purpose. Better for that than a school, according to Father Mackey.

But in 1978, he and Brother Quinn moved to Jigme Sherubling High School. The word *sherab* can be translated as "knowledge" or "learning" and *ling* is generally a "pleasant, self-contained place." Father Mackey translates Sherubling (or Sherabling) as "place of learning." *Jigme* means "fearless," but probably became part of the name in honour of the late King.

The school was intended to accommodate classes 6, 7 and 8 in the first year. But because of a shortage of room in southern schools, Father Mackey also received a class nine made up of students from Southern Bhutan.

At first, the two Jesuits lived in small houses near the present-day gymnasium, as Dantak officers were living in the small bungalow they would have later. This was at the top end of the campus, where the hillside grew steeper, and overlooked the school and the valley. Inside were a small dining room-reception room, two bedrooms and a tiny kitchen. Later, the Jesuits built a separate kitchen outside. A larger house was built for the Sisters, on their own design. It was a two-storey building with good-sized bedrooms, a large dining area and a large chapel. Quarters were also built for the rest of the staff.

Khaling did not have much of a town site, and still doesn't. There were a couple of shops on the main road where the bus would stop, and a few houses. But the rest of the community was scattered. There was no post office, no wireless station, and no telephone. The way the postal system worked could be annoying. The mail was carried on a bus that passed right through the town, just below the school, but outgoing mail was collected only by the bus going up to Tashigang.

There the mail was sorted and sent on — even mail for Samdrup Jongkhar and beyond. And because of the timing and logistics, a letter destined for Wamrong, about an hour's drive south of Khaling, would take three days. When the opportunity presented itself, mail or messages would be sent with anybody who might be travelling, but traffic was light on that road.

For some time, the nearest wireless station was Tashigang. If a message for Khaling arrived at Tashigang post office before four o'clock, it would be sent down on the next day's bus. Otherwise, it would take an extra day.

As at Sherubtse, a diesel generator supplied electricity. Dantak had brought one while building Jigme Sherubling, and left it to the school. As this generator was quite old, Father Mackey decided to get a new one from Tashi Commercial Corporation in Phuntsholing, the largest commercial enterprise in the country (owned by Ugyen "Rimp" Dorji).

He ordered it through the department of education, which paid for it. It arrived on a truck and was set up by the experienced generator man, an Indian chap who had been running the old generator. The new machine ran, but gave some trouble. Father Mackey wondered at this: "We shouldn't have trouble with a brand new generator."

Brother Nick, working at his training and research farm, had a Dutch volunteer working with him, a trained mechanic. He came down and looked at the faulty generator, and said: "This is not a new machine."

"Well, I bought it as a new machine."

The mechanic took out his pocket knife, scraped off the shiny paint and found two layers underneath. The bottom layer indicated that the generator was obviously an old machine. Father Mackey was furious. He blasted off a message to Tashi stores (as it was called). The people there insisted they'd sent a new one from Phuntsholing.

When Father Mackey complained to the department, they said, "Oh, don't worry about it. These things happen."

He never did solve this particular mystery. And he was left with two old, run-down machines.

The school had no telephone and Father Mackey pressed for one, as the Dantak line ran right through Khaling. In addition to conveying his own messages, he would be able to keep up on other news, as the line was just like one long party line. But he was refused for years, and the only option available in an emergency was to climb a telephone pole and tap into the line. This was possible because the main Dantak camp at Gomchu, a few kilometres up the road, included a telephone line repair crew.

One rainy evening, when Father Mackey and Brother Quinn were working in their quarters, they noticed that the lights had not come on when they usually did. Father Mackey looked out the door and saw that none of the school lights were on. He waited and waited, but still no lights. He called to Sonam, one of the servants, "Where's that darned generator man?"

A few minutes later, Sonam came back white and breathless to report: "He's hanging from a beam!"

Father Mackey got Brother Quinn and they ran through the rain to the generator house. Perhaps the man wasn't dead. Maybe they could revive him. They cut him down and Brother Quinn tried to resuscitate the lifeless body. But it was no use. The man was dead.

Father Mackey got Prem, his driver, and set out in the jeep for Gomchu. He found the telephone repairman and told him what had happened: "I have to call Tashigang." The telephone man drove them to Barshong, a tiny village on a mountain spur a few kilometres further up the road. There the telephone line passes very close to the roadway.

With the rain still pouring down, the man climbed the pole and connected a handset to the line. He got through to Tashigang and handed the phone to the Jesuit. Father Mackey got the message through for the Dzongdag and the police, and returned to Khaling.

These nights he was sleeping in what he called the "box room," a small room within the boy's dormitory. There was no telling when the police would show up, so Father Mackey went to bed, leaving the outside dormitory door locked. He was fast asleep when the police arrived around eleven that night. When they asked for the principal, they were sent to the dormitory.

They knocked and then pounded on the door, but Father Mackey was in the far end and heard nothing. As for the boys, they had heard that the generator man had hung himself, and had no intention of opening the door in the middle of the night. The death meant a devil or at least a ghost was floating around the campus, and they weren't going to let that in. Father Mackey slept peacefully through the night's investigation.

Brother Quinn, on the other hand, was harangued and admonished. The police found him in his quarters and bawled him out: "Why did you cut it down?"

As an ex-Mountie, Brother Quinn understood police interests, but he said, "You and your crazy rules. If I can save a life, I'll save a life. I didn't know whether there was any life in him or not. There's only one way to find out and that was to put him on the ground and work on him. I tried for an hour or so, until he was cold, and then I stopped. Then we just left him there."

"But you shouldn't cut him down without the police!"

"That's your rules. I was a policeman for many years, and I was told to use my head."

The day after the late-night investigation, the students found a large hole dug near the bridge, where they often went to "swim" and play in the Jirichhu. When they asked about it, the police told them that the dead generator man would be buried there.

He was a Christian from Kerala. Trying to contact his family could take many days. It was warm in Khaling and hot down on the plains. Keeping the body or shipping it home was out of the question. As a Christian, the man should be buried, not cremated, so Dantak said: "Bury him and forget it. We'll send word to the family."

When Deda Tashi, the police chief from Tashigang, came to finalize the report, his two sons studying at Jigme Sherubling assailed him. "What are you doing, spoiling our swimming place? You put a dead body there! We're not going to swim there now, a *doen* might pull us into the river!"

He complained: "I didn't do it, it was Dantak!"

"No, you did it!" And they were right. Dantak had decided on burial, but the police chose the spot.

A week went by with no swimming, but the days grew hotter. Finally, it got too hot to worry about a dead body in the ground, and the boys returned to their swimming hole, jumping and splashing and yelling.

* * *

Father Mackey ran Jigme Sherubling as he had run Sherubtse. He established a library, stocked initially with books from Sherubtse. Father Leclaire, the new Sherubtse principal, agreed that his predecessor should take the books that were appropriate to the lower high-school classes moving to Khaling. Father Mackey built up the library with donations and purchases, and Brother Quinn carried on, as he had before, binding books when necessary.

As before, Father Mackey used student librarians, lab assistants, and so on. And he introduced all the programmes, including sports, concerts and plays, he'd pioneered at Kanglung and Tashigang. He tried to ensure that the school staged at least two functions each month.

Jigme Sherubling, however, was too far away from Tashigang to draw an audience from there. Occasionally, Dzong officials attended special events. The local community was invited to the shows, of course, and this new school was within walking distance of villages further south. Besides providing entertainment, school activities raised interest in education.

The constant activity kept most students from getting into trouble. But here, again, a few went astray, committing offences that varied from theft to uttering threats. The theft involved food from the kitchen. Each night the cooks would put out the supplies for early morning tea — tea leaves, sugar and milk powder — and quite frequently it wouldn't be there in the morning.

The room was secure. It was locked, albeit on the outside, with a padlock. At first, Father Mackey suspected the cooks, as they had the best opportunity. "You put the darned stuff out and you've got the key, so how does the stuff go? It doesn't just fly out the window."

They pleaded innocence and Father Mackey was inclined to believe them. Then he considered Bola, the sweeper, who had the lowest job on campus. Bola said, "No, no, it's not me!"

Again, Father Mackey gave him the benefit of the doubt.

The stealing went on for over a month and Father Mackey got fed up. He warned everyone around the kitchen, including Bola, that if it happened again, he'd get rid of the whole bunch of them.

A couple of nights later, Bola had a bout of diarrhoea that got him up and outside. While outside, he heard noise in the kitchen. He sneaked up and saw three boys. He could see their faces by the light of their flashlight, and he dashed off to wake Father Mackey. By the time Father Mackey arrived, the boys were back in their dormitory. He called them out. When they saw Bola, they realized how they'd been caught and wanted to kill him.

Father Mackey said: "Because of you, I wanted to fire the whole staff! Now, I'm not taking any nonsense. You three have until tomorrow morning. But by eight o'clock, you're off this property. I don't care where you go, pack your stuff and out you get!"

Next morning, all three came to plead for leniency. Two were class-nine boys. One was the son of a Bhutanese labour officer on the road works, a good friend of Father Mackey's. The second had come first in all of Bhutan in the previous year's class-eight exam, but he came from an extremely poor family. The third was a class-seven boy who should not have been in the class nine and ten dormitory. He was a rather useless fellow, "a real *badmash*," as Father Mackey described him, but the half-brother of one of the school's Bhutanese language teachers.

Their pleadings elicited an emphatic no from Father Mackey. He was outraged about the blatant theft, which had caused so much trouble and bad feeling. The boys disappeared. But next morning at ten o'clock, he spotted them on campus and flew into a fury. The youngest boy's half-brother, Lopen Tshewang, had taken them into his house, hoping that Father Mackey would soon relent.

The Jesuit rarely got really angry, but when he did it was something to see. His face would turn bright red and one could imagine steam coming from his ears and fire from his nostrils. He blasted Lopen Tshewang, who finally realized that there was no changing Father Mackey's mind.

While there was no way the boys were going to remain at Jigme Sherubling, Father Mackey did not cut off their education. The top student he sent with a letter to Father Miranda, who was now head of Punakha High School. He explained the situation and said, "He's a very clever kid, and a poor devil, but I can't bring him back here. I'd be most grateful if you could put him in Punakha." The boy was admitted and did well in his exams. He went on to enter the Indian National Defence Academy.

With Father Mackey's recommendation, the second boy got into Paro High School. The third boy had nothing to his credit worthy of the priest's intercession. He found work, but later ran afoul of the law and wound up in prison for smuggling.

Lopen Tshewang wouldn't speak to Father Mackey for nearly three weeks after this incident, but he was the one who took the hard line when a student named Pema became a new father. For quite some time, this boy had been visiting the School for the Blind, just below the high school and across the main road. He'd gotten involved with the daughter of the cook at the school, and she had given birth to Pema's child.

Pema was in class eight and had important exams coming up. Father Mackey thought to keep the matter quiet and let the boy carry on. In rural Bhutan, marriage is usually the simple acceptance that a man and woman are "married," with no ceremony, and they co-habit from that point on. In this case, everyone concerned accepted the situation and said nothing about it. But then the *lopens* picked up the story, and Lopen Tshewang took a very righteous position: "This cannot be accepted!"

"Okay, Lopen, but what to do? He's class eight, we must let him write his exams."

"No! He must be thrown out!"

This time Father Mackey had to recognize that his opponent would not be dissuaded. Once Lopen Tshewang dug in his heels, nothing would move him. Father Mackey called the boy and said, "Get your things, we're going to Tashigang."

At Tashigang, he explained the situation to the headmaster, promising that if Pema passed his year, he'd get him back in at Khaling. Pema did well at Tashigang, both academically and in sports, setting up his own gymnastic team.

The class eight exams were held at Khaling that year and Pema passed. Father Mackey sent a private note to Parsuram Sharma, the man in charge of the board of examinations, saying, "I'd be grateful if you could send this boy to Jigme Sherubling for class nine."

When Lopen Tshewang learned that Pema was returning to Khaling, he inquired. Father Mackey, with a look of angelic innocence, said, "Lopen, the department is sending him here. I can't say no. They know about the case, because I reported it." He didn't say to whom, or how he'd reported it. "If it's been reported, and if the government sends him back, I can't turn him away."

The boy did well, completed class ten, and, with Father Mackey's help, went on to become a teacher: "It's often the scoundrels who turn out to be the good people, so you help them."

* * *

Father Mackey faced a similar problem when one of the Sisters told him that somebody had been in the "box room" upstairs in the girls' dormitory. This room, like the one in which Father Mackey often slept in the senior boys' dormitory, was occupied by a servant girl. One of the Sisters slept downstairs near the dormitory entrance.

Father Mackey inspected the room and deduced that whoever was coming in had used high-school science. A boy could climb up the large plumbing pipes on the outside of the building, but should have been prevented from entering by half-inch iron bars across the windows. But a pair of bars on the girl's window had been bent apart far enough to allow a boy to squeeze through. The discolouration on the horizontal bars and the wax on the window sill showed that the boy had heated the bars with a candle. When the night-time lover left the girl's room, the bars could be turned so they appeared normal to a casual observer.

Father Mackey was not terribly concerned about the situation, but the Sisters were adamant. The culprit had to be found and expelled. The Jesuit used some investigative science. He'd heard a class-nine boy called the "second-storey man," and put two and two together. A few days later, he called this "second-storey man" into his office. He said, "I'm afraid you're on your way out. We know what's been going on. The boys have known about it, but I didn't get it from them. We knew someone was getting in and I was pretty sure who it was. Now, you probably didn't notice when you went in last night, but we had some white powder spread around, to see if we could get a footprint. In fact, there's probably still a bit left on your shoes now."

The boy cast a guilty look down at his shoes.

This boy was the son of Father Mackey's driver, Prem, who was away in Thimphu. When Prem got back and learned what had happened, he was furious. Father Mackey said, "Prem, if something like this happens, I have to step in. There's no waffling on this one. He's out. If I let him come back in, I'd lose Sister Leonard. Mother Peter would step in and that would be the end of the Sisters. And I don't think your son is worth losing three Sisters, so we have to get rid of him."

As in nearly every other case, the boy continued in another school and went on to complete his class ten.

* * *

The most serious discipline problem Father Mackey ever faced involved a young Anglo-Indian teacher named John. He had been referred by his old colleague, Father Stanford in Darjeeling. Coming from a broken home, John had been raised mainly by the Sisters, who had paid for him to go to good schools in the Darjeeling area, including North Point.

But he had some kind of a breakdown and may have been on illicit drugs. At Jigme Sherubling he was a fairly good teacher when he was "on," but when he wasn't, according to Father Mackey, he was childish and would sometimes do strange things. Father Mackey described him as "queer," meaning strange.

John often had difficulty controlling study period, at which every teacher had to take a regular turn. So Father Mackey was not surprised one evening when he came running up to the Fathers' mess, where Father Mackey was eating, and said: "The boys won't obey me. They're causing trouble in the study. Will you come down?"

As they left the mess, the young teacher asked, "Do you want me to come in?"

"No, that's not necessary. You can go on down and relax. I'll take care of this."

The first part of evening study was a reading period, where the boys read their library books. It was normally a very peaceful time. About forty-five minutes into the study period, the little boys would be sent off to bed and the older boys would stay on to do homework. This evening, apparently, just before the little boys were sent off, something had happened.

As soon as Father Mackey stepped into the study hall, the room went silent. But the priest did nothing. He didn't even dismiss the small boys, and by now it was their bed time. Forty-five minutes later, when the older boys were normally dismissed, he still did nothing. The boys worked in silence and Father Mackey walked up and down the rows.

By this time the smaller boys were falling asleep. If a little boy was asleep as Father Mackey approached, an older boy would give him a dig in the ribs. The little boy would sit up in a daze and then slump back into sleep. Father Mackey said nothing. Finally, everyone was sleepy and he sent the boys off to their dormitories. He knew their excitement was completely dulled and there would be no talking or fooling around that night.

Father Mackey left it at that. He didn't know what had happened and didn't much care. He believed in letting a teacher solve his own problems. If John needed more help, he could come to Father Mackey, but he didn't.

End-of-term exams were coming up and everyone was preparing for them. Then, as exams were about to start, John came to Father Mackey and said he wanted to go to Thimphu. Father Mackey told him he could go if his English exam papers were ready. The exams would be given and Father Mackey would collect the completed papers. John could correct them when he returned.

Father Mackey knew something was up. He went to discuss it with Lopen Ngawang, the assistant principal, who said: "Father, he's cracked. He was telling the other teachers that he wanted to change schools."

Next day, Father Mackey sent a wireless message to education headquarters. He said that John was coming to Thimphu, and asked that he be transferred to another school, as he had been causing problems. When John reached Thimphu and asked for a transfer, the director of education immediately agreed.

John asked about getting his belongings.

"Don't worry, we'll have them sent to you. You report to your new school."

John never returned to Jigme Sherubling.

This left Father Mackey with the problem of John's unmarked exams. Everybody had a heavy load, so he decided to mark the papers himself. There were four of them, two papers each from classes seven and eight. One of the class seven students had written an essay entitled, "Three Dangerous Boys."

As Father Mackey read it through, he realized that it was based on a real incident. He was sure of the identity of two of the boys, and saw that he faced a serious disciplinary problem that had to be dealt with as soon as possible.

The students had been given a long weekend to go home after writing exams. But they had to return for their marks and be present for National Day, which usually marked the end of the school year. Many of the smaller boys who lived far away stayed in the school because it wasn't worth while to go home for just a few days. Father Mackey sometimes used the little boys as a kind of information bureau. He chatted with them in the dormitory: "Hey, what about those three dangerous boys in class seven?" He had identified two of them, and so had an air of knowledge. The little boys confirmed his deduction and provided the third name.

The students came back on Monday. Tuesday morning on his way to the office, Father Mackey stopped at the student dining room and made an announcement: "The following three boys, please bring your books, your uniform and report to the office." Everyone knew what that meant. The three boys were on their way out.

Father Mackey had prepared a letter for each of them. The letter, to their parents, explained what had happened — that they had attacked a teacher — and said that, by way of a warning, the boys were being sent home for two weeks. At the end of that period, the parents were to bring the boys back and Father Mackey would lay down conditions for their re-entry into the school.

However the teacher had provoked them, the three boys had seriously threatened him. They had held *chowangs*, large knives with thirty-centimetre blades. Although students did not carry these at school, nearly everyone in rural Bhutan — men, women, even children — carry these for various purposes in a wooden sheath tucked in the tight belt everyone wears. And although it could be deduced that the teacher, acknowledged to be "cracked," had given the boys reason for anger, such a violent threat could not be tolerated.

The first boy came in, head down, picked up his letter and left. The second boy was similarly humble and subdued. But the third boy was defiant. He did not deserve punishment. He refused to take the letter. Father Mackey asked, "You don't want this?"

"No."

"Very good." Father Mackey put the letter down on the desk. From his desk drawer he withdrew a thick, soft-covered book that looked like a book of large coupons. It was a transfer certificate book. The boy knew what it was, everybody did. He was going to be transferred from Bhutan's best high school to God-knows-where.

Father Mackey started filling out the certificate: the boy's name, his father's name . . . The boy grabbed the letter, turned and hurried out.

The parents were to report with their boys on a Saturday morning. The first boy came back on the Friday night with his mother. Father Mackey had known the father, an ex-monk who had been known as the "*gelong rabjam*" having also been a *rabjam*. He had left the monastery, married and had a family, but had since died. This boy was a very intelligent student. From appearances, it was obvious he had been punished by his mother — an old-fashioned beating. And she was obviously very concerned and sincere when she said, "Father Mackey, his father is dead and he needs education. Without education he can't do anything. I'd be very, very grateful if you could keep him in the school."

"I'm not getting rid of him," Father Mackey replied. "I just wanted him to realize, and for you to realize, that this was a serious offence."

She was relieved, but said: "Father, you mentioned a *chowang*. He didn't have a *chowang*."

Father Mackey turned to the boy. "What did you have?"

"I had a compass."

There is no word in Sharchopkha for this mathematical instrument with its sharp point, and Father Mackey had difficulty explaining it to the mother. He managed to get the idea across to her. The boy was re-admitted to school and all was well. His mother left Father Mackey a bag of apples from her orchard.

The next morning, the second boy arrived with his father, a *drimpoen*, or sergeant-major, at the nearby army base at Yonphula. Again, the boy had received a beating, this one even worse than the first boy's. He slunk behind his father. The *drimpoen* said, also in Sharchopkha: "Father, I'm a *badmash*, I'm a difficult one, I'm a rascal. Three times I've been promoted to *drimpoen*. First time I was promoted, I did something wrong, down to the ranks. Worked my way up again, then back down to the ranks. Worked my way up again." He looked intently at Father Mackey and continued, "Father, you have full permission to do anything with this kid except kill him. Anything else, you can do what you like. And if he doesn't behave, he'll get it from me too."

So it was settled. Father Mackey knew his message had been received and the second boy was back in good standing at the school.

The rest of Saturday morning passed with no sign of the third boy. His father had also been a *drimpoen* in the army, but had been hired by Father Mackey years before to look after the food and run the kitchen at Sherubtse. The afternoon went by, and finally, about six in the evening, the boy and his father arrived in the College car. Having told them to be at the school by ten o'clock, Father Mackey was not in a conciliatory mood. The attitude of the boy's father didn't help. It was obvious that he cared not at all for the boy's welfare or education, but was concerned for his own reputation: "What are people going to think of me? My kid being thrown out of school?"

Father Mackey became angry. "I don't care about you. This is about your darned kid!"

The father took an arrogant stance and said, "Well, you can do what you like."

"Very good." But Father Mackey was still smouldering. "Come with me," and he led them to the class-six room. It had been fitted with a newfangled glass chalk board (painted black), which now had a small hole in it and a couple of cracks running from the hole. He went after the father: "Who did that? Your son. Last year. Throwing marbles. He wanted to see if he could break the thing. Well, if that's the kind of children you have, I don't want them around the school."

The boy stood uncomfortably through this tirade. But he no doubt remembered the day the offence had occurred. Father Mackey had come into the room and seen the broken glass. "Who broke that board?!!!"

The row of girls in the centre of the class was quick to inform: "He did!"

Father Mackey fetched his yak tail. Someone had taken Lopen Shing (his regular punishment stick), and he was substituting the hefty "handle" end of a real yak tail to administer corporal punishment. He called the boy to the front of the class, bent him over and lifted his *go*. The boy wore no underpants. Father Mackey gave him three good licks with the yak tail. The boy hardly felt the yak tail, all he could think of was the row of girls looking at his bare behind. He had been mortified.

Now, his father made a feeble attempt at lessening the more serious charges. "Father, he didn't have a *chowang*."

"Oh?" Father Mackey turned to the boy. "Did you have a *chowang*?"

"Wasn't mine."

"That's not my question. Did you have a *chowang*?"

"Wasn't mine."

"Did you have a *chowang* in your hand?!"

"Yes."

The exchange had taken place in Sharchopkha, so the boy's father understood. Father Mackey turned to him again. "Is this your son? Is this the way you train your children? To cheat and lie?"

Reasonably satisfied, Father Mackey ushered the father out and reinstated the boy. All three boys went on to college, graduated and joined the civil service.

21/

During his years in Eastern Bhutan, Father Mackey had little contact with other foreigners — Indians weren't considered "foreigners" — because so few were present. But the numbers did grow from zero when he arrived in 1963, to two dozen or so by the time he left Khaling twenty years later. The Norwegian Santal Mission had a leprosy hospital at Riserbu, about thirty kilometres south along the road to Samdrup Jongkhar. It also ran a basic health unit at Khaling. Another protestant mission ran the school for the blind.

Health services in the area were extremely limited. The government hospital at Tashigang could not really service the large and highly populated Tashigang Dzongkhag. Doctor Anayat had expended a lot of effort fighting leprosy, but it remained a scourge in Eastern Bhutan. The protestant organization called The Leprosy Mission set up a hospital in the neighbouring *dzongkhag* of Mongar, but with the limited transportation facilities this was not of much assistance to Tashigang.

Dantak had a hospital at Deothang, to the south, but that was primarily for their own personnel. So Father Mackey and his colleagues were happy to see the medical missionaries move into Tashigang Dzongkhag. The Riserbu hospital functioned as both leprosy and general hospital.

A few of the Protestant medical missionaries, however, were less enthusiastic about the Jesuits. They had a strong suspicion of Catholics, especially Jesuits, and questioned whether these priests were even Christians. This attitude was much less so in those who brought the Norwegian Santal Mission into Eastern Bhutan, Doctor Edel and Reverend Magnus

Haugstad, and a nurse, Asbjorg Fiske, who was the main health worker through the early years.

These people got along well with the Jesuits. And, in fact, with some effort on both sides, through mutual professional respect and joint Bible study sessions, the two communities developed good relations.

Father Mackey speaks in glowing terms of Miss Fiske (as she was called), who worked tirelessly for the rural people, and who would not hesitate to step in and help even if the "patient" was a cow having difficulty in delivering its calf, at any hour of the day or night. She was probably as much a doctor as a nurse much of the time.

But Father Mackey's closest association with the Protestant missionaries came through Einar Kippenes and his wife Reidun. They were Norwegian missionaries, working for the Swedish organization known as KMA (Female Missionary Workers), who started and ran the school for the blind. Like most foreigners living in rural Bhutan, they experienced some hardship in this region, so different from their Western home.

The Kippenes family lost one child in a car accident, but raised two other children in Khaling. The younger spoke better Sharchopkha than Norwegian. The parents got on well with the Jesuits at the high school and the communities cooperated.

Mr. Kippenes was the one who started the Bible reading sessions. Once a month, the Norwegian missionaries and the Jesuits would get together to share thoughts on readings from the Bible. They would take turns hosting the gathering, choosing the text, reading it to the group, developing it and then leading discussion. This went a long way in breaking down prejudices. The participants learned that the others were also devout and knowledgeable Christians, and also human beings.

For the most part, the members of the two communities became good friends. The notable exception was a Doctor Melbostad, head of the hospital at Riserbu. He was a very hard-working doctor and made a considerable contribution to the hospital. But he was also conservative and prejudiced against the Jesuits. When the government wanted the missionaries to build a big hospital next to the College at Kanglung, he apparently blocked the project.

Many feel it was because he did not want his hospital next to a Jesuit college. In his mind, Catholics were virtually allied with the devil himself, and contact between the communities did little to alter his attitude. Not even the joint Bible sessions helped. On one occasion, Brother Quinn was discussing human suffering and the suffering of Christ. He drew on a Biblical teaching that something positive could come from suffering.

Doctor Melbostad furiously opposed this idea: "No, suffering is completely evil!"

Brother Quinn said, "Physically it's evil, but sometimes it can be worthwhile, a good thing." He had in mind a teaching of St. Paul, but couldn't put his finger on it. "St. Paul mentions somewhere that suffering brings us closer to Christ. That our suffering complements the suffering of Christ, and if it's evil, how can it complement Christ's suffering?"

"That's not in the Bible!" The Protestants knew their Bible, and could usually cite chapter and verse.

Brother Quinn said with his quiet authority, "It's there."

Father Mackey backed him, but neither Jesuit could come up with the reference on the spur of the moment.

Later, back in his quarters, Brother Quinn went through the writings of St. Paul and found the reference. Next meeting, he showed it to Doctor Melbostad. The Doctor remained adamant:

"That's not in the Protestant Bible!"

"May I see your Bible, please?" Brother Quinn flipped to Colossians in Doctor Melbostad's Bible. "This is your Protestant Bible. Here, what does this say?"

Doctor Melbostad conceded with only a low harrumph.

Father Mackey's broad views also offended Doctor Melbostad — specifically, his interest in Catholic philosophers like Teilhard de Chardin and Hans Kung. Father Mackey would lend their books to Doctor Melbostad and try to discuss theology, but to no avail. Even the new ideas coming out of Rome offended the doctor, like those of Vatican II, which acknowledged the value of non-Christian religions.

Doctor Melbostad felt that Protestant Christians had the only true way, and no good existed in anything else. Further, Protestant baptism was the only salvation available to humankind. For that reason, he required that all his staff be baptized. This was at odds not only with Bhutanese government desires, but Father Mackey's refusal to convert and baptize Bhutanese nationals.

Then there was Buddhism. Father Mackey found the Buddhists around him fit his view of devout belief and life, and that his study of Buddhism gave him insight into his own religion. He tried, probably unwisely, to explain this to Doctor Melbostad.

As if to compound these heresies, he lent the good doctor *The Divine Madman*, the biography of Drukpa Kunley, a beloved, though unorthodox, Tibetan Buddhist saint of the sixteenth Century. The book's back cover says of him, "In contrast to other more ascetical teachers of the East who teach negation of the body and its desires, Drukpa Kunley used desire, emotion, and sexuality to arouse disillusionment, insight, and delight in all he encountered."

Father Mackey found *The Divine Madman* to contain deep spiritual teachings, but presented in ways that might shock readers — especially monks and lamas who stood too much on their dignity. Drukpa Kunley could also teach the common people by catching their attention with his lively stories, and the book was very popular among the Bhutanese.

When Doctor Melbostad had read the book, he called Father Mackey a heretic, said he was damned to hell, and refused to speak to him any further.

Mr. Kippenes apologized to Father Mackey for the doctor's behaviour, and the doctor's wife remained friendly and gracious. But even when Doctor Melbostad was finally leaving Bhutan, and Father Mackey went to say goodbye, the doctor refused to speak to him. Father Mackey's assessment is: "Fantastic doctor. Would walk miles and miles. But just a narrow, narrow, narrow mind. He had blinkers on his eyes and couldn't see beyond the end of his nose on things religious."

* * *

Early in 1981 on a visit to Sherubtse, Father Mackey learned that Lopen Jamphel was very sick. The *lopen* had been one of his most important staff members at Sherubtse, a vital counsellor and good friend. Now Father Mackey had his driver take Lopen Jamphel to Gauhati, where he was admitted to hospital. About ten days later, a lecturer from the College went to Gauhati on business and visited Lopen Jamphel. The attending physician told him Lopen Jamphel was in the last stages of cancer. "We can do nothing. Get him back to his home as soon as you can."

The lecturer had the College jeep and he brought Lopen Jamphel back to Kanglung. As they passed Khaling, Lopen Jamphel wanted to see Father Mackey. They stopped, and Lopen Jamphel said, "Father, please come up with me."

"Lopen, I can't get away just now. I'm sorry. But we'll get Lopen Ngawang to go with you."

They went to see Lopen Ngawang, who now headed the school for the blind. But his response was, "I'm sorry, I'm tied up too. But I'll come over the weekend."

Father Mackey then sent for Lopen Jamphel's daughter, a bright young girl in class five or six. He told her to go with her father. They proceeded to Kanglung and were dropped at the College gates. While his own house was under construction, Lopen Jamphel was staying in a house behind Zangdopelri, the temple just across the road. Lopen Jamphel walked slowly to his home with his daughter. Inside, he lay down. Ten minutes later he was dead.

Lopen Jamphel's cremation drew many important people, including lamas, the Lam Neten and the monk body from the Dzong. He was cremated on Sherubtse campus, just above the football field where the first boys' degree hostel was later built. Father Mackey and Lopen Ngawang, both of whom had missed sharing Lopen Jamphel's final hour, came up together, bringing rice and some money to help out with the cremation.

They were there when the old *lopen's* body was brought and placed on the pyre. He was still a big man — 180 pounds (about eighty kilograms) or more — even after the weight loss caused by his disease. The pyre was large: it would take a lot of heat to burn this body. Along with Lopen Jamphel's remains, the bodies of three small children who had died recently were also placed on the pyre to be cremated. By being cremated with this important *lopen*, they would also receive the benefits of the prayers said for him by the monk body.

The cremation went normally until those in attendance realized that the big man had broken the ropes that bound him and was sitting up among the flames at the top of the pyre. Some people were shocked and disconcerted, but most realized what had happened. Sometimes in a cremation the gases in the stomach react and expand, creating a strong outward force. In Lopen Jamphel's case, this force was great enough to break the binding ropes and push the body into an upright position.

Now the concern was that, perched on top, the body was too much out of the heat and would not be properly consumed. It had to be moved back down into the fire. With long poles (for it was about three metres up), people tried to push and beat the old *lopen's* body back down, much to the consternation of some of the guests. The Bhutanese were not bothered, but some of the Indian professors and the Jesuits began to feel very uncomfortable as their dead colleague was beat about the head while the flames licked from below. Father Mackey, typically, was not bothered. He had seen this sort of thing before and was "enjoying the fun."

Finally, the body settled down into the flames and the cremation proceeded. But when it came time for the meal — hosted by the deceased — some of the guests had lost their appetite. Eating at a body burning was difficult enough, but the sight of Lopen Jamphel's body rising and being beaten back down was just too much for the delicate tummies of the non-Bhutanese. They were queasy and afraid that any food they ate would come back up. There was an awkward pause as some of the main guests hesitated to take food. Then someone asked Father Mackey if he would begin the meal and he obliged, "I'll always eat, boy."

The others then slowly followed.

As the cremation was drawing to a close, someone pointed out a distinct ring around the sun. There was nothing to explain it. Father Mackey is certain it was not an effect or illusion caused by smoke from the fire or anything like that, and it was a distinct ring. The Bhutanese assumed that it was connected with the cremation of Lopen Jamphel, whom they held to be a very holy man. Father Mackey doesn't know if there was a connection or not, but he found it very impressive.

* * *

Father Mackey's sister Tess, who had visited him in Darjeeling, wanted to see him in his Bhutanese home. She was now into her seventies, but still hearty and ready to challenge the rigours of rural Bhutan. She brought with her two friends who were only slightly younger. They flew into Gauhati and were met by a friend of Father Mackey's, a businessman whose company supplied science equipment to schools.

He would also arrange transport for them to Samdrup Jongkhar, where Father Mackey would be waiting. The flight into Gauhati was usually early in the morning, so Father Mackey was expecting the women by mid-day, but lunch-time came and went. He waited a bit longer, then assumed that the flight hadn't arrived and went off to have a siesta. He was staying with Chabeldas Moth, of Moth & Co. He had a good long nap through the warm afternoon, and it was past three o'clock when his host woke him to say, "Your sisters are here."

Father Mackey emerged to greet the women and was surprised to see that the science supplier himself had brought the ladies: "What happened?"

The Indian gentleman answered, "Oh, I took them around Gauhati and gave them a big meal in a hotel and then brought them through."

Tess and the other two were keen to get to Khaling as soon as possible: "Can we get there tonight?" Father Mackey did a head count and looked at the pile of luggage they had brought. He had only the school jeep.

Tess' friends, both in their sixties, were sisters-in-law, having married two doctors who were brothers. Father Mackey describes the younger woman as a "petite French Canadian" and the other as a "big, tall, lanky English girl from Toronto, about twice the weight of the younger one." He put the big Torontonian and the medium-sized Tess in the front of the jeep with the driver. Father Mackey and the French Canadian squeezed in the back with the luggage, said goodbye to Chabeldas and the man from Gauhati, and set off.

They reached Khaling about eight o'clock. As was often the case, it was rather cold and miserable, and Father Mackey put on the electric heater. He showed them their beds and had a meal brought. The women were exhausted, but before they retired Father Mackey asked, "How are you going to go to the bathroom? It's all squatting toilets, you know."

When Tess admitted they'd been worried, he said: "Well, come on. I'll show you what I've got."

A year or more before, Father Mackey had experienced trouble with his prostate gland. And in January of 1980, he'd had old-fashioned major surgery in Calcutta. It was a month before he could even walk again, and "going to the bathroom" had been very difficult.

His regular toilet was of the Asian squatting style that makes so much sense, especially where facilities are difficult to maintain and keep clean. But this was uncomfortable in his post-operation condition, and he'd had a toilet seat set in a wooden box. Placing this over the Asian toilet, he could sit in the Western style and do his "business."

When he showed the ladies his improvised sit-down toilet, they were delighted. The French Canadian told him to sit down and pulled out her camera. Father Mackey obliged, the camera flashed and she had a memorable shot of the Jesuit on the wooden toilet seat.

As the visitors were guests of Father Mackey, the people of Eastern Bhutan couldn't do enough for them: their's was like a royal tour. There were concerts and shows and the students, especially the girls, really warmed to the three elderly ladies. Tess, the eldest, was called "Abi," which means grandmother. The next eldest, the tall Torontonian, was called "Ama," or mother; and the small French Canadian was called "Usa" — sister.

The women were not averse to the occasional drink, so Father Mackey introduced them to *ara* served hot with egg cooked in it. Politely, they wondered if there wasn't anything else. Father Mackey didn't have much of a liquor cabinet, but Apsoo rum, the old standby, was always available in the bazaar.

In India, most foreigners and many Indians consider rum to be the best commercially distilled spirit — dark and smooth and quite sweet. Apsoo, a similar Bhutanese product, is not the best grade of rum but is very potable, especially in tea, coffee, cola or even hot water, which was how the women drank it.

The three took an interest in the neighbouring school for the blind and the small health unit. And when it came time for a classic picnic, the visitors insisted on paying for the compulsory pig, boiled with hot chillies. The sprightly French Canadian even went swimming with some of the girl students in the Jirichhu, the small clear mountain river that flows past Khaling.

The women spent a good deal of time with the girls, chatting in their dormitory. The visitors learned much about Bhutan and the girls a lot about Canada. Friendships developed, and even years later, when the girls were grown, correspondences flourished.

Father Mackey took his guests to Tashigang and the other towns in Eastern Bhutan and to villages and homes a little off the road. They climbed the simple ladders or stairs up into village homes, sat on the small carpets laid out for them and ate the simple meals or drank the tea or *ara* the village people served.

In Tashigang they met the Lam Neten and toured the Dzong. Officials like the Dzongdag and the police chief, Deda Tashi, treated them to classic Bhutanese hospitality, including grand meals. The visitors found some of the dishes very strange, and had trouble adjusting to the hotness of the chillies.

On one of the trips to Tashigang, Father Mackey brought the women to meet Phongmey Dungpa, who was working on the new temple in Kanglung and living in a house not far away, near Kangma. He insisted that they eat with him. As they were on their way to see someone in Tashigang, they agreed to stop on the way back and have dinner. Tess had heard stories about Phongmey Dungpa for years, so she might have known what to expect, but she may not have relayed her knowledge to her friends.

About four o'clock that afternoon, Father Mackey stopped at Kanglung and picked up Phongmey Dungpa. They were all crowded in the closed jeep and Phongmey Dungpa got into the back and sat next to the Torontonian. As they drove up to Kangma, not one to miss an opportunity, he put his arm around the big Canadian woman and gave her a squeeze. To her French Canadian companion next to her, she said in French, *"Au secours, au secours, au secours!"* ("Help, help, help!")

The response, roughly translated, was: "Ah, leave him alone. He hasn't had a chance like this in years."

Once at Phongmey Dungpa's house, the guests were ushered in, taken to the nicest room in the house, the altar room, and served *ara*. Father Mackey was pointing out things around the room and Tess was shocked to see her own photograph on the wall. "What's that doing there?!"

Father Mackey explained that when his friend saw the picture on his desk in Tashigang, he picked it up and said, "Ah, she's beautiful." He took it and Father Mackey never got it back. Phongmey Dungpa kept that picture of Tess hanging on his wall, and saved others taken on that visit, until he died some years later.

Before leaving about nine o'clock that night, the departing guests were presented with gifts of hand-woven cloth, turned wooden *gorbus*, *bangchungs* and other traditional Bhutanese items. Then Phongmey Dungpa escorted them up the steep path to the vehicle. He was just behind the French Canadian and when she slipped a bit, he gave her bottom a pinch and she took off up the slope. That Christmas, in her letter to Father Mackey, she said, "Tell that friend of yours I'm learning judo for my next trip to Bhutan."

Summing up the visit, Father Mackey said: "They caused a sensation and we caused a sensation for them. I don't know who caused the greater sensation."

* * *

Stray dogs have always been a problem at schools in Bhutan. They feed on scraps thrown away at the kitchen, and the students and staff also toss scraps to the dogs. The problem, of course, is rabies. But reducing the number of dogs is extremely difficult, practically impossible in some situations. This is mainly because most Bhutanese, who are Buddhist, consider killing animals unacceptable. Nor is sterilization practised, as no one owns the dogs.

As schools like Sherubtse and Jigme Sherubling grew, so did the dog population (a larger kitchen and student complement could support more dogs). But anyone who had the means and the inclination to shoot the dogs risked fierce opposition from both the community and students. It was not worth the risk.

Father Mackey tried various other methods, starting with poison. It seemed impossible, however, to poison more than one dog at a time. He might have the cooks or the sweeper put out ten "servings" of poisoned food, but get only one dog. Somehow the other dogs sensed that the food was bad and wouldn't touch it.

Father Mackey tried exporting the dogs to India. If he learned of an empty truck going to the border, he'd round up a bunch of dogs and have the driver dump them. His driver Prem had an even better idea. If he was going down to Samdrup Jongkhar or Gauhati in the jeep, he would round up any puppies on campus and take them along. As a puppy, just about any dog is fluffy and cute, and he'd set up shop just across the border at Mela Bazaar and sell the pups as Apsoos: "Oh, Apsoos, Bhutanese dogs, ten rupees, ten rupees!"

Brother Nick, the wild Dutchman, took a single-minded approach to dog eradication. His method was simple, usually quick and effective. He used a length of pipe that he kept under the seat of his vehicle. A single blow on the head from the hefty Jesuit Brother usually took care of any dog.

On one occasion, however, Brother Nick's approach caused an embarrassing and grisly scene. Father Mackey was meeting in the Jigme Sherubling staff room with several teachers and guests. Brother Nick, outside, spotted a stray dog and went after it with his lead pipe. Unfortunately, he struck only a glancing blow and the dog, blood flowing from a nasty gash on its head, ran for refuge and found it in the staff room, under the table, among the feet of those assembled.

Shock, anger, disgust, embarrassment and confusion ensued as Brother Nick followed the dog into the room and tried to get it out. Eventually he drove the dog from the room and finished it off.

When Father Mackey reached the end of his patience and resources in trying to control the "pup-ulation," he called upon the assistance of his old friend, the home minister. On one occasion the home minister arranged for someone from animal husbandry to help out at Jigme Sherubling. A Bengali gentleman arrived armed with needles, syringes and injectable poison. As the man was alone, a problem presented itself. When they went out on the campus grounds and found the first dog, the fellow said, "Okay, you catch the dog and hold it and I'll inject it."

Father Mackey didn't like that idea at all. "You give me the needle," he said. "*You* catch the dog and *I'll* inject it."

As neither man, nor anyone else in his right mind, wanted to catch and hold a half-wild stray dog while it got poked with a needle, the dog population remained undiminished.

The home minister tried again, asking the army at Yonphula to send sharpshooters to kill the dogs. Two men arrived carrying one old rifle. They went out onto the campus and found stray dogs gathered near the dining hall. One of the soldiers raised the rifle, aimed, fired — and missed. The animals fled. The men trudged around the campus with the rifle. Every time they found a dog, one of them would fire a shot in its general direction.

By late afternoon, the men had fired twenty or more shots and hit not one dog. Father Mackey was fed up. The exercise was not only disruptive, especially since the students didn't like the idea of people trying to kill the dogs, but totally ineffective. He had his afternoon tea in his quarters at the top of the campus and then walked back down to the classroom block.

Passing the girls' dormitory, where the girls were having a study period, he spotted a group of dogs. He hurried to the staff room where the soldiers were having their tea. He took them back up to the dormitory and pointed at the dogs. "Now look, you haven't shot a single dog yet. There are three dogs there, now shoot!"

The man with the rifle raised it, aimed and fired. The bullet went over the heads of the dogs, through the dormitory window, between two girls hard at work, and out the window on the other side. Father Mackey still had no dead dogs, but he did have two broken windows, a lot of frightened girls and a very angry Sister Leonard, who came running out of the girls' dorm.

That was the end of the dog-shooting exercise.

* * *

Father Mackey was happy as principal of Jigme Sherubling and had no intention of retiring. But in 1982, the Bishop and the Jesuit Superior came from Darjeeling to see him. Father Mackey was sixty-seven. He had been running schools in Bhutan for nineteen years. And his superiors felt he was doing too much. They wanted to turn the high school over to a younger man, with Father Mackey staying on as an assistant.

Father Mackey was not one to hang on to a position of authority for its own sake. And despite his rather loose style in dealing with official Church matters, he had always taken his Jesuit vows and obligations to Jesuit authority very seriously. So while he would have preferred to stay on as principal, he did not oppose the proposed changes and brought the Bishop and Superior to Thimphu to discuss matters with Nado Rinchen, the director of education.

They told him Father Mackey needed a rest and proposed another Jesuit Father to take over Jigme Sherubling: Father John Perry had taught at Sherubtse, Punakha and Khaling, and was presently teaching at Punakha.

The director agreed and in 1983 Father Perry became principal of Jigme Sherubling, with Father Mackey his assistant. Besides helping to guide Father Perry in the running of the school, Father Mackey continued to teach mathematics. Father Perry relieved him, however, of most of the extra, non-teaching jobs, and the long hours spent in the dormitories. Father Mackey was able, however, to keep up some of his gymnastics and other sports activities.

Later in 1983, the director of education visited Father Mackey and invited him to Thimphu to become an advisor. In mid-July, the school gave a farewell programme in honour of Father Mackey, who then moved to the capital.

22/

T himphu had become the capital of Bhutan in every way, and was home to all government departments and foreign agencies. Even so it was small, with a population of about 20,000. Much of the government administration was located in Tashichoedzong or in low barrack-type buildings just outside, to the south of the Dzong.

The education department was split, with the pure administration situated just outside the Dzong, and the rest, including Father Mackey's office, housed in a three-storey building near Changangkha school. This was north-west of the bazaar area, south-west of the Dzong, and about a kilometre from each, up the moderately sloped hillside that most of Thimphu occupied.

Proximity brought Father Mackey into close contact with the whole government administration. At official gatherings or social functions, he could chat with just about everyone. The upper levels of government comprised a tightly-knit group of thirty or forty people, among whom he knew many already, like Dawa Tshering, the foreign minister, and Nado Rinchen, director of education, and former Darjeeling students like Pema Wangchuk, director of agriculture.

When officials invited Father Mackey to education headquarters, they'd intended to name him advisor to education. But senior Indians in the administration didn't like the idea of a non-Indian being called "advisor." The government deferred and Father Mackey became Secretary of the Bhutan Board of Examinations and, soon after that, Coordinator of the Textbooks and Syllabus Committee.

This was certainly not retirement or even the work reduction Jesuit authorities had suggested the previous year. At Jigme Sherubling, Father Perry had tried to restrict Father Mackey's activities to teaching and sports. But in Thimphu, with the board of examinations — responsible for all the class six and class eight exams in Bhutan — plus the textbook and curriculum division, Father Mackey had two full-time jobs.

He carried this double load until 1985, when he retired officially, traded his two jobs for two others and gained Bhutanese citizenship. The oddest event of the three, perhaps, was his retirement. That year, Father Mackey turned seventy years of age, and with a retirement law coming into effect in Bhutan, he had to be retired. On the 25th of October, he was awarded a gratuity of 40,000 *ngultrums* (about $4,300 Canadian) for "21 years" service. The *ngultrum* is the basic unit of Bhutanese currency, equal in value to an Indian rupee.

The day after he was retired, however, he was rehired. The same thing happened to his friend and colleague, Lopen Nado. While the law necessitated their retirement, apparently nothing said they couldn't then be rehired. Father Mackey observed to Lopen Nado, "Say, this is a pretty good deal. We should retire again."

Over the years, the matter of school inspections had never been addressed beyond nominal gestures. If problems arose in a school, someone from headquarters might visit and try to sort things out. But neither classroom inspections, nor broader school inspections, ever took place systematically. In the earlier education policies that Father Mackey and Dawa Tshering had written, they'd stressed the need for regular inspections. Now, Father Mackey was again working on a draft education policy that emphasized this need. When the director, Nado Rinchen, read the draft, he agreed and told Father Mackey: "Okay, you're the chief inspector of schools."

Father Mackey was certainly the most qualified person in the country — educated, experienced, understanding and respected. At first, this job was simply added to his others, but he and the director soon realized this was too much. Father Mackey handed over the Bhutan Board of Examinations to someone else, and the Textbook and Curriculum Division was reorganized.

At the end of 1985, Father Mackey became Chief Inspector, Inspectorate of Schools, though he'd actually already begun the work. He was also made Chief Coordinator, Curriculum Development Division, though he did not retain this position for long.

Father Mackey explained to the director that one man could not do the whole job of inspecting. There were just too many classrooms, even though initially only high schools and junior high schools would be inspected. Then there was the matter of different subjects. Father Mackey probably had the broadest education in the department, but he didn't want to be responsible for inspecting teachers of all academic subjects. He would need a small team of inspectors.

Unfortunately, Father Mackey did not get to choose the team, and its makeup was not what he'd hoped. He would have looked for experience, as well as a sensitive and sympathetic ear. The department's criteria were unclear. The team was of mixed quality, but reflected the nationality mix of teachers in the country: apart from Father Mackey, the inspectors were all Indian except the one responsible for Bhutanese language.

An experienced high school principal handled English and history. The Jesuit respected his ability and they became good friends. Father Mackey handled science as well as maths until a science man, a good one it turned out, was found. Father Mackey was able to maintain good relations with the other members of the team, but they lacked the qualities of good inspectors. Some felt that these men had been placed on the team because there was no other place for them.

Becoming chief inspector meant still more work, though Father Mackey found it interesting and invigorating. He liked dealing with people and schools first hand. The inspections allowed him to get back into the classroom and work with teachers, and even to teach the occasional class. Initially, all of the schools under the inspectorate were "on the road." But travel on that road was (and still is) never completely predictable, and could be very unpredictable during the rainy season. When roads got washed out or blocked, delays could last days.

Trouble was, given the time frame of the school year, inspections had to be done in the rainy season. Theoretically, school opens about the tenth of March, but students and even teachers trickle back slowly. Very often, new syllabi, books and materials have not arrived. Staff transfers may still be taking place. Finalizing the timetable takes a major effort, and it may be April before things are running smoothly. Some primary schools could be even later. There is little point inspecting a school before teachers have actually been at work for a few weeks.

At the other end of the year, final exams begin in late November or early December, and a lot of teaching time is lost in November to exam preparations, the celebration of the King's birthday and finalization of sports programmes. This leaves about six months of full-time active teaching. In the original set-up, the single team of usually four inspectors would have to inspect all the high schools and junior high schools during this period.

The rains that make travel so problematic from early June and on into October also make some areas of the country difficult and unpleasant, even if roads stay open. Parts of the country at low elevations, especially valleys within the mountains of south-central Bhutan, turn into tropical jungles: hot, humid and teeming with leeches.

School inspection wasn't simply a matter of sitting in classrooms observing teachers at work, but included many hours on the road, time in the classrooms, time with students, full use of listening skills and, where possible, problem solving. Sometimes he did his most valuable work after class, sitting and listening to the headmaster and teachers. Some remote schools would be cut off from the rest of the world for months, and the staff needed human contact. As Father Mackey pointed out, "They needed friendship. They needed someone who was interested in them to sit down and listen, let them do the talking."

Father Mackey found there was often a great gap between what the teachers were experiencing (sometimes directly related to department policy) and the understanding at headquarters. While it was his job and desire to bring the reality back to Thimphu, he knew that frequently nothing would come of his reports, and that his listening was an important end in itself.

While visiting schools, Father Mackey would often end up sleeping in the classrooms on the floor, benches or tables. Other elements of life-on-the-road were just as basic: dining, toilet, bathing. Father Mackey has always taken rough conditions in stride. And where many people find travelling Bhutan's winding mountain roads terrifying, with his driver-friend, Mindu, at the wheel, Father Mackey found it recuperative.

Leaving a school, he would usually be tired, but a couple of hours in the four-wheel-drive vehicle would revive him. This was hard for some people to believe, and the workload and working conditions for a man moving into his late seventies made the Superior say, "You're doing too much." And to the department, "You should give this man an easier job."

But as long as he could handle the work, Father Mackey was happy to continue. As he moved into the 1990s, he did acknowledge that he was less physically able — he couldn't climb mountains as well as before, and his eyes felt tired when he used them all day at the office. But otherwise, physically, he continued to feel fine: "I think I'm probably doing more work than a lot of people."

* * *

Father Mackey was often called upon to be chief guest at school functions and to attend receptions and other quasi-official events. One of the oddest functions he attended after moving to Thimphu arose not long after he arrived. For a couple of years around 1984, there was a Miss Thimphu pageant. It was a fund-raising event for some good cause, and everyone was expected to attend.

Nobody would have wanted to miss it anyway. Conservative by Western standards, the pageant was good fun. The young women would appear in classic beauty contest format, in traditional Bhutanese dress (one could expect exquisite hand-woven *kiras*) and a Western dress. Bikinis were nowhere to be seen, for while the Bhutanese are not prudish, showing a lot of uncovered body is not their way.

Father Mackey enjoyed the show, and clapped and cheered with the boisterous crowd. Everyone knew everyone else, including the young women on the stage. Paljor Dorji, or Dasho Benji as he is generally known — the son of the late prime minister — was master of ceremonies. Father Mackey thought he heard him say, "Father Mackey is wanted on the stage immediately."

As the Jesuit didn't respond right away, his friend, Lyonpo Tamji Jagar, sitting nearby, leaned over and said, "Father, they want you."

"What do they want me for? I'm not beautiful!"

"I don't know, but you'd better go up."

So Father Mackey went up on stage and behind the curtain, where he found himself in a contest to choose the best knees in Thimphu. The men were all wearing the knee-length *go*, and those chosen to compete were lining up across the stage behind the curtain. The curtain would be raised to show just the men's knees, and as the master of ceremonies indicated each pair of knees, the audience would register their choice with applause.

Father Mackey protested: "This isn't fair. Everybody will know me because my legs are white."

Actually, his knees were well-tanned from wearing his *go*. But he was up against some stiff competition. Captain Kado (of the Royal Body Guard, and married to Ten Dorje's "clever" daughter) for example, he described as having "huge elephant knees." The officials rejected his excuses and put him in the line-up.

Kado's knees won first prize, but all the contestants received certificates thanking them for their participation in the beauty contest. Father Mackey sent his to sister Tess, who responded with astonishment: "What were you doing in a beauty contest?!!"

* * *

Over the years, like every other foreigner, Father Mackey had been subject to Indian restrictions on travelling in India and entering Bhutan. Only during his last few years in Eastern Bhutan did crossing back and forth within the country become an option. And even then the route was long and unreliable. Most Bhutanese still chose to go through India if they had to travel between, say, Tashigang and Thimphu.

Generally, Father Mackey's schedule was fixed by the academic programme and he could plan his travel well in advance. When he moved to Thimphu, however, his schedule became less predictable. If his work required him to go to Samtse at short notice, as it often did, he was out of luck. It took at least six weeks to get an Indian transit permit. This would make inspecting schools very problematic too.

One day, Father Mackey mentioned these difficulties to Dawa Tshering, who had been foreign minister for some time. Lyonpo Dawa responded: "Why don't you become a Bhutanese citizen?"

A Bhutanese official would not propose such a thing without knowing in advance that it would be approved. Lyonpo Dawa must have discussed this with the King. Father Mackey paused, a little surprised, then said, "Well, then, get me citizenship."

The official government document, the Kashog of Citizenship read: "We are pleased to accept Rev. Fr. William Mackey as our loyal subject from this day and we do hereby confer on him all the rights, privileges and duties of a citizen of Bhutan." It was signed by the King of Bhutan on the 8th of March, 1985.

Bhutanese citizens cross the Bhutan-India border and travel in India freely. But Lyonpo Dawa foresaw that Father Mackey's Bhutanese citizenship might be questioned by Indian authorities at the border and, in addition to an identity card, he gave him a passport to carry. Normally, Bhutanese are issued passports when they travel abroad (beyond India), and keep them in their own possession only while they are outside the country. While a Bhutanese is inside Bhutan, his or her passport is held by the Ministry of Foreign Affairs.

Furthermore, for the first trip that arose — a long-planned trip to Samtse for which Father Mackey had requested a transit permit — Lyonpo Dawa suggested he use the permit, reasoning that Indian border officials had probably not yet been notified of his citizenship.

Father Mackey did so. But on his next trip, again to Samtse, he travelled as a Bhutanese, without a permit. He decided to stop at the Indian check post and explain the situation. He said he'd been stopping at this check post for twenty years, but this was the last time. Now he was a citizen of Bhutan. He pulled a copy of the *kashog* out of his *go* and showed it to the border official. As a gesture of cooperation he meant to leave the copy at the check post.

The man looked at the *kashog* without comprehension: "But you, you, you can't be Bhutanese."

Father Mackey's good humour began to wane: "Well, if you don't like it," he said — and he took back the *kashog* and stood up. "Does a Bhutanese have to come through here?"

"No."

"Well, I'm a Bhutanese and I won't be stopping anymore."

"But you're not."

"What in hang is this?" He pulled out his passport. "This is a pukka Bhutanese passport."

"You can't have such a passport."

"I can't? Who are you to say I can't have a Bhutanese passport?"

The man thought for a moment: "Well, yes, okay. You have the passport. I must write it down."

"Well, do. Write it down if you like, no problem. But I'm not stopping again."

"No, no, no. Please. You must report."

"Look, a Bhutanese citizen does not have to report. Why should I report?"

"We have no instructions from our headquarters."

"What instructions do you need? You don't check Bhutanese."

"Yes, but you're not Bhutanese."

"Look, what does this say?" In exasperation Father Mackey again held up the passport.

The man's rigid training hadn't prepared him to handle anything so out of the ordinary: "Please. When you come back, please let me know. I just want to know your movements."

Father Mackey relented: "Look, I'll stop in on the way back from Samtse, but after that I'm not coming here any more."

A few days later he checked in as promised, but said as he left, "This is the last time."

After that, Father Mackey drove right past the Indian check post. The traffic is usually so heavy on that street in the chaotic border town that an individual vehicle, even with a white-skinned man in it, is not noticed. Only on one occasion was he noticed and stopped by a guard at the Indian customs check post located a hundred metres down the road from the immigration office in Jaigaon. The guard stepped out of his sentry box and waved the vehicle to stop. He came to Father Mackey's window and said, "Papers."

"What papers? I'm a Bhutanese."

The guard looked at Father Mackey. Did this white man think he was stupid? "Papers."

Father Mackey showed him the Bhutanese passport.

The guard looked briefly at the passport. It is quite possible that this fellow, an ordinary policeman, did not read English, and certainly not Dzongkha. He said, "Come with me."

Father Mackey sighed and said, "Look, you go into that place." He pointed to the immigration office. "They've got a copy of this, the number of this passport, all the details. They know I'm a Bhutanese citizen. A Bhutanese citizen doesn't have to report. You go in there and ask for the file on Father Mackey of Sherubtse school, Khaling school, and Thimphu. You've got a huge file in there. They know everything about me. I'm not going in." He took his passport from the guard's hand. "Thank you very much."

He told Mindu, his driver, to go ahead. The guard watched them drive away, then ambled back to the sentry box.

On a later occasion, Father Mackey encountered a more difficult official. He had been in south-central Bhutan and was returning to Thimphu, going out though Geylegphug, across to Phuntsholing and then home. As he approached the Indian check post at Samtibari, across from Geylegphug, he found three vehicles lined up and the border guard lowering the barrier between vehicles.

This suggested that the officer was new and unfamiliar with regular procedures. When they got to the barrier, Mindu got out, went to the officer and said, "Bhutanese."

The man could see Father Mackey in the Land Cruiser and said, "He's not Bhutanese."

"Yes, he is."

"No."

Mindu came back and shrugged his shoulders. Father Mackey went in to the officer. He showed his Bhutanese identity card. "See this? I am a Bhutanese."

"No. Can't be."

"Look, I'm not arguing. What's your name and what is your authority?"

The man ignored the questions. "Sign here," indicating a form on his desk.

"I'm not signing anything. No Bhutanese has to stop here." He picked up his I.D. card. "Good afternoon." As he was leaving he said, "Now, open that gate." He returned to the Land Cruiser but the barrier remained down. There were vehicles lined up behind them now. He went back to the official. "Unless that gate is opened I report to your Ambassador. Give me your name and tell me what authority you're working under."

Father Mackey's tone and bearing carried the day, and the official told the guard to lift the barrier.

The Jesuit was destined to meet opposition at every main border crossing. The first time he crossed into Bhutan at Samdrup Jongkhar after getting Bhutanese citizenship, he was stopped at the Darranga check post, possibly the most insignificant frontier post in India. He walked up to the small office about seventy metres from the road. The makeshift office had no proper desk or other office furniture, just a low table, some chairs and a cot in the corner.

Father Mackey sat down opposite the Indian immigration official. "Look," he said, "you've got my name. I've been in here many times. I was the second person to cross through this check post when it opened. I'm number two in the book. I've been coming and going for twenty years, but now I don't have to come any more. I'm a Bhutanese citizen."

This man was more reasonable. He looked at Father Mackey's documents and accepted his claim: "Yes, okay."

For some reason, however, the same man was not in charge when Father Mackey exited Bhutan by the same route a week or so later. A guard at the Indian check-post gate refused to lift the barrier for the vehicle. Father Mackey showed his identification, but the guard didn't even move.

Father Mackey turned to his driver: "Mindu, take this and go see that guy in there, will you?" He assumed the same officer would be in the small office. But another man came to the gate and said Father Mackey had to come in. It appeared that Mindu was now stuck inside, unable to come out. Father Mackey stormed up to the office.

Inside, he grabbed the I.D.: "My identity card, thank you! Now, what is this? A Bhutanese identity card? Very good. That's all I need. Now, this is being reported to your ambassador in Thimphu. What is your name and what is your authority?"

Again the threat of reprimand made the officer relent and, reluctantly, he let the Jesuit pass.

"It's just bureaucracy," Father Mackey says. "These guys are given orders and they can't take a decision. If something like this is not written down in their rules, they're frightened stiff in case they make a wrong step and get demoted or something."

23/

When Father Mackey arrived in Thimphu, he had no vehicle, except for official use, and would walk to his office. This wasn't too far unless it was pouring rain, and occasionally he would get a lift from someone driving by. One rainy day, Ashi Dechen, the King's sister who was Father Mackey's main support for many years in Eastern Bhutan, saw him walking and had her driver pull to a quick stop. "What are you doing walking?"

"I'm enjoying it, Ashi."

"Where's your car?"

"Well, I haven't got one."

The next day he had a beautiful new Toyota station wagon. Ashi Dechen had her husband, Dasho Thinley, give up his car to Father Mackey. Dasho Thinley had to go back to a jeep for a few months while Father Mackey used the Toyota. Then, when he heard that Brother Nick was going to receive a new vehicle from John Goelet, Father Mackey wrote to the man and explained that he had a borrowed vehicle and could use one of his own.

The millionaire responded and, even before Brother Nick got his vehicle, Father Mackey received a new blue short-wheel-base Toyota Land Cruiser. This was Father Mackey's vehicle, though it carried government registration plates and the department paid for repairs and diesel fuel. The priest also got a government driver.

This driver, Mindu, became his right-hand man. He was a short, stocky Drukpa with a round face and a serious look, though he was capable of smiling, particularly if sharing a joke with Father Mackey.

When Father Mackey arrived at headquarters, an old jeep was assigned to him for official transport and Mindu was the driver. Mindu became devoted to Father Mackey immediately. He was quite upset when the priest acquired the car from Ashi Dechen because it came with one of her drivers.

When Father Mackey got his Land Cruiser and the education department offered a driver, he asked for Mindu. By this time Father Mackey had learned that Mindu was not only an excellent driver (in a country of notoriously bad drivers) who took great care of the vehicle in his charge, but also a loyal and devoted servant and friend.

Mindu lived in the bazaar where he had a small piece of property and a simple house — really a sturdy shack. He lived there with his wife and children. He kept the vehicle at his place. Each morning at eight o'clock, he would pick up Father Mackey at his quarters. The Jesuit would have prepared and eaten his breakfast of coffee, bread and perhaps an egg. He'd bring a sandwich to the office for lunch. In the evening after work, Mindu would drive Father Mackey home and cook supper for him before returning to his house in the bazaar.

Father Mackey's first residence was up the hillside beyond Changangkha, in the area called Motithang. But Ashi Dechen didn't like the building. She arranged for Father Mackey to move into one of the new bungalows built to house foreigners working for the United Nations Development Programme (UNDP). These were located less than a kilometre north of Changangkha, just above the Bhutan Hotel.

These bungalows were quite nice, but Father Mackey was uncomfortable there. For one thing, he was "the odd man out," as he puts it — the only non-UNDP person there. Besides, he was more accustomed to living among Bhutanese and Indians than highly-paid foreigners. The UNDP enclave was like a mini-suburb, a cluster of small bungalows all alike. Father Mackey would have preferred a more Bhutanese setting, with more rooms and more of a view.

After a year or so, he found a Bhutanese house for rent up the hillside from the Memorial Chorten, south-west of the town centre. It was owned by a daughter-in-law of Ten Dorje, his old friend in Tashigang. By this time Mindu was spending most of his time with Father Mackey, cooking, washing up, and generally trying to look after the priest, as well as being his driver. Mindu's wife and children still lived in the bazaar.

Thus far, Father Mackey had not had a home that could accommodate another family. And he didn't know much about Mindu's wife and children. However, during a short period when Mindu was sick and stayed home, Father Mackey visited and got to know Mindu's wife, Kunzang Chhoedron, and the children. Mindu and Kunzang Chhoedron had two little girls, aged about four and five, and a son who was about eight years old in 1985.

Father Mackey took to the whole family. Kunzang Chhoedron was short with a medium build, an attractive face, and wore the standard Bhutanese woman's haircut — straight and fairly short. In contrast to Mindu, she had a ready smile and offered a steady stream of talk, with plenty of jokes. The girls were pretty, lively and bright. The boy was quiet but clever.

Mindu and Kunzang Chhoedron had arranged to sell their property, which was right in the heart of Thimphu and so relatively valuable. But they had no definite plans about where to move. Father Mackey suggested they join him on the hill. Kunzang Chhoedron could take over the cooking and household management.

His house was a single-family dwelling, but he suggested building a house next door. With the help of the department of education, he had a simple house built, and helped Mindu make it comfortable. So began an arrangement that has greatly benefitted all concerned, and continues today in different quarters.

Father Mackey and the family moved to their present home in 1988. The priest was forced to leave the house above the Chorten, and then his next one north of Thimphu, when rents increased beyond his budget. This happened through the latter half of the eighties, as an influx of foreigners working for aid organizations drove up the market value of rental units. It became difficult to find a nice house for less than 5,000 *ngultrums* (about 400 dollars), and this was too much for Father Mackey's salary.

About this time, following a change in government policy on housing for civil servants, a number of government houses became available. Father Mackey learned of a good-sized house, more or less in the Bhutanese style, just north of Motithang High School. It was two storeys high, with the bottom half made of concrete and the upper half of wood.

The upper floor was big enough to provide a large bedroom, a large chapel, a dining room and a central area that could serve as a living room or a lounge. There was also a small kitchen and a bathroom. Downstairs, the ground floor had an entry area at the front, with stairs leading to the upper floor, and four rooms, one of which was converted to a bathroom. Besides these rooms, there was a large room and a multiple-use entry area at the back of the house, exclusively for Mindu's family. At the back, there was also an outside stairway to the upper floor.

Some time before, Father Mackey had taken in Brother Nick. Then the government put an end to non-Bhutanese headships at educational institutions, and two more Jesuits joined them. Father Leclaire arrived after transferring from Sherubtse to education headquarters — the Jesuits had already left Jigme Sherubling — and Father Miranda, who had been principal at Punakha, came as well. They moved into the house, but within about a year, all three were gone from Bhutan.

This left Father Mackey and Mindu's family to live a full and comfortable life on their own. The priest is well-served by Mindu and Kunzang Chhoedron, and he loves them and their children. He helps the girls with their schoolwork and helped get the boy into Tongsa Junior High School and then Punakha High School, which would serve him better than staying in Thimphu.

For Mindu and Kunzang Chhoedron, Father Mackey is a good employer — but the situation is more that of an extended family. Mindu can use the vehicle for his own or family chores, and never abuses this privilege. Father Mackey treats the children like grandchildren, and Mindu and Kunzang Chhoedron virtually "mother" the priest. They demonstrate great concern for his health.

They make sure he is well-dressed when he goes out (Mindu helps him put on his *go*), both for his health and his appearance, as dressing properly is important in Bhutanese society. And they think very badly of anyone who uses Father Mackey's good and generous nature — though that does not stop them from cheating a bit in the friendly and boisterous games of rummy that precede just about every evening meal.

The family eats separately, but that is a matter of tradition and convenience. Kunzang Chhoedron is an excellent cook and prepares a variety of meals for Father Mackey — Bhutanese, Indian and Western. The family eats Bhutanese, and so will sometimes share dishes cooked for Father Mackey. The priest eats seated at the table. The family eats Bhutanese-style, sitting on the floor. Father Mackey likes to eat and retire early, whereas the family often prefers to eat later.

Father Mackey likes a drink of Scotch or Bhutanese whisky before dinner, and always has something on hand for guests — usually Scotch or Cognac, given to him by friends, as well as Bhutanese liquors and Indian beer. Here again, if Kunzang Chhoedron feels like a drink (Mindu doesn't drink at all), she opts for her own home-made *chang* (traditional Bhutanese "beer") or *ara*. If a guest of Father Mackey's desires a traditional Bhutanese drink, she draws upon her stocks.

On Sundays, Father Mackey says Mass for the small foreign Catholic congregation at 10:30 in the morning and sometimes again at six in the evening. The morning service is by far the greater, as thirty or more people pack the largest room in the house, which is laid out as the chapel. Kunzang Chhoedron brews up tea to serve everyone after Mass, and provides a snack as well. None of the family members attend Mass. They are Buddhists, with their own altar downstairs where they say their prayers, and Father Mackey would never consider interfering in their religious life.

* * *

For Father William Mackey, the eighties brought honour and celebration. In 1982, he went back to Canada to celebrate fifty years as a Jesuit. Five years later, he was informed that he had been elected to the Loyola High School Hall of Merit. Loyola's *raison d'être* is "education, understood in larger than purely academic terms; namely, that full growth of the person which leads to action in the spirit of Jesus Christ, the Man-for-others."

While a high school hall of merit may not sound like much, this is a small and prestigious collection of people that includes the late Father Bernard Lonergan, S.J., a distinguished theologian, and the late Georges Vanier, a former governor-general of Canada.

The induction ceremony was held on April 22nd, 1988, and Father Mackey arrived wearing a *go*. As it happened, six Bhutanese teachers and teacher trainers were studying at the University of New Brunswick, and were able to attend the ceremony, also wearing Bhutanese traditional dress. Jigme Thinley, Bhutan's permanent representative to the United Nations, came up from New York.

Father Mackey called this the most enjoyable trip he had ever made to Canada, and the presence of the Bhutanese at this very happy occasion contributed hugely. The organizing chairman later wrote to Father Mackey: "It was very obvious to all of us how very much at ease you are with your chosen people and they with you."

Father Mackey had brought a small wooden *chorten* from Bhutan. He said that four years before, the students of Jigme Sherubling had built a full-size *chorten*. He explained a bit about *chortens*, and then gave the small *chorten* to the High School in thanks for what he had received from

Loyola — both the education and the family spirit, which he said had helped him during his forty-two years of work in the Himalayas.

In late 1987, before he learned of his election to the hall of merit, Father Mackey had planned a trip to Canada. He intended to spend Christmas with his family and didn't want to cancel out. So he decided to go both times. The first trip had included an unexpected diversion, as he flew Air India via New York. He had decided to visit some old friends, an Italian-American family in Brooklyn. While there, he called another old friend — Jigme Thinley, who was heading Bhutan's delegation to the UN.

The permanent representative was delighted to hear from Father Mackey and invited him to the UN. After greeting him, Jigme Thinley had to excuse himself for a short while, as he had a meeting to attend. But he said, "Why don't you go to a General Assembly session?"

Father Mackey thought this a great idea. He obtained the necessary clearance and accompanied two Bhutanese representatives for the occasion. In the assembly hall, the Bhutanese delegation had three seats, plus more behind for visitors or observers. As there were only two delegates, they sat Father Mackey in the front with them. He found the proceedings fascinating and watched as the delegates voted, using a system of buttons on the desk-top in front of them. There was one button for "Yes," another for "No" and a third for "Abstain." He said to the delegate in charge: "Look, next time you vote, let me push the button. Just tell me which one to push."

When the next item came to a vote, Bhutan's position was to abstain. So Father Mackey pressed the "Abstain" button and was thrilled to see the results board light up: "Bhutan — Abstain."

The biggest celebration of all took place back in Thimphu on August 19th, 1989. By Bhutanese reckoning, Father Mackey was seventy-five. The party was organized by a group of his former students and was called his Platinum Jubilee Birthday Celebration. The idea was to congregate as many of Father Mackey's former students and friends as could come together at the swimming pool complex in Thimphu.

Around four o'clock in the afternoon, scores of well-wishers began to gather in front of the main hall to be on hand to greet the Jesuit at four-forty-five. When he arrived, the Royal Bhutan Army pipe band, in a rare public appearance, piped him into the compound. Father Mackey wore a rich hand-woven *go* in the pattern most often chosen for a ceremonial garment.

Many people came forward to offer *katas*, which they draped around his neck. As Father Mackey walked from the gate to the hall, he acknowledged the well-wishers in his friendly, casual fashion. He was surrounded by the organizers, with whom he laughed and joked while waving to the people lining the driveway. At the steps of the hall, the procession stopped for photographs and Father Mackey was surrounded by scores of friends, among them teachers and business persons, government ministers and foreign dignitaries, people who had known him for forty years and a few who had met him only months before.

As the party entered the building, organizers and senior government officials led the way to an ante room to the left to view an exhibition of photographs. These dated back to 1963, and included photos depicting some of those people who'd organized this party — people like Jigme Tshultim, who had been known as Radi Jigme, and had been punished for sneaking into girls' accommodations, and later served as translator between Father Mackey and the Umdze. Some of the photos had been borrowed from Father Mackey and, unfortunately, never found their way back to him.

After the chief guests had viewed the photo exhibit, refreshments were served. It was, after all, past five o'clock — tea time. When the two hundred or so guests were seated in the hall, the Bhutan Pledge was read. This was a piece from some now forgotten source that Father Mackey had come across and adapted for use in the schools in Eastern Bhutan. It read: "Bhutan is my country, all Bhutanese are my brothers and sisters. I love my country, and I am proud of its rich and varied heritage. I shall always strive to be worthy of it. I shall give my parents, teachers and all elders respect and treat everyone with courtesy. I shall be kind to animals. To my King, I shall pledge my devotion. In his well being and prosperity lies the happiness of my country."

Jigme Tshultim then gave the welcoming address, and this was followed by the distribution of the Students' Memoir book. It comprised more than eighty pages of photos, student memoirs and other memorabilia of Father Mackey's life in Bhutan.

Then came an hour of entertainment. People read poems they'd written for the occasion, and a small musical ensemble played a variety of tunes from Bhutan and elsewhere. But the most popular acts featured old students recreating the early days in skits, gymnastic "displays" and the singing of old school songs, some updated to include notable personages in the audience, like "Lyonpo Dawa Had a Farm." Ex-students poked fun at Father Mackey and just about everyone else. The audience roared its appreciation and no one laughed more than Father Mackey.

At seven, with the stage lights dimmed, young men carried two gigantic, three-tiered birthday cakes ablaze with candles to the front of the hall. The organizers had arranged one, and the Queen Mother had sent another to make sure there would be enough to go around. Her intuition proved correct, as the hall was packed. Then the official birthday gift was presented by Ugyen Tenzin of the organizing committee. U.T., as he was commonly known, had been a student of Father Mackey, and was the same Ugyen Tenzin who led the Indian police on a mad chase while bringing Father Mackey to Samdrup Jongkhar after his harassment in 1976. He was now deputy secretary in the ministry of finance.

The gift was a complete set of the best quality Bhutanese dress: hand woven *go* and belt, raw silk *kabney*, *toego* (shirt) and hand-made Bhutanese boots. This was followed by other gifts and short speeches, among them one by Dago Tshering, deputy home minister, whom Father Mackey had taught at St. Robert's. Paljor Dorji, the son of the late prime minister, gave a short but moving tribute, imagining what his father would have said about Father Mackey's work — the work begun when the prime minister invited Father Mackey to Bhutan. Dasho Benji imagined his father looking down at the celebration and saying to Father Mackey, "Well done, man!"

The senior official at the celebration, and one of Father Mackey's oldest friends and colleagues in Bhutan, was Lyonpo Dawa Tshering. If any of the assembled well-wishers, apart from some of the students who had spent ten years with Father Mackey, could speak of the Jesuit's work from personal experience, it was Lyonpo Dawa. And he had a perspective different from the students. As a government official, he had followed Father Mackey's work, often more closely than anyone else in the kingdom, from the day of his arrival in Paro in 1963.

While managing to match most of his comments to the light atmosphere of the evening, Lyonpo Dawa pointed out some remarkable aspects of the celebration itself: a cake sent by the Queen Mother; senior government officials, some with middle-aged paunches, stripping down to light shorts to perform skits in public; and he pointed out something that few in the audience knew. A few years earlier, someone had stolen Father Mackey's Druk Zhung Thuksey Medal. This was the medal presented to him by the King when he was pronounced "Spiritual Son of Bhutan."

Father Mackey had tried to keep the loss a secret, but when celebration organizers insisted that he wear the medal on this occasion, he had to admit that it was gone. Someone said he should ask the King for another, but of course Father Mackey said he couldn't. The situation did get mentioned to the King's private secretary, however. And as Father Mackey was getting ready to leave his house for the celebration, the head of the Royal Body Guard drove up with a case of various bottles of the best liquor, from His Majesty. Then he placed a card and something else in Father Mackey's hand.

Father Mackey asked, "Is this what I think it is?"

"Yes, Father." It was a Druk Zhung Thuksey Medal.

Lyonpo Dawa pointed out that receiving a Druk Zhung Thuksey Medal was a very rare honour, but here was Father Mackey, surely the only person to receive two such medals.

After the gifts and speeches, people sang Happy Birthday. Then it was Father Mackey's turn to speak. He ran loosely through the chronology of his life in Bhutan, rambling a bit and poking fun at old students along the way. But it was clear to the audience that he felt strong pride and appreciation regarding his life in Bhutan, and was moved by the show of appreciation directed at him on this occasion. The formal part of the evening ended at about seven o'clock, as one of the organizers said thanks to all concerned.

Next came the dinner, always an important part of a Bhutanese celebration. As the buffet-style meal was laid out, people had time for drinks and conversation. The meal itself matched the success of the earlier programme. All the classic Bhutanese dishes were arrayed: a variety of meat dishes including one adorned with a hog's head; *hemadatsi*, the quintessential Bhutanese dish of fresh white cheese (*datsi*) cooked with hot green chillies (*hema*); red rice, apparently grown only in Bhutan; Bhutanese salad or *eze* made of crumbled *datsi* and finely chopped onion and chillies; and much more. There were also Indian-style curries and dhal. And there was beer and soft drinks to wash it all down. It was a feast.

Having finished their meals in the main hall, the Bhutanese gathered spontaneously in front of the stage to do traditional dancing. The dances, performed in a large circle, to the rhythm of the dancers' own singing, usually consist of rhythmic steps — some forward, some back — with hand movements and turns of the body. To the uninitiated spectator, the dance looks slow and simple. But on such occasions visitors are encouraged to join in, and once in the circle, the visitor realizes how deceptive appearances can be. The steps and hand movements are intricate, and the slow rhythm is difficult to follow. Fortunately, the Bhutanese accept an outsiders' awkward movements with grace and good humour.

The final event of the celebration was the traditional closing dance, called Tashi Lebey, in which everyone takes part. Most of the participants were Bhutanese, of course, and what they were feeling — who can say? But to the author of this book, the dance, a classic way to end a Bhutanese evening, felt perfect and more than a little moving. The Tashi Lebey brought everyone together in a communal action that climaxed a heart-felt, five-hour out-pouring of national love for a deserving man of God and the people — Father William Mackey.

EPILOGUE

Traditionally, the Bhutanese don't celebrate birthdays. At birth, Bhutanese are considered to be one year old, and thereafter, they become one year older at each Losar, or New Years. Hence, East and West met when the Bhutanese celebrated Father Mackey's 75th birthday in 1989.

The Jesuit remained chief inspector of schools until 1992. By then the education department had expanded the inspectorate to three teams, but also expanded its mandate to cover all schools in the country. With the addition of off-the-road primary schools and community schools (one-room schools providing the first four years of schooling in the most remote areas), inspectors would have to walk for hours, even days.

Father Mackey did make small concessions to his advancing years. He rode ponies more often and left the distant off-road schools, especially those that required days of trudging through steamy jungles, to younger inspectors. Still, with more teams and more schools, as head of the inspectorate, he had more reports to analyze, synthesize and discuss.

In 1991, Father Mackey made a rush trip to Canada in response to a report of sister Tess' imminent demise. The news reached him on tour, in Eastern Bhutan, and Mindu drove twenty-two hours straight to get to Thimphu. After a few hours there, pulling things together, the two were off again on the eight-hour drive to Siliguri. Father Mackey flew to Delhi, then on to Canada.

To his relief, but some chagrin, he found that Tess had suffered little more than a bad fall. Father Mackey took the opportunity to make a regular tour, and caught the end of the major 1990-91 Jesuit celebration: the 450th anniversary of the formal approval of the Society of Jesus by Pope Paul III, and the 500th anniversary of Ignatius Loyola's birth. Father Mackey was the oldest participant in a six-day pilgrimage around Midland, visiting the sites where the Canadian Martyrs had died. The longest leg was twenty-six kilometres. He found that while he and the missionaries based in India took the walking "in stride," many Canadian-based Jesuits were "too well fed" to enjoy it.

In 1992, the Jesuits flew Father Mackey to Canada to celebrate his sixty years with the order — a landmark not many achieve. On his way back to Bhutan, he visited Ireland. In Dublin, the Irish overseas volunteer service, the Agency for Personal Service Overseas (APSO), took the opportunity to fete him. They had been sending volunteer teachers to Bhutan, and recognized and respected Father Mackey's work.

Later that year, the Bhutanese government again honoured Father Mackey. This time it was a unique appointment — honorary advisor to education, for life. The Canadian government also came through with a useful gift — a new Isuzu Trooper. Father Mackey had said that his old vehicle, like him, was beginning to feel its age. By now, age seventy-seven, he was visiting only those schools that were "on the road." But, in addition to inspecting schools, he had remained involved in teacher in-service courses and workshops, and in producing and evaluating texts and teacher manuals.

Having stepped down as chief inspector, he had a little more freedom and began writing a bit, on things like the history of Bhutanese education. The education department head now referred to him as his "Roving Ambassador." Father Mackey still loved to rove, and said nobody listened to his advice anyway, so he was happy with this role, which incorporated both travel and work. The Jesuit still often serves as a school inspector, and travels with one of the teams.

For almost a decade the University of New Brunswick has been helping with the higher education of Bhutan's education personnel. It has built a reputation as the Bhutanese home in Canada. In 1994, the university awarded Father Mackey an honorary Doctor of Letters degree. One of those who wrote in support of his nomination was Pierre Trudeau, the former Canadian prime minister. It was his younger brother, Charles, who had shouted *"Mon Père"* as he tossed a mouse at a young Bill Mackey at Brébeuf some fifty-five years before.

* * *

As a citizen of Bhutan, Father Mackey could have remained in the country no matter what, but his lifetime appointment ensured him of an income even when he was no longer able to work. When he was made honorary advisor for life, he said, "I feel honoured that I can spend the last days of my life in a country I respect and among people whom I appreciate and love, and with whom I have spent twenty-nine years of my life."

While most of Father Mackey's oldest friends and colleagues have passed away, he still has a great many friends. Many are old students, but there are others who have shared his life in Bhutan as adults, among them the Queen Mother, Ashi Kesang; His Royal Highness, Namgyal Wangchuck; and Lyonpo Dawa Tshering. Such people not only share his company from time to time, but also show concern for his welfare.

Given his irrepressible vitality, sense of humour and interest in life, Father Mackey is constantly in demand at official and private social events. He sometimes entertains official visitors at his home. And his friends feel free to drop by any time. It may not be the simple life of Tashigang in the mid-1960s — when the community lived and worked together as a big family and everything, especially entertainment, was home-made — but it is still a good life.

In and around Bhutan, Mindu remains his driver and right-hand man. Mindu's wife, Kunzang Chhoedron, runs the household, and the home is happy and comfortable. Every Sunday, Father Mackey says one or two Masses for his small flock in his simple chapel.

When he reflects on the life he has lived, Father Mackey sees very few unhappy stretches like the one that preceded his move to Bhutan, and which a Jesuit superior in Rome once described as "that blessed difficulty with the government." The best of the good times have been the years in Bhutan, and the best of the best were the early years in Tashigang.

Three main reasons stand out.

First, Father Mackey enjoyed the people he lived among. Tamji Jagar personified the attitude and values that Father Mackey identifies with those early days, and his first experience with the traditional life in Bhutan. The Jesuit greatly appreciated Tamji Jagar's wisdom, loyalty, generosity and warmth, and describes him as a faithful servant to the King and the people.

Father Mackey's friend, Phongmey Dungpa, also exemplified dedication to duty and traditional values. Obviously not driven by material motives, he acquired no financial wealth in a lifetime of service. Father

Mackey also fondly recalls other representatives of a kind of nobility that, with regret, he saw largely pass away as modernization took hold in Bhutan. Among them were Babu Tashi and Ten Dorje, Mr. Kharpa and Lopen Jamphel. Of these, only Dasho Ten Dorje survives, now retired.

Among the non-Bhutanese, Father Mackey relished the company of Doctor Anayat and Lingshay, and of his fellow Jesuits Brother Quinn and Father Coffey. All worked hard, but in addition to being good colleagues, they were people of joy and warmth. Father Coffey died in 1993, and Brother Quinn is in declining health in Canada. Doctor Anayat and Lingshay, however, are still going strong.

For his part, Father Mackey was accepted by the Bhutanese, and the others, not because of his hard work or spirituality, but because he accepted them as they were. He respected and appreciated their way of life, their values and their religion. He came without condescension and without any sense of being a saviour, religious or otherwise. Indeed, he was eager to learn, and to be enriched by what he found.

The second reason Father Mackey remembers the early years so fondly was the work. In Tashigang and on into the years at Sherubtse, he ran his own show. He had the qualifications, the experience and the aptitude to do the job, and also the freedom to do it as he saw fit. He made good use of the letter from Ashi Dechen that affirmed her support for whatever he wanted to do. He enjoyed the work immensely, and the results of his efforts, including the products of his earliest labours in Tashigang, have justified the trust the Bhutanese placed in him.

Although Bhutan is in many ways a society of protocol and etiquette, Tashigang functioned as a world unto itself. With modernization came bureaucracy and red tape. By the time he left Sherubtse, Father Mackey was no longer free to operate as he chose. In retrospect, he sees his move to Jigme Sherubling as partly an attempt to recapture the simpler pre-college days of running a relatively ordinary school. But that era had passed.

Once in Thimphu, of course, Father Mackey had to fit into a restrictive bureaucracy — often unresponsive and indifferent to human concerns — that included more modern aspects than one might think. Soon the department introduced computers, and — thirty years after arriving in Bhutan, when there wasn't even electricity — Father Mackey acquired his own desktop computer.

Regarding Bhutan generally, "it's hard to realize the change that has taken place in thirty years," Father Mackey says. "We've jumped from a medieval Tibetan Buddhist society that ran without money, into the modern, educated, sophisticated, money bureaucracy." He sympathizes with the present King, as he did with his father, and describes the job of leading contemporary Bhutan as "steering a bobsled down the icy, twisting, snow-covered, steep mountain path of modernization." Every moment requires a decision for which there is little time or opportunity for preparation, but for which a wrong choice could spell disaster.

Father Mackey's primary concern remains children and their education, which he defines as "not merely memorizing information, but learning to relate to one's environment in particular and the world in general in a creative and intelligent manner." The Jesuit also poses the question of how the system can deepen the cultural and religious roots of the children. He agrees with some of the many changes that have taken place, feels others need adaptation, and regards a few as totally out of place in Bhutan. But if no one listens to his advice, as he jokingly asserts, the Jesuit Mackey takes it philosophically, providing assistance where he can and taking life as it comes.

The final reason Father Mackey remembers the Tashigang years with such fondness was the prevailing atmosphere of spirituality. The depth of spirituality he found in Bhutan is probably the main reason he has been so comfortable with the proscription against proselytizing. In the Buddhists of Bhutan, as in the Hindus of Darjeeling and Southern Bhutan, Father Mackey has found people whom he believes are as close to God as he feels.

"I am a better Jesuit, a better priest and a better human being because of my years in India and Bhutan," Father Mackey has declared. "I am convinced of the real presence of the Spirit in Hinduism and Buddhism. He is very much alive in the peasant people of Bhutan. Bhutan has taught me how to pray. I had been trying to grasp God with my mind. It can't be done. The ordinary Bhutanese taught me to grasp God with my heart, to experience God in prayer and in every detail of my life.

"I am perfectly at home in a Buddhist *lhakhang*, a Hindu temple or in a Christian church. The Holy Spirit is at work in many strange ways. We must not let man's narrow thinking try to minimize God's love for every man and woman in this world. My own Christian faith has been enriched and come alive through contact with these people. They have taught me to accept myself and others as we really are, as God made us and not as we think ourselves to be.

"We need greater trust and faith in human nature. All men are trying to find their way towards God in a very complicated, often disturbing, mysterious world. No one can remain sane without real faith — it is God's gift to every man and woman in this world. May we all respond to God's faith in us, in human nature — His gift to creation."

Given these sentiments, some will no doubt ask if Father Mackey has succeeded at all as a conventional missionary. He would probably say, as he did on one occasion, that if he has brought people closer to himself, to education, to Buddhist values, to love of country and culture, then he has certainly brought them closer to what Christ stands for — love of God and neighbour. And for those who have questioned his Christianity, given his attitude towards Buddhism, he has said: "Many think I am a heretic. However, I am convinced that the Lord loves me. That is all that matters."

Glossary

The following definitions and the attributing to specific languages are very simplified.

ama - term of address: Madam, Mrs., Missus; mother (Tsangla)

anna - coin in former system of Indian currency, one sixteenth of a rupee

Apsoo - breed of Himalayan dog; brand name of a rum made in Bhutan

ara - alcoholic beverage, distilled from fermented grain (Dzongkha, Tsangla)

ashi - princess, lady of noble extraction (Dzongkha, Tsangla)

Avalokiteshvara - a Buddhist deity symbolizing compassion

badmash - rascal (Nepali, Hindi, Urdu)

bangchung - double basket of woven split bamboo, the two halves of which fit tightly together to form a closed container (Dzongkha, Tsangla)

Bidung - small village about four hours' walk east of Tashigang

BOAC - British Overseas Airline Corporation (predecessor of British Airways)

Bumthangkha - language of Bumthang region

Changangkha - place name in Thimphu given to a primary school

chappal - Indian-made rubber sandal (like the Canadian "thong"), originally made of leather (Hindi, Urdu)

charpoy - simple Indian bedstead made with light rope webbed across the wooden frame (Hindi, Urdu)

cha-walla - Indian seller of brewed tea (Anglo-Indian)

chhu - river (Dzongkha)

choedrom - low (about 50 cm high) rectangular Bhutanese table, closed on front and sides, open at back with shelf inside, often decorated (Dzongkha)

Choekey - Classical Tibetan (language)

chorten - religious monument of variable size and style, but most usually in Eastern Bhutan in the Tibetan style, built of stone and whitewashed, with a square base about 3 metres on a side, narrowing to a point, about 5 or 6 metres high; complex in significance and composition (objects built into the structure); dedicated to the Buddha, symbolizing his mind (Dzongkha, Tibetan, Tsangla) (stupa in Sanskrit, Hindi, Nepali); Chorten Kora is exceptional in its size and style.

Dantak - Indian paramilitary road-building organization which built roads in Bhutan

dasho - "excellent one"; person honoured by the King of Bhutan for meritorious service (but more or less automatic in the case of high members of Royal Family), somewhat like knighthood; signified by being given by the King, and thereafter wearing, a red *kabney* and sword; title used in addressing such a person or a highly placed person (director level or higher in the government) even without "the red scarf" (Dzongkha, Tsangla)

dekshi - cooking pot (Hindi, Urdu)

dhal - a type of pulse or lentil; a spicy stew made of these lentils

Diwali - Hindu autumn festival of lights (Hindi)

doen - devil or demon (Dzongkha, Tsangla)

dorje - thunderbolt; object representing same, having great religious significance; symbolizes Tantric Buddhism (Dzongkha, Tibetan, Tsangla); commonly used as personal name, also spelt Dorji

driglam namzha - Bhutanese code of traditional etiquette (Dzongkha)

druk - dragon (Dzongkha, Tibetan, Tsangla)

Druk Yul - "Land of the Dragon"; Dzongkha name for Bhutan

Druk Zhung Thuksey - "Spiritual Son of Bhutan"; an honorary title, along with a medal, given by the King of Bhutan

Drukpa - originally, followers of the Drukpa Kagyupa school of Tibetan Buddhism, the official religious school of Bhutan; whence the name given to the people of the interior of Bhutan (Dzongkha, Tibetan, Tsangla)

dungkhag - sub-district (Dzongkha)

dungpa - chief administrator of a *dungkhag* (Dzongkha)

dzong - fortress; seat of civic and religious power, especially of a *dzongkhag* (Dzongkha, Tibetan, Tsangla) *dzongdag* - "master of the *dzong*"; present-day chief administrator of a *dzongkhag* (Dzongkha)

Dzongkha - "language of the *dzong*"; official language of Bhutan; indigenous to Western Bhutan; derived from Tibetan

dzongkhag - administrative district (Dzongkha)

dzongpoen - "master of the *dzong*"; former term for chief administrator of a *dzongkhag* (Dzongkha)

gelong - ordained celibate monk (Dzongkha, Tibetan, Tsangla)

go - Bhutanese man's garment; very full, ankle-length robe gathered, raised and tied tightly at the waist to produce a knee-length skirt of the bottom half and a voluminous blousing top (Dzongkha)

gompa - monastery (Dzongkha, Tibetan, Tsangla)

gorbu - turned wooden bowl (Tsangla)

guluphulu - rascal, fool (origin uncertain)

Guru Rinpoche - respectful Bhutanese way of referring to Padmasambhava, 8th Century Buddhist saint and Tantric master, credited with bringing Buddhism to Bhutan

Jigme - "fearless" (Dzongkha, Tibetan, Tsangla); commonly used as personal name, also spelt Jigmi or Jigmie

kabney - ceremonial scarf; for men: twelve feet long and two feet wide, of raw silk or cotton; for women (also called *rachung*): six feet long (folded to half this length), one foot wide (folded to third of this width), hand-woven of silk or cotton (Dzongkha)

kashog - official proclamation or document (Dzongkha, Tibetan, Tsangla)

kata - ceremonial white scarf offered as an auspicious gesture (Dzongkha, Tibetan, Tsangla)

Keralan/Keralite - person from south Indian state of Kerala; of or from Kerala

kira - Bhutanese woman's garment; single rectangle of fabric (often hand-woven), four to five feet wide (shoulder to ankle) and six to seven feet long; wrapped around the body in a particular way, fastened together at the shoulders, and held tightly at the waist by a belt (Dzongkha)

la - mountain pass (Dzongkha, Tibetan, Tsangla)

Lam Neten - abbot of a regional state monk body (Dzongkha)

Lepcha - Tibeto-Burman ethnic group of the Sikkim-Darjeeling area

lhakhang - Buddhist temple (Dzongkha, Tibetan, Tsangla)

Lhotsampa - people of southern Bhutan, of Nepali origin (Dzongkha) *lopen* - (*lopoen*) "master"; title given to anyone who has received a traditional (monastic) education; teacher, educated person (Dzongkha, Tibetan, Tsangla)

Losar - Bhutanese New Year, falling in February-March (Dzongkha, Tibetan, Tsangla)

Lyonpo - minister (of government) (Dzongkha, Tibetan, Tsangla)

Mountie - member of the Royal Canadian Mounted Police

Muskoka - region of Northern Ontario favoured for summer vacations

Ngalong - people of Western Bhutan, original speakers of Dzongkha (Dzongkha)

ngultrum - Bhutanese currency unit; tied, at par, to the Indian rupee (Dzongkha)

nyerchen - tax collector and quartermaster of district (Dzongkha, Tsangla)

poenlop - title formerly given to the main regional governors of Bhutan; the title "Tongsa Poenlop" now designates the Crown Prince of Bhutan (Dzongkha, Tsangla)

rabjam - head clerk, assistant, "right-hand man" to *dzong* officials like *thrimpoen* or *nyerchen* (Dzongkha, Tsangla)

Radi - small village about four hours' walk east of Tashigang

Rinpoche - "Great Precious"; honorific title for a high reincarnated lama (Dzongkha, Tibetan, Tsangla)

rupee/dollar exchange - the Indian rupee was worth about 33¢ Canadian in 1947, 20¢ in '59 and '63, 14¢ in '68, 13¢ in 78, 12¢ in 83, 10¢ in 87 and 7¢ in 1990.

saag - a type of spinach (Hindi)

Sharchopa - people of Eastern Bhutan, who speak Tsangla (Tsangla)

Sharchopkha - commonly used name for the dominant language of Eastern Bhutan, the real name of which is Tsangla

suja - "butter tea"; made with hot water, butter, a type of tea leaf, salt and bicarbonate of soda, mixed together in a special churn (Dzongkha, Tsangla)

tati - stool, excrement (Nepali, Hindi)

thrimpoen - "master of the law" (Dzongkha, Tibetan, Tsangla); chief administrator of Tashigang district when Father Mackey arrived

Tsangla - dominant language of Eastern Bhutan

Tshechu - annual festival honouring Guru Rinpoche (Dzongkha)

Umdze - choir master in a monastic community (Dzongkha, Tibetan, Tsangla); acting head of the monk body in Tashigang Dzong when Father Mackey arrived

villager - Bhutanese peasant

Note on pronunciation of Bhutanese words:

Vowels:

"a" is usually quite broad, about midway between the "a" in map and the "a" in father;

"e" is usually pronounced as the "ay" in say; or the French "é"

"i" is normally pronounced like the "ee" in see, or the "i" in sit, but not like the "i" in fire;

"oe" is pronounced much like the vowel sound in bird;

"u" is pronounced as the vowel sound in too or cute, but not as in run.

Consonants:

"h" (in combinations such as chh, dh, kh, lh, ph, th, tsh) usually only indicates that the previous vowel is aspirated, and for native English speakers can be disregarded, as most consonants tend to be strongly aspirated in English; this produces a rough approximation of the proper sound which is very difficult for native English speakers to achieve.

Notable exceptions are "ashi", "dasho", "guluphulu", "kashog", "Tashigang", in which the "sh" or "ph" combinations are pronounced as in English.

The "ch" combination is pronounced as in English.

"ng" is somewhat like the "ng" in king.

For the combinations of "dz" and "ts" (and "tsh" is virtually the same), the speaker should just try to make the sound indicated by the letters.

"zh" is like the "s" in measure.